THE THROW THAT FAILED

Britain's Original Application
To Join The Common Market

by

Lionel Bell

© Lionel Bell: 1995

British Library Cataloguing in Publication Data
Bell, Lionel

The Throw That Failed

First published by New European Publications Limited, 1995
14-16 Carroun Road, London SW8 1JT.

ISBN 1-872410-03-0

Typeset by Data Print, Blackthorns, Springfield, Oxted, Surrey.

Printed and bound in Great Britain by Biddles Limited,
Guildford, Surrey.

614482

CONTENTS

INTRODUCTION

The British government's 1961 application to join the Common Market, though initially unsuccessful, did achieve the creation of a new orthodoxy in established, respectable opinion in this country. In this climate the very arguments which formerly weighed within government could be routinely derided and their proponents treated with bullying and contempt. The establishment's commitment to 'Europe' has persisted for more than thirty years; it even succeeded in recruiting Gaitskell, who had opposed entry up to the time of his death, posthumously into the ranks of the great and good. The success of the new orthodoxy has tended to push into oblivion the extent to which it amounted to a revolution in political thought; in a short period at the beginning of the sixties entry to the Market was turned from an impossibility into an imperative. How was this possible? The argumentation that was the public accompaniment of the decision, with its fluffy metaphors and soporific generalisations, was scarcely compelling. While the Common Market could be supposed to make some contribution to containing the advance of Soviet Communism it could hardly be argued that its performance or potential in this regard was such as to require the sacrifice of any British interests, either to enhance it or to prevent its disintegration. Nor could it be seriously advanced at this time that its existence was what prevented the countries of Western Europe from going to war with each other, let alone that British membership was necessary to enable it to bring off such a feat. Politicians might be forgiven for seeking to prevent the last war but they should be expected to relate the insurance premium to the size and nature of the risk.

Nor was the economic case any less superficial. Membership might improve the United Kingdom's poor performance by simultaneously exposing it to greater competition and offering it greater access to the continental market, but since the bargain involved restrictions in respect of the much larger world market it required little thought to recognise that economic success was far from an inevitable outcome.

It was possible, however, that the reasoning that really drove the government was not something that it would have been politic to acknowledge openly. Now that more than thirty years have passed it is possible to examine the government's own papers, which show at least what it was saying to itself. It should not be supposed that the public record is free of debating points and dissimulation, or that it contains a single consistent and coherent argument. There was no paper presented to Cabinet in 1961 with a cool and sober assessment of advantage and disadvantage, of risk and opportunity. The decision was, rather, the culmination of a continuing process, a search through a succession of avenues for a solution to the problems for the United Kingdom that appeared to be presented by the development in part of Western Europe of a new economic and political entity.

The purpose of this work is to establish the government's reasoning, principally by examination of its own records, to evaluate the quality of that reasoning and, finally, to test it in the light of later events. Because Macmillan's application was unsuccessful those later events include a period of non-membership, which will afford some opportunity for comparison, though there are obviously far too many variables for such comparison to do more than proffer suggestions.

The general background will not put in much of an appearance in these pages. It needs to be borne in mind, however, that this was a period of fear and turmoil. Looming over everything else on the international scene was the Cold War, with its accompanying threat of nuclear annihilation. The process of decolonization might at any moment present the world's governments with a new battlefield. Consideration of the future place and role of the United Kingdom, or of Western Europe, vital though it was, could proceed only in the context of all these other pressures. It will be for the reader to decide how to bring them into play in judging the events that are presented here.

Chapter One

In Their Own Words

Establishment of the European Economic Community

On 25 March 1957 the Six (France, the Federal Republic of Germany, Italy, Holland, Belgium and Luxembourg) signed the Treaty of Rome and thereby chose to seek political integration by the route of customs union. Their objective was to prevent a recurrence of the internecine warfare of the European nations that had had such disastrous consequences for them and for the whole world, the same objective that had earlier led to the creation of the European Coal and Steel Community. Britain had stayed out of that organisation on the grounds expressed by Harold Macmillan that 'We would not allow any supranational authority to close down our pits and steelworks' [1]. The political aspect of the Treaty of Rome was fully understood by the British government, which had been briefed in 1956 to the effect that:-

the Messina Powers want... to achieve tighter European integration through the creation of European institutions with supranational powers, beginning in the economic field ..... The underlying motive of the Six is, however, essentially political.[2]

This only confirmed what was being said in public, e.g. by Professor Hallstein of the Federal Republic. 'It may be the last chance for the nations of Europe to maintain their old positions in the world or even for them to survive at all' [3]. Because of this, because of a belief that the enterprise might well fail and because in any case major British economic interests were seen to lie elsewhere, the United Kingdom stood back from the negotiations that led to the Rome Treaty.

A European Free Trade Area

Nevertheless, it was felt that the creation of a protectionist zone within Western Europe might hinder the desirable expansion of trade or, to put it another way, deprive this country of access to an increasingly profitable market. The suggestion of a major change in the United Kingdom's European policy appears to have originated with Macmillan, who became Chancellor of the Exchequer at the end of 1955. By the middle of the following year Ministers had approved the idea of an industrial free trade area[4] and during the discussions on the continent that led to the Treaty of Rome the concept received some support[5]. But the French and the British seem not to have understood the free trade area in quite the same way. The proposal put to the Organisation for European Economic Co-operation (OEEC) by the UK government, which it knew as Plan G, was for the gradual abolition of tariffs on all trade, other than agricultural produce, in Europe outside the Soviet bloc. The customs union of the Six would thus be contained within the industrial free trade area, an arrangement which would permit the other European nations in OEEC to continue their existing agricultural support and other practices. The plan thus met British economic interests, which were defined at the time by Sir H. Caccia as retention of the full liberty to trade across the Seven Seas[6], in contrast to the Treaty of Rome, whose signatories bound themselves to a common external tariff and transferred their power to conduct trade negotiations to the supranational Commission.

It was difficult, however, to produce proposals that were generally acceptable[7]. As it was expressed in the Cabinet a free trade area, unlike a customs union, would have no common external tariff, and the United Kingdom as a low-tariff country would be offering competition for the high-tariff countries in the Community. The French, who had got a high price out of the Treaty of Rome, were entirely hostile to a free trade area. Their policy was based on a deep-seated protectionism and a violent jealousy of Britain[8], whereas a free trade area was tailor-made to meet British requirements. The United Kingdom would have to make no agricultural commitments, it would be free to maintain its special relationship with the Commonwealth and would not be subject to any harmonisation of industrial, commercial and social policy.

By November 1958 it was becoming clear that the negotiations for this free trade area were in serious difficulty, particularly because of the attitude of France. Macmillan contemplated[9] breaking off the discussions and seeking the support of the United States for a free trade area alongside the Common Market, as the Community established under the Treaty of Rome was generally called; he also suggested that consideration be given to denouncing the Western European Union and that Adenauer might be induced to influence de Gaulle towards a political solution. Even trade discrimination against the Six might be contemplated. But these remarks were signs of his frustration rather than plans for active pursuit. In the event the French declined to continue these discussions.

The British felt that after the return to power of General de Gaulle the will to conduct the negotiations to success had disappeared and that the French were simply not prepared to accept the fundamental principle of a free trade area[10], while the French felt that Britain was seeking specific industrial benefits without offering comparable concessions in respect of agriculture, let alone the social policies on which France had insisted in negotiating the Treaty[11]. They were also unhappy about Britain's determination to retain preferential treatment of imports from the Commonwealth[12]. The British, on the other hand, took the view that a free trade area had been promised them[13] - the idea had appeared to find favour in both France and Germany - and they had become convinced they were wanted in Europe. It was a shock to find they were not[14], though nothing to what they later had to endure at the hands of France.

The breakdown in negotiations created considerable concern among those Western European countries who were outside the Six, despite the fact that France had announced that the tariff cuts to be made under the Treaty would be extended to all members of OEEC and the General Agreement on Tariffs and Trade (GATT). The British even contemplated offering a bribe to the French in the form of special economic treatment [15]; there is no evidence that this was taken any further.

There was no consideration given at this time in government discussions to the possibility of resolving the perceived difficulty by accession to the Community. As Heathcoat Amory (Chancellor of the Exchequer) put it to the Cabinet in February 1959 there were four fundamental difficulties in the way of that approach [16]. The common commercial policy of a customs union would damage the Commonwealth and he noted that three-quarters of UK trade was with the world outside Europe, whereas three-quarters of the trade of the Six was within Europe; the Common Agricultural Policy of the Six would not make it possible to safeguard Commonwealth interests; the Treaty of Rome was aimed at political union and in joining the United Kingdom would be implicitly accepting the objectives of its signatories; the commercial aims of France would make it impossible for the United Kingdom to safeguard the position of the Commonwealth. At the same time he thought the existing institutions of the EEC fell far short of being supranational and were not the obstacle they had appeared in 1955.

The European Free Trade Association
Shortly after this discussion it was agreed by those outside the Six that they should seek to hang together in a separate European Free Trade Association (EFTA). The countries concerned, apart from the United Kingdom, were Sweden, Norway, Denmark, Austria, Switzerland and Portugal (the Seven). EFTA was thus intended in the first place as an economic defence mechanism; whether it could develop as an alternative route to prosperity or provide a means of negotiating a suitable form of association with the Common Market was for the future. But it represented at the same time a decision not to join the Community or, rather, a re-affirmation of the earlier decision[17].

The view taken of EFTA for public consumption was well expressed in a Board of Trade briefing for the Minister of State's PPS (Neil Marten, who was to become a consistent opponent of British membership of the Common Market) as follows [18] :-

We believe that the EFTA will be a strong and progressive economic group which will bring trade benefits to all its members. It is an association of countries with a combined population of about ninety millions, with high living standards and highly developed industrial and agricultural skills. Its formation has helped to preserve cohesion in the European economic system and it has demonstrated that it is possible for the U.K. to belong to a purely economic European association consistent with our Commonwealth membership.

To the head of the European Economic Organisations Department of the Foreign Office writing at about the same time affairs looked rather more complicated [19] :-

As late as November 1959 the Foreign Office went on record with other Departments as saying that "the...negotiations broke down in December 1958 mainly for economic reasons". During most of 1959 attention was concentrated in this country on mitigating the feared economic consequences of the breakdown of the negotiations. This was the primary purpose of the Stockholm Plan. The "building of a bridge between the Six and the Seven" was indeed one of our declared aims, but no indication was given nor indeed was any clear idea formulated as to how such a bridge should or could be built. This probably explains the marked reluctance of Ministers and officials alike to take any bridge-building initiative. EFTA was formed primarily as an economic defence organisation and the simile of a bridge-head would in fact have been more apt than that of the bridge. In any case, it was still the aim that the bridge should lead, by a different route, to the European Free Trade Area which had been fought for from 1956 to 1958. Foreign Office attempts to substitute the more general (and more political) objective of "the achievement of a permanent and comprehensive settlement between the Six and the Seven" as the aim of policy met with little success.

It was not that the British government was unaware of the political angles of the question. In October the Prime Minister wrote to Selwyn Lloyd (then Foreign Secretary) [20] :-

Clearly one of the most important tasks of the next five years will be to organise the relations of the United Kingdom with Europe. For the first time since the Napoleonic era the major continental powers are united in a positive economic grouping, with considerable political aspects, which, though not specifically directed against the United Kingdom, may have the effect of excluding us both from European markets and from consultation in European policy. For better or worse, the Common Market looks like being here to stay, at least for the foreseeable future. Furthermore, if we tried to disrupt it we should unite against us all the Europeans who have felt humiliated during the past decade by the weakness of Europe. We should also probably upset the United States, as well as playing into the hands of the Russians. And, of course, the Common Market has certain advantages in bringing greater cohesion to Europe. The question is how to live, with the Common Market economically and turn its political effects into channels harmless to us.

The difference was that while Ministers understood that the Economic Community could have political consequences on the grand scale officials were conscious that it had political objectives, including political institutions, and that it would not be possible to negotiate effectively with the Community without subscribing in some way to those objectives.

In a purely internal discussion in the Foreign Office at about this time[21] officials considered the possibility that, given the views of President de Gaulle, the Six might not faithfully apply the Treaty of Rome and might move in a confederal direction. If so, they felt, it would remove one feature of the Community which was considered incompatible with Britain's own position in the world. It might then be possible to contemplate some formal relationship with the Six, but there was no advocacy of accession.

The Foreign Secretary's view at this time, expressed in a minute to the Prime Minister [21], was that support should be given to the political integration of the Six, but he also did not advocate membership. What was necessary was to prevent the Six from supplanting the United Kingdom as a principal influence on United States policy. There was a general feeling in government that the political ground needed to be cleared before any progress could be expected on economic issues.

The close involvement of the United States with the economic regeneration of Western Europe after the war and with its defence thereafter made its attitude to these developments particularly significant. It has been seen that Macmillan thought of enlisting American aid. The visit in December 1959 to the United Kingdom of Douglas Dillon, Under-Secretary of

State, therefore excited some apprehension. It was reported to the Cabinet [22] that the United States did not regard a Seven/Six agreement as necessary (politically or economically) or desirable, which must have been something of a disappointment for the government. This report went on:-

The attitude of Mr. Dillon may be summed up as follows:-

(i) The United States support the Six for political reasons, i.e. to see a strong and cohesive Power in Western Europe. They have always been prepared to accept disadvantages to United States trade in order to get this political objective. They do not see why the existence of the European Economic Community (EEC) should create a political split in Europe - all can work together, they say, in the North Atlantic Alliance (and of course in the Organisation for European Economic Co-operation (OEEC)).

(ii) The United States will press the Six with increasing strength to adopt a liberal trading policy - the more firmly established are the Six, the harder the United States will feel able to press. They would clearly welcome support from us and from the Seven.

(iii) Although unenthusiastic, the United States accept the Seven. When the European Free Trade Association (EFTA) Convention comes before the General Agreement on Tariffs and Trade (GATT), they will want to satisfy themselves that it is in accordance with the international trade rules.

(iv) The United States do not oppose in principle a Free Trade agreement between the Seven and the Six, provided that is in accordance with GATT. But they do not positively want to see an agreement, because they see it as widening and increasing the discrimination against them and so they will not press the Six to come to agreement. They do not believe that the Six will be prepared to negotiate anyway, until they feel stronger and assured that a wider European agreement would not frustrate the development of the Six.

(v) The United States therefore consider that the best course is to make a big effort in the coming GATT tariff negotiations to reduce the common tariff of the Six, and they welcomed our statement that we were considering with the Seven whether we should ourselves negotiate with the Six in this conference.

The report was by no means despondent about the economic aspects:-

First, how serious is the potential economic damage to us from the Treaty of Rome? It would be unwise to draw conclusions too quickly, but there are three points that I would mention at once:-

(i) The position is greatly affected by what happens to the Seven. If we are able to hold the Seven together, this will limit the danger (and provide some gains to offset our losses). If, on the other hand, the Seven were to fall apart, and the rest of them inevitably come within the orbit of the Six, our position would be greatly weakened. The Six take one-seventh of our exports: the Six and Seven and peripherals take one-quarter.

(ii) It may be that the effect of the Treaty of Rome will be to make our problem of maintaining a satisfactory balance of payments during the next decade somewhat more difficult, and correspondingly somewhat to worsen our prospects of economic growth. But this depends very much upon the policies of the Six and of the United States and of ourselves and the Commonwealth; and I think we must await a more thorough review. We must not forget that our economy is changing fast all the time; it has shown itself in recent years very adaptable, and we should not take a defeatist view.

(iii)The worst danger is that the Six might adopt policies which would make other countries revert to restrictive policies, and damage the whole fabric of international trade rules, leading to a general situation of quotas and tariffs and preferential arrangements that would be very bad for us indeed. Generally speaking, the consolidation of Western Europe economic power in the EEC inevitably reduces our influence in the formulation of the world trading rules and puts us at risk accordingly. It could likewise become a magnet tending to attract our industry and capital from the United Kingdom into Europe - and thus leaving us in a backwater. There is no certainty, and not necessarily a likelihood, that such damaging results would follow - but the possibility is there. These dangers, again, would be much greater if the Seven were to fall apart.

The dangers are not certain. They may become serious and they may not. What is certain is that we should lose the benefits that we had hoped to gain from the all-European free trade area.

The project was a very favourable one in our interests.

This view was based on an examination by officials of the economic impact of the European Economic Community on the United Kingdom [23].

This report to the Cabinet concluded:-

To sum up, in my view our objectives should be:-

(i) To consolidate the EFTA

(ii) To go on trying for a wider Seven/Six agreement, while accepting that at best we shall not make progress very fast.

(iii)To join in readily in a general move, in association with the

United States and the Seven and the Commonwealth, in the OEEC and in the GATT, to reduce tariffs and bring pressure upon the Six to adopt a liberal policy.

Heathcoat Amory (Chancellor of the Exchequer), who was responsible for the memorandum, added in discussion that although the population of the EFTA Countries was only 90 millions, compared with 160 millions in the EEC Countries, in terms of national incomes the former group were two-thirds, and in terms of foreign trade three-quarters as large as the latter. The establishment of the EFTA, in addition to its importance as a means of facilitating an association with the EEC, provided valuable commercial opportunities for the United Kingdom. While other members of the Cabinet pointed out the dangers of the diversion of investment into the Common Market and of the competition of the Common Market countries outside Europe, together with Commonwealth fears that an association between the EEC and the EFTA would harm the preferential treatment of their exports to the United Kingdom, the immediate objectives set out by the Chancellor were accepted.

The Cabinet was not allowed to forget the wider framework. The Prime Minister expressed the view that [24]:-

The economic problem with which we were faced in Europe could not be satisfactorily settled until we had reached a political understanding with the French Government. A united Europe was, on balance, in the best interests of the free world. We had no wish to deprive France of her natural leadership of Europe. But we had to bear in mind our special relationship with the United States, and also the value of our position in the Commonwealth. It would be necessary at some future time to consider how best to proceed to discuss these questions with the French President.

For the time being, however, international discussions would have to concentrate on the major questions of the proposed East/West Summit, of Germany and disarmament.

Sixes and Sevens: January to May 1960

But such considerations did not mean the cessation of trade discussions and it was agreed in January 1960 to set up a Trade Committee containing representatives of the eighteen member countries of the OEEC, the United States, Canada and the

European Commission.   Its mandate included the need to examine the relationship between the EEC and the EFTA.

At a meeting of EFTA Ministers in Vienna on 11 and 12 March to prepare for the Trade Committee at the end of that month Reginald Maudling, the President of the Board of Trade, found his colleagues in good spirits and inclined to take a tougher line with the Six than he liked. As he reported to the European Economic Association Committee of the Cabinet [25] he was able to head them off, but his further analysis of the situation is of some interest:-

> The reasons why our EFTA partners were taking such a robust line, rather in contrast with what some of them were saying a short time ago, are two-fold:-
>
> (i) The growing prosperity of trade generally in Europe has taken the sharp edge off discrimination for them for the time being.
>
> (ii) They are very disillusioned about the attitude of the Six. They do not expect anything useful to emerge from the Paris Trade talks and, therefore, they are rather more concerned with dramatic gestures, particularly ones that have some internal political appeal, than they are with working compromises.
>
> I am inclined to share their cynicism about the immediate outlook. We all agreed in Vienna that any acceleration of the operation of the Treaty of Rome would be provocative because it would mean increasing Benelux and especially German tariffs against us. The Six do not seem to have made up their own minds yet and so I am hopeful that we shall be able to avoid acceleration, but I think the chances of achieving anything more than this are slight. The best that may emerge from the Paris meetings is likely to be that on 1st July the Six and the Seven will proceed with their discriminatory tariff reductions in accordance with the Rome and Stockholm Treaties.
>
> I should like to emphasise the gravity of the situation that is emerging in Europe. I do not believe it is yet generally recognised how serious and far-reaching are the problems that we shall be facing. The men who are in control now in the Six, mainly the French Government, the European Commission and the German Foreign Office, are all determined to build up the Six as a major economic, and therefore political, force, and they consider that the exclusion of the United Kingdom from the European scene is an essential part of the process. The two elderly gentlemen who control the policies of France and Germany are wedded to the Bonn-Paris axis, each in the belief that in the long run his end of the axis will prove the more important. So long as they remain united

in this determination, the prospects of a satisfactory settlement for us are small.

The effects upon British trade, and indeed upon the whole position of Britain in the world if we are excluded from the heart of continental Europe will, I am convinced, in the long run be of the greatest gravity. The community of the Six which is now developing will be on the scale of the United States in population and industrial skill. It will be the greatest importing community in the world and the second greatest trading community after the USA. The effect on our trade and our political position will be the same as if a second United States had developed alongside us, with roughly the same level of tariff protection as the United States but with a wage level no higher than our own. It is easy to see what the consequences will be:-

(i) There will be growing difficulties with our trade with the heart of continental Europe, the most rapidly growing market in the world.

(ii) The Six will grow in power, both as exporters, because they will have a broader industrial base than we have, and as importers. Their trading influence, therefore, will continue to grow more rapidly than ours and we shall face stiffening competition throughout the world, including the Commonwealth, where the buying power of the Six would be increasingly felt.

(iii)Dwarfed by this giant economic rival, Britain will steadily lose power and influence and in particular our relations with the United States will be undermined.

I admit that these are long-term considerations. It is true also they may be falsified if the Six should break up: but this possibility itself would be a disaster for us also for other reasons. Nevertheless I believe that we should proceed on the assumption that this is the way the world will develop and that we should shape our policies to meet a problem of major national concern. It will be very difficult indeed to find our way into Europe and it may cost us a high price in political terms. But I have no doubt that a high price will be well worth paying.

I believe we should now start a serious reassessment of the whole problem. When July 1st has passed and the Six and the Seven have started to go their separate ways, the time will then soon come for a new and radical approach. The original idea of a 17-nation Free Trade Area, embracing and engulfing the European Economic Community and the EFTA countries alike, will not gain acceptance. Instead I believe we should develop the concept of a single European market, formed by a treaty between two Groups who would retain their own identity. When we have developed this idea, we shall have to discuss it with our EFTA partners and then try and obtain for it support in the Commonwealth and the United States and acceptance in the United Kingdom. We may have to face internal political difficulties, but it must be remembered that the effects upon our industry and our commercial life generally of the present European situation are gradually becoming known to articulate opinion, and we must expect, in the absence of some initiative, growing political criticism of a kind that in the long run is more serious than the protests of outraged sectional interests, which have been all that we have heard so far. In any case the considerations of long term national interest will be so great that we shall have to be guided by them.

This was a particularly forceful expression of the pessimistic prognosis for the United Kingdom and one made by a Minister who was not regarded as particularly European in his sympathies. The proposed solution, indeed the whole final paragraph, belies the assertion made later within the Foreign Office (in the paper quoted earlier) that at this date the only aim of policy was still an all-embracing free trade area. The point is not in itself particularly significant but it illustrates the difficulties inherent in trying to establish what were at any moment the views and policies of such a widespread mechanism as the British government.

Maudling's view was consistent with that which he had expressed in Cabinet, though there recorded less forcefully, at the same time as the Chancellor, in reporting on the Dillon visit, had deprecated defeatism. There is no reason to make much of such a difference between Ministers; what is more important is that at this time Maudling sought the solution for the difficulties he foresaw within the framework of Six-Seven relations. It is also worth noting that Treasury officials strongly supported the Maudling view, expressing the hope that Ministers would not impose any limits on re-assessment of the problem. It was felt that it would be necessary to pull up and look at some roots which hurt, agricultural roots and Commonwealth roots. We would not achieve the position we wanted in Europe without paying a heavy price [26]. They saw the same problem but seem to be hinting at a more radical solution.

Meanwhile Macmillan had visited de Gaulle and had sought, without success, to persuade him to give up the acceleration of tariff reductions and the accompanying increases in the external tariff of the low-tariff members of the Community[27].

De Gaulle's attitude was that the Treaty of Rome was a commercial treaty - he would not have signed it but he acknowledged that it had forced French industry to be more competitive. He thought it should be possible to make a commercial bargain between the Six and the Seven.

The British government was immensely concerned by the loss of eighteen months of negotiating time in which some alleviation of the threat to their trade might be found. It regarded this acceleration as a hostile move away from the search for a settlement [28]. Macmillan took his concern about the effect of the acceleration to the United States, where he sought to persuade the Secretary of State that there were great political dangers in the Six. Unless the whole of Europe could be co-ordinated in some manner that provided for European unity the situation of 1940 (a hostile Western Europe), against the creation of which our two nations had fought twice this century, might be repeated. The object of the exercise was to secure American support for pressure on the Six to keep trade channels open; interestingly, Sir Frank Lee and others in the Treasury, which was to supply figures to back up the Prime Minster's case, felt that the United States was more likely to be swayed by political than by tariff arguments, even if the latter could be quantified [29].

Macmillan returned to his theme when meeting de Gaulle, who was on a state visit to the United Kingdom, at Buckingham Palace in early April. The essence of his argument [30] was that the United Kingdom economy was so delicately balanced that a difference of even £100m could be significant and that for this reason the discrimination between the Six and the Seven, which was now to come into effect on 1st July, had to be avoided. De Gaulle, who was hardly likely to be persuaded by problems in the UK balance of payments, then asked if the United Kingdom could not contemplate coming into the Common Market. Macmillan's reply was that this was unfortunately impossible.

He went on to say that while the idea of a Europe-wide free trade area might be too ambitious, he remained anxious that there should not be a deep economic division. His concern, as expressed earlier to the Cabinet[31], was about the possible political consequences of a permanent economic division, but one must assume he regarded the economics as very important, given the prominence he affords them in his autobiography[32]. This assumption is borne out by the Treasury's seeking to persuade him that the Americans would be more likely to be influenced by political than by economic arguments. What all this does indicate is the impossibility of disentangling political and economic arguments. Macmillan's own analysis of his conversations with de Gaulle appears in his report to the Queen:-

> I think he would accept that Britain should be her (France's) partner and in return for close co-operation with us he would be prepared to mitigate the effects of the Treaty of Rome.

Meanwhile, in parallel with Cabinet Ministers, officials meeting in the Economic Steering (Europe) Committee were going over this ground. At their first meeting[33] at the end of March they noted that there were substantial difficulties about the removal of discrimination between the EEC and the EFTA. The United States favoured the political integration of Western Europe and feared that a looser association might imperil the opportunity. The United Kingdom did not necessarily accept this political view since the integration might not in any case occur and if it did it might be dominated by Germany. They contemplated without enthusiasm the possibility of retaliation against the EEC if the latter did not relax the Treaty of Rome[34]. A little later in their proceedings the view was expressed that it was impossible for the United Kingdom to join the EEC without renegotiation of the provisions of the Treaty of Rome since its presence would upset the balance. This is an argument that continued to be raised from time to time and in due course was simply discarded. The need to retain the existing form of Commonwealth trade was emphasised; the objective was to do this and at the same time benefit from the removal of trade barriers in Europe.

Looking at Roots - A Cabinet Rejection: May to June 1960

The difficulties exposed in these explorations led Sir Frank Lee to develop a proposal which was first put orally to Ministers in a special Sub-Committee of the Cabinet, chaired by the Prime Minister, on 23 May. He had taken the precaution of circulating his ideas, on a very limited basis, in a personal memorandum.

One of the recipients was Lord Gladwyn, H.M. Ambassador in Paris, who welcomed it as in line with the views he had himself been putting forward for years, saying [35]:-

I believe that we rather tend to exaggerate the horror of our one day actually joining the Common Market. For instance if we ever did so we should be no more committed to the prospect of an actual Federation than is the Government of General de Gaulle, that celebrated nationalist. Indeed, I think that if a harmonisation plan is ever safely negotiated it will be almost inevitable that we shall form part of the Common Market before many years are past.

At the beginning of the meeting itself [36]:-

THE PRIME MINISTER said that he had called the Meeting to look at the problem of relations between the European Economic community (EEC) and the European Free Trade Association (EFTA) in the light of the failure of the Summit Conference. A change in the world political scene was bound to affect the approach to economic problems. The European economic problem was two-fold; whether there was the political will for a solution, and secondly, whether arrangements could be devised which would be acceptable to third countries, especially the United States, having regard to the General Agreement on Tariffs and Trade (GATT). Recent events might have lessened the difficulties on both scores. There were indications that some sectors of opinion in France were coming to accept the desirability of an agreement with EFTA, and it was possible that United States objections to a European regional settlement would not be pressed so hard.

After some general discussion:-

SIR FRANK LEE then described a proposal at present being studied by officials for an arrangement between the EEC and EFTA which would go as far as possible towards acceptance of most of the essential features of the Common Market. This would involve a common external tariff (though perhaps preserving, at least to a limited extent, Commonwealth free entry); agreed arrangements on agriculture and horticulture (perhaps involving managed markets for some agricultural commodities and tariff reductions on some horticultural products); some harmonisation of social charges;

membership of the European Coal and Steel Community and the European Atomic Energy Community; some understanding about Commonwealth agricultural exports to Europe and about the sale of tropical products; and, finally, some political content, e.g. acceptance of majority decisions on trade matters.

In the course of discussion of this proposal, the following were the main points made -

(d) It no longer seemed possible that we could reach agreement with the EEC for free trade in industrial goods only. To achieve a settlement now, we should have to pay a higher price - in some surrender of our sovereignty, a weakening of our Commonwealth links, and concessions on agriculture, tariff policies etc.

(e) In any negotiation with the EEC it would be essential to carry our EFTA partners with us. It would also be essential, before any public approach was made to the EEC, to assure ourselves by a bilateral approach to the French that agreement would be possible.

(f) Before decisions could be reached studies ought to be made of the comparative economic and political advantages and disadvantages of drawing nearer to the EEC and of letting the EEC and EFTA run their separate courses.

(g) It should not be forgotten that when the United Kingdom Government last considered joining the Common Market there appeared to be excellent reasons for not joining it. Only some 14 per cent of our trade went to EEC countries and it was questionable whether we should realign our whole economic and political relations for that. Perhaps the most difficult aspect of the proposal for coming closer to the Common Market were the arrangements for agriculture and horticulture. It might be that managed markets would not be unacceptable to our farmers; but any change in the present pattern of protection for British agriculture would raise most serious political difficulties.

(h) On the other hand it was argued that there would be increasing pressure from industrial and other interests in this country for an accommodation with the EEC.

(i) The immediate problem was what response should be made in the meantime to the offer by the EEC for renewed negotiations. The Foreign Secretary would be attending a meeting of Western European Union on 15th June and would have to indicate our view. There would previously be a meeting of the Trade Committee of Twenty Governments on 8th June at which we would try to establish whether the EEC countries genuinely wanted a long-term settlement.

Summing up the discussion, THE PRIME MINISTER said that Ministers would soon have to decide which of two courses was the better for the United Kingdom. The first would be to go on with EFTA and let the division in Europe continue. What would we suffer economically, in investment as well as trade, if the two groups continued their separate ways?

Was the United Kingdom strong enough to withstand discrimination against her exports to Europe? Could the investment losses be mitigated in any way by greater freedom of capital movements and by joint capital groupings? The second course would be to enter into a close association with the EEC. What would the effects of this be on our agriculture and on our trade relations with the Commonwealth? These were some of the fundamental economic questions posed by the alternative courses. But the political questions were even more difficult. What would be the effect on the United Kingdom's standing in Europe, in NATO and in the world generally of staying outside the EEC, and what would be the political advantages of joining it? The Government would have to decide, on a judgment of the balance of both political and economic advantage, between the two courses. They would have to take into account the difficulties of carrying a radical change of policy through Parliament. If the Government were to decide in favour of drawing closer to the EEC it would be essential to obtain agreement at the highest level with the French beforehand: this was more likely to be gained when France was strong politically.

It was agreed that the Ministerial Committee on European Economic Association should resume their consideration of these questions later in the week on the basis of a paper prepared by the Economic Steering (Europe) Committee.

The Meeting -

Took note that the problems of closer economic association with the EEC would be considered further at a meeting of the European Economic Association Committee later in the week.

This is the point at which one can see the tide beginning to turn, but there was still a long way to go.

On the 27th the Ministerial European Economic Association Committee met to consider the memorandum from the Economic Steering (Europe) Committee of officials entitled *The Six and the Seven : Long Term Arrangements.* It was very largely Sir F. Lee's work and the full text appears at Appendix B.

The essence of his argument, even at this early stage, was that the disappearance of trade barriers between the Six would provide a dynamic impetus to their economic performance. It was, in fact, an argument that only large-scale players could be successful in international competition; it was therefore necessary for the United Kingdom to get inside some larger European market. It was also suggested that political integration would follow and that the consequence would be the emergence of a new Great Power on the world stage, to the disadvantage of this country. The paper recognised that the time was not, perhaps, ripe for immediate action, but urged the Committee to decide on the broad objective and make plans that could be put into operation when the political will for a settlement could be perceived.

Relations with, indeed obligations to, EFTA partners, the Commonwealth and the United States would very much need to be taken into account. After rehearsing the difficulties inherent in other solutions the paper suggested that joining the Market would be economically advantageous but would create difficulties within EFTA, involve the risk of a commitment to a federal Western Europe and weaken the Commonwealth. The device that was therefore recommended was one of "near-identification with the Common Market", which meant taking on as many of its obligations as were necessary to be accepted by it (nearly all the major ones) but without formally joining.

With hindsight it can be seen that this proposal was heavily spiced with wishful thinking, both about its own viability in general and about what might be achieved for the Commonwealth in particular. This is not to say that those who prepared it deceived themselves - but they may well have felt it necessary to aim to retain existing arrangements in any approach to the Six if Ministers were to be persuaded to sanction it. Certainly it was the view of the Head of the European Economic Organisations Department of the Foreign Office that the logic of the argument indicated that the best course would be to accede to the Treaty of Rome [38], while as early as February the rather more cautious view had been expressed inside the Treasury [39] that:-

We may be willing to gear UK policy towards an all Europe single market even if it means the additional policy changes involved in accepting a customs union.

Equally certainly, as will be seen, the Cabinet was not ready for radicalism of this order.

The Committee had before it at the same time, but does not seem to have discussed, except tangentially, a report from Maudling on an EFTA meeting in Lisbon. He himself was not present at this meeting. The details are not significant but his conclusions are worth recording [39]:-

(1) We must seek a long-term negotiation and press the Six to take a negotiating position.
(2) Any proposal must leave the political cohesion of the Six unthreatened.
(3) Any solution must preserve the political independence of the member countries of the Seven.
(4) We must safeguard United Kingdom and Commonwealth interests.

Any suggestion that the Seven apply to join the EEC is ruled out by (2) and (3) quite apart from the problems raised by (4). The concept must be a treaty between the Six and Seven as separate entities to work in partnership for a single European trading system that will prevent the division that now threatens.

The Seven are anxious to start such a negotiation. Our starting point is clearly something like the Free Trade Area which we still believe to be the ideal solution. But we are willing to see if by negotiation a compromise can be reached. First we must hear from the Six what they would regard as an acceptable treaty of partnership. "Joining the Six" is clearly ruled out but there is no reason why the Treaty of Rome principles should not be taken on the side of the Six as their basis for negotiation just as the Free Trade Area is ours. Only in this way can we get the confrontation of ideas that is necessary first to identify and then to solve the practical problems.

This was clearly some way from what the officials were proposing and the Prime Minister did put some questions along these lines when he opened the Committee's discussion, of which the text is also at Appendix B. But as far as one can tell from this type of record his own view was that "near identification" would create more difficulties than would membership. Every direction was seen to involve dangers and the difficult choice with which he left them was between dramatic change and traditional policy. At least they could be got to agree that more research was needed and that it should be carried out under Macmillan's own direction. This was the first time that there was authorisation at Cabinet level of the examination of what might be involved in drawing closer to the Common Market.

What Macmillan chose to do was to draw up a list of questions to which officials would provide answers[41]. The discussion was now to be taken to the Cabinet itself, which would be faced with the broad choice of whether to seek a close association with the Six or to continue to remain aloof while doing all we could to mitigate the economic and political dangers of the division in Europe.

The officials' answers, in the form of a Cabinet memorandum, appear in Appendix C, followed by the record of the Cabinet discussion. The officials acknowledged the difficulties caused by current uncertainties about the development of the Community and suggested there would be little substantial difference between joining the Community and forming a close association with it. This was because they felt the insertion of the United Kingdom would be bound to modify provisions of the Treaty of Rome. They emphasized the newly apparent foreign policy advantages of accession but noted that the economic benefits would flow only to a United Kingdom that was fully competitive - which it would in any case have to be. Similarly, the political advantages would be derived only insofar as the United Kingdom was genuinely involved in the political aspects of the Community. It cannot be said that the memorandum left any major questions untouched, though much of its content was, of necessity, both generalised and vague.

It will be apparent to the reader that the Cabinet memorandum, presumably in anticipation of the difficulties that would be felt by Ministers, continued to contain a generous helping of wishful thinking, together with inescapable uncertainty about some crucial issues. In the first category the history of previous negotiations should have put a very large question mark against the possibility of modifications to the Treaty of Rome, modifications which can be identified by remarking those features which were described as inconceivable, unthinkable and out of the question; however much the Six might appreciate the political value of the Commonwealth it was never likely that they would yield anything of substance to support it; the idea that the United Kingdom would be able to exercise a claim to be a world Power by performing a balancing act within the Community between Germany and France needs only to be stated to be implausible, while the likelihood of the Community being steered to support specifically British interests (a worthwhile version of leadership) was truly negligible. It might be only hindsight that singles out a potential gain to the Exchequer of £160m annually from changing the form of agricultural support, but one cannot help remarking on it as one of the more evident ways of getting things wrong. Finally, it is not easy to see why, given that the difficult behaviour of France had been experienced at every turn since 1957, anybody should have supposed that it would be possible to ensure that acceptable terms would be available before launching an initiative to join or to seek close association with the Community.

As for the vagueness, the initial, and well-justified, proviso that it was not possible to judge how great British influence would be inside the Community should have tended to dilute the optimism expressed at a number of points in the paper and it may well have affected the discussion in the Cabinet. It should certainly have ruled out the assumption (question 22) that the United Kingdom would be a leading member of the group and one with a powerful influence. Given this uncertainty about the extent of British influence if on the inside, the unpredictability expressed in the first answer about the development of the most important aspects of the Community should have occasioned serious concern. Similarly, the perception that the United Kingdom within the Community might be obliged to prejudice vital interests in a manner difficult to foretell and might have to change its own view of its interests must, or should, have been a worrying one. Other speculative comments in the memorandum, or its refusals to speculate, could reasonably have been tolerated.

It is also right to draw attention to some of the hard-headed points that were made. There was certainly a prospect that the Community would develop into a powerful and effective player on the world stage. If world power can be regarded as a zero-sum game that would mean a decline in the rating of other contestants, particularly if, like the United Kingdom, their status was already reduced. However, given that power can take different forms, the uncertainty as to whether such a development would take place and the difficulty of foretelling (question 4) in what direction such power might be exercised there could be no clear calculation of the appropriate reaction.

The memorandum was certainly wise to stress that the economic advantages of joining the Six would be no more than potentialities, that the United Kingdom would have to be fully competitive with the Six and that this would depend on the maintenance of appropriate economic policies by the UK government. Given this perception and the fact that at the same time additional limitations would be imposed on the formation of economic policy it is, perhaps, a little surprising that the paper goes even so far as to say (answer to question 7) that association with the Six should make us economically stronger and able to wield influence through trade and aid.

Finally, there is the advice that there must be political content in a UK application to join the Six, preparedness to enter into the institutional arrangements and in any development towards closer political integration. That this point was very much in official minds at the time is made clear in a despatch from Sir Roderick Barclay, head of the UK delegation to the European Commission in Brussels [44]. He stressed that the aim of the Community was not merely harmonisation but the unification of policies in every field of the economic union, i.e. economic policy, social policy, commercial policy, tariff policy and fiscal policy. That this was not pie in the sky needed to be made clear to the politicians. The Six positively did not want anything to do with the United Kingdom because of their conviction that it would seek to dilute the Community. There needed to be a complete will to establish a real economic Union and unless the political masters were abundantly seized of this there might well be honest misunderstandings which could lead to serious and damaging recriminations if they came to light afterwards. The expression of Barclay's views might well have been coloured by his accreditation to the Commission, whose officials were understandably devoted to the fullest and fastest integration, but they were fundamentally sound and the Cabinet memorandum could have been even harder-headed on this issue.

The format of question and answer imposed by Macmillan was probably responsible for some of the internal inconsistencies that have been noted. There is no evidence as to why he should have opted for this rather than the advantages - disadvantages, opportunities - threats format which one might have supposed was appropriate. He may well have been averse from a procedure which influenced Cabinet members in the direction of making a firm decision, preferring at this stage to test the water. A somewhat similar caution may have induced him not to open the discussion, despite having chaired the Committee which originated the memorandum and being personally responsible for its form, although one would have supposed that he would not have had the slightest difficulty in keeping back at that stage any views he may have formed.

The record of the discussion is best described as judicious, without any trace that any of the Cabinet took really firm positions. Heathcoat Amory set out both the advantages and disadvantages in broad terms and opted for the combination of entry and preservation of the Commonwealth, while Maudling, taking a similar line, emphasized the prior need for a political will to be present in the Community. Home argued for involving the Commonwealth countries with the negotiations at every step, while Hare was pessimistic about the possibility of a settlement on food and agriculture. The recommendation of 'near identification' (a policy which was regarded in the Foreign Office as having no disadvantages compared with membership, but easier presentationally[45]) was not put to them. Faced with this challenge the Cabinet was unable to arrive at a basis for substantive action. After all, they had been advised that 12 to 18 months would probably elapse before a settlement might be negotiable and it was understandable that they did not feel pressed to make the "broad choice". It is not, therefore, surprising that their decision was no more than that a public statement should be prepared. On the other hand, the tenor of the record is of an underlying hostility to entry, which Macmillan acknowledged in his summary. It does appear that had a firm question been put the answer would have been negative and Butler later expressed the view that the Cabinet had agreed that there were insuperable difficulties in accession; the format of the discussion was a prudent one for anybody who wished to promote entry. Heath was to describe it as a discussion of principles; it by no means looks like it but there may have been more said than was recorded.

There were those officials who were not impressed with this performance. The head of the European Economic Organisations Department completed his notes for his successor [46] shortly before the Cabinet meeting, describing application for entry to the EEC as the logical result of Sir Frank Lee's analysis. He felt that near-identification lacked the political element necessary for a successful application and that the answers to the Prime Minister's questions (which he saw in draft), while bolder, continued the wishful thought that something less than full membership would provide a solution.

On the other hand a minute on these notes takes a different angle:-

> If it were impossible to obtain true intimacy in the Councils of the Six without serious disruption of our relations - both economic and political - with the Commonwealth, then we are better off outside ..... I am for joining the Community, if terms taking proper account of our extra-European (and of course EFTA) obligations and interests can be negotiated, primarily because I believe this is a simpler course for us and provides certain automatic correctives and stimulants to any weaknesses in our body economic. But if we decide not to try there is no reason to be doubtful of our economic future, provided we accept the degree of discipline and develop the sense of purpose which will be required to hold EFTA and the Commonwealth together.

Elsewhere in the Foreign Office the Cabinet's decision to postpone the decision (which we have seen it was carefully not asked to make) was regarded as unsatisfactory [47]. What was sought was a decision in principle that the objective was membership of the Common Market provided some fairly substantial modifications to the Treaty of Rome could be negotiated. It is understandable that civil servants who have been hired to make deals with foreigners become fractious if they are not allowed to make deals or that if they are there to execute decisions they feel frustrated by their absence; in this case the immediate problem appears to have been the Foreign Secretary, who in Cabinet decided to set aside that part of his brief from the Office which said that a decision of principle was needed urgently.   What is, perhaps, a little curious is that in this memorandum and the associated papers the idea of coming by a political path to an economic unity is put forward. It is not unlike the Chancellor's comment in Cabinet; that comment itself is unlikely to have been available inside the Foreign Office, but the notion may well have been going the rounds. From this point of view the objective is economic benefit but to get it it will be necessary to take political steps; from which it is only a small step to saying it is necessary to pay a political price. It should be noted that this is logically quite different from saying the Six have a political objective and unless we can whole-heartedly support it there can be no progress; it does look as though we are in the area of trying out different arguments for different audiences, but the differences contain the seeds of the future recrimination of which Sir R Barclay in the Foreign Office and Sir D Walker-Smith in the House of Commons warned.

The New Team Presses on Regardless: June to December 1960

Be that as it may, in the summer of 1960 the way was still clear to search for solutions to the apparent problem. But first it was necessary to change the Cabinet.

The translation of those fervent Europeans, Sandys, Soames and Heath to the crucial Departments of Commonwealth Relations, Agriculture and the Foreign Office respectively has been noted elsewhere [48] as a manoeuvre in the direction of Brussels.   Heath as Lord Privy Seal was given special responsibility for European negotiations, which were transferred from Maudling, President of the Board of Trade. Bought back to the Cabinet, though in the less significant Aviation post, was Thorneycroft, who had written in 1947 of European Union:-

The people must be led slowly and unconsciously into the abandonment of their traditional economic defences, not asked .....[49]

A curiosity of the reshuffle was the replacement of Walker-Smith at the Ministry of Health (outside the Cabinet) by Powell. Both of them later appeared as prominent opponents of the European accession towards which the government was then inching its way.

The search for solutions in the second half of 1960 had to be pursued with some delicacy. Ministers were uncertain in their minds and not wholly agreed among themselves[50], but the door had to be kept open and the Six convinced that the United Kingdom genuinely sought an association. The Foreign Secretary (then still Lloyd) felt able to acknowledge in the House of Commons on 25 July that the objective involved a political relationship, though he was cautious about the form it might take, whereas Maudling put some emphasis on pressing ahead with the development of the EFTA.

A meeting between Macmillan and Adenauer on 10 and 11 August gave the Economic Steering (Europe) Committee something to work on. The Germans had indicated that at that stage the best way to proceed would be by examination of the economic difficulties that stood in the way of any arrangement and seemed to be suggesting that an economic association, for which there was provision under the Treaty of Rome, might be appropriate. They were, of course, speaking only for themselves. This limitation, the Committee noted, did not fit in with the long-term foreign policy objective which it had earlier put forward, that of being in the inner Councils of the Six, but it was prepared to concentrate on the economic front for the time being. The Committee continued to hold the view that a political solution would involve an extensive re-negotiation of the Treaty of Rome; nevertheless they emphasised that it should still be sought and saw difficulties in the notion of a purely economic association[51] :-

Nor indeed could we refuse a purely economic association if satisfactory terms for it could be negotiated. We suggest, therefore, that we should fall in with the German approach and proceed to an examination of the economic difficulties and try to find an answer to them. An acceptable economic association might well lead in due course to a satisfactory political relationship with the Six. It is difficult to see how we could achieve any economic association unless it were accompanied in some degree by harmonisation of policies and common acceptance of appropriate institutions. Indeed it may well be that while the Germans may feel that an economic association is easier to negotiate than our entry into the Community, other members of the Community would be reluctant to negotiate on any basis other than that of accession with certain derogations to the Treaty of Rome. Both in the debate of 25th July by implication, and in the Bonn talks more explicitly, we indicated that we were prepared to consider accession to a modified Treaty of Rome if changes could be made to meet our difficulties. It seems important that in further discussion with the Germans we should be prepared to reaffirm our readiness to consider joining a modified Treaty of Rome which would provide appropriate safeguards for our basic interests and for EFTA.

The Committee went on:-

OUR BASIC INTERESTS

We must always bear in mind our relationship with the Commonwealth and its value as a stabilising factor in the free world.   In large part the political relationship with the Commonwealth depends upon the economic relationship, i.e. the Commonwealth preferential system, based on a wide measure of free entry into the United Kingdom.

Secondly, we must bear in mind the interests of U.K. agriculture and horticulture.   There are explicit Government pledges here.

Thirdly, we have to take account of the interests of - and our obligations to - our partners in EFTA.

Here it is sufficient to say that unless - which we do not believe - something like the old Free Trade Area proved practicable, concessions will have to be made, and some sacrifices accepted, in respect of free entry (with repercussions on our own preferences in Commonwealth markets), our autonomy in matters of commercial policy, agriculture and horticulture and - though this is less clear - to some extent by those members of EFTA who, for one reason or another, are unable to secure acceptable terms for joining an economic association with the Six.   What Ministers are asked to decide is:-

(a) the general basis on which we should be prepared to negotiate an economic association;

(b) the line which we should take with the Commonwealth in discussing these matters with them at the end of next month, and

(c) the line which we should take with the Germans (and possibly the French) in the immediate future as a follow up to the Bonn talks.

At a later stage decisions will be required on the ultimate sticking points on which we can on no account move, particularly as regards Commonwealth free entry, even if it means that the negotiations founder once more.

When the European Economic Association Committee of the Cabinet met on 30 August [52] to discuss the officials' paper they concentrated on economic rather than political aspects and were attracted by a proposal that had been put before them, with some diffidence, as follows:-

We have however considered another approach, which is set out below. There has not been time to examine it in detail and it is full of difficulties which are set out in the Annexes to this paper.

(i)   Common Tariff on Manufactured Goods

We think that we could accept the Common Tariff on manufactured goods without placing intolerable strains on the Commonwealth. As partial compensation for some Commonwealth countries, particularly India, Pakistan and Hong Kong, we should seek to secure from the Six some easement of their restrictions on imports from the low cost countries generally - though we must recognise that our own attitude to imports from Japan would be a complication. In the view of the Commonwealth Relations Office and the Colonial Office the imposition of the Common Tariff on cotton textiles would mean the ending of the present voluntary restrictions on exports to the United Kingdom of these goods from India, Pakistan and Hong Kong, and it would be impossible to replace them with other types of quantitative restriction. The Board of Trade, however, consider that this is a matter for decision when the time comes. In general, the fact that "reverse preferences" would be involved would accentuate the difficulties of the Commonwealth.

(ii)   Raw Materials

This would be somewhat easier and we that we could accept the Common Tariff on the whole range of raw materials with the exception of vegetable oils, woodpulp, aluminium, lead and zinc, for which it seems essential, for both Commonwealth and domestic reasons, to retain duty free entry. There has not been time to consider raw materials in detail, and others (e.g. those on which smaller colonial territories rely heavily) might have to be added to the list.

(iii)   Tropical Foodstuffs
It might be possible to get the Six to agree to a bargain in this field. Our tropical overseas territories (dependent or independent) and those of the Six produce in general the same kind of foodstuffs, and a broad bargain might be possible under which they would allow duty free entry to certain tropical foodstuffs from the Commonwealth and we would allow free entry to certain products of their overseas territories. Such a bargain should be beneficial to the Commonwealth countries concerned, taken as a whole, whether dependent or independent.

(iv)   Temperate Foodstuffs
It is here that the most difficult problems arise. It seems out of the question that we could accept the Common Tariff or the other protective devices of the Six for these products, even from foreign sources, because of the impact on the Commonwealth, the damage to our trading relations with third countries - in the case of the United States a breakdown of the Trade Agreement - and the consequences for food prices here. For these reasons we think we must in present circumstances make it a sticking point* to maintain free entry for all temperate foodstuffs from the Commonwealth and the existing free entry or the present low tariffs on such foodstuffs from third countries. We should also try to maintain the preference on tobacco, particularly for Rhodesia.

Agriculture and Horticulture
If, as we have suggested, we are going to insist, at any rate in present circumstances, on maintaining free entry for our imports of foodstuffs, it follows that we cannot accept a common agricultural policy of the Six involving in addition to other protective devices, high rates of duty for agricultural imports. We should, therefore, seek to secure separate treatment for agriculture - the Six would go their own way and we would go ours, maintaining our existing agricultural support policies intact. The fact that the Germans are at present dissatisfied with the agricultural policy proposed by the Commission may make them sympathetic to our approaching the matter on these lines.

---

* If, subsequently, acceptable arrangements for temperate foodstuffs from the Commonwealth and foreign countries could be made within the framework of managed markets it might be possible to modify our attitude.

On the other hand, we must recognise that any accommodation with the Six must have some agricultural content - something to satisfy the agricultural producers within the Community. We did not succeed in excluding agriculture entirely even from EFTA and it is unrealistic to suppose that we could do so in any arrangements with the Six. We might well be able to keep our basic agricultural policy intact, but a closer association with the Six would increase the apprehensions of our farmers about our ability to deal with larger imports from Europe. Moreover, given the importance to some members of the Six of trade with us in horticultural products, we are clear that an agreement would not be possible unless we made concessions in this field. But we have not yet considered in detail what these might be.

Commercial Policy

We should wish to retain independence in conducting commercial discussions and negotiations with the Commonwealth, not only because of the practical implications, but also because the cohesion of the Commonwealth depends in part upon the established practice of economic and commercial consultation. We could not, however, expect to retain independence insofar as we had accepted a common tariff; for the part of our trade covered by such a tariff, we should be bound to subscribe to the agreed common policy. Even the maintenance of independence in other fields might meet with objections from the Six, since discussions with, for example, Australia and New Zealand about our imports of foodstuffs from them would inevitably involve consideration of the preferences which the United Kingdom enjoys in those markets; and in bargaining to maintain those preferences we should be affecting the trade prospects of our partners in the customs union.

This, it will be seen, was a proposal for association based on the partial acceptance of a common tariff. While Ministers would have preferred to see the Six join the EFTA as a unit, they recognised that the Six were unlikely to accept an idea that so closely resembled the old free trade area. Indeed, it had originally been put forward by Macmillan in 1956 as part of the exploration of the free trade area [53]. Quite why they, or some among them, should then have toyed, as they did, with the optimistic assumption that the Six themselves might put forward such a notion is beyond fathoming.

The Committee concluded that:-

A settlement on the lines proposed would probably give us the economic advantages of full membership of the European Economic Community. We should be part of the European market for manufactured goods, and would attract investment at least equally with continental Europe. Although the association would have no manifest political content, political consequences would no doubt flow from it.

The general view of the Committee was that, although a solution under which the Six as a unit might join the European Free Trade Association was preferable, we should not rule out the possibility of a settlement on the lines discussed and that it would therefore be necessary to obtain the views of other Commonwealth Governments upon it. A message should be sent to them saying that the matter would be discussed at the meeting of Commonwealth Finance Ministers on 20th and 21st September. This message would have to be sufficiently explicit to stimulate a worthwhile reaction, but it would be dangerous to unfold anything like a considered plan or to allow the impression to gain ground that the United Kingdom was preparing to abandon Commonwealth free entry on a significant scale.

The suggestion that a message be sent to Commonwealth governments in advance of the September meeting of the Commonwealth Economic Consultative Council had formed part of the officials' memorandum. Although much emphasis continued to be put on the importance of the Commonwealth the United Kingdom was now contemplating the imposition of the common tariff on manufactures, a step which would clearly cause great resentment, particularly as it would involve reverse preferences in favour of Europe against the Commonwealth. In the event, this meeting, which took place on 20 and 21 September, passed off without too much difficulty. Selwyn Lloyd, by now Chancellor, reported to the Prime Minister [54] that any acceptance of a common tariff without extensive derogations providing for Commonwealth free entry would involve great difficulties for Commonwealth governments. There was a greater realisation of the long-term political importance of the United Kingdom's being closely associated with Europe and bringing the European economic division to an end. Commonwealth members recognised, said Sandys [55], that the question was one for the United Kingdom to settle itself but they avoided committing themselves to any specific sacrifices of their special position in the UK market. Canada and New Zealand were the most resentful.

The situation at this point in the process of European negotiation illustrates the difficulties of tracing continuous and consistent threads of reasoning in the whole affair. The Community had come into existence as a putative economic union for fundamental political purposes; the British, recognising an economic threat and an economic opportunity, had tried to bring about an essentially commercial agreement and had failed through unwillingness to subscribe to the political covenant; in contemplating this failure some Ministers and some officials, at any rate, had been induced to believe not merely that there were inevitable political consequences but potential political advantages in drawing closer to the Community. Yet here they were concentrating on a wholly economic proposal at the suggestion of a German Chancellor who was devoted not simply to the political but to the supranational element of the Community.

The advantages of the common tariff proposal at this point were twofold. Domestically, i.e. among the handful of people involved, it offered some hope both to those who would wish to go no further and those who felt desirable political consequences could be made to sprout from it, while externally it kept the door open by indicating that the United Kingdom was prepared to make some movement towards an agreement. But something extraordinary would have had to happen to induce the French to accept what was on offer here.

Heath was briefed by the Foreign Office in advance of the talks with the French at the beginning of October [56] that the French attitude was likely to be discouraging. He was advised to emphasise again that the economic division of Europe must endanger its political unity. The French no doubt felt that they were sitting pretty and could wait for the United Kingdom to run after them; to do so, however, would only be to make them stiffer on such matters as the harmonisation of tariffs, social obligations and agriculture. In the event, it was reported [57] that they had, perhaps, shown more interest in relations between the

Six and the Seven. The discussions had been concerned mainly
with political questions arising out of de Gaulle's ideas about co-
operation in Europe which he had first put forward in July.

What he had sought was a degree of political co-ordination
among the Six through a committee of Heads of Government, a
device which put to one side the supranational institutions of the
Communities, for which he had a less than scant regard [58]. The
Italians had reacted by suggesting that the United Kingdom
should be included and the Dutch shared their concern about the
creation of a body to form political policy without British
participation.

No progress was made with the French in October on
economic questions but they appeared to accept the importance
of British economic relations with the Commonwealth and were
content that possible solutions should be explored with the
Germans.

The talks at official level with the Germans, in Bonn at the
beginning of November and London at the end, were thus a
search for ideas to deal with trade difficulties rather than for a
broad framework which might lead to a settlement[59]. Some
sympathy was shown by the Germans to the proposition that
Commonwealth countries should continue to enjoy free entry to
the UK market [60], thus nourishing the idea that Great Britain
could have it both ways. They kept the French informed of what
was discussed but had to report back that the latter had had no
comment to make [61].

The search for a resolution *via* concentration on the
economic aspects of Six-Seven relations thus produced nothing
of consequence. For their part the British government was
uncertain how best to tackle the French. The Germans, Dutch
and Italians had shown themselves to be sympathetic to British
difficulties [62] but the obstacle was always going to be France.
One view from the Netherlands was that French opinion did not
now want to see the United Kingdom in Europe. Diplomatically
the problem was that to tackle France head-on risked a damaging
rebuff, while to seek solutions *via* the other members, such as
Germany, who might then put them to France risked both
ineffectiveness and accusations of duplicity. In any case the

German Chancellor, reported HM Ambassador to the Federal Republic, was unlikely to be willing to press the French [63]. And in all this it was essential not to fall out with the EFTA and the Commonwealth. The British continued to hope they might achieve large derogations from the Treaty for the benefit of the Commonwealth and UK agriculture [64] and discussions continued to be on an EFTA basis [65].

The government's position at this time was summarised by Sir Roderick Barclay for the benefit of Sir Harold Caccia, then HM Ambassador in Washington, as follows [66]:-

We have been deliberately concentrating on the purely economic aspects of the problem - how to maintain Commonwealth free entry and our own system for supporting agriculture if at the same time we accept, at least in part, a common or harmonised tariff for industrial goods and raw materials, and how to fit in the other members of E.F.T.A. in any such economic arrangements. We have left on one side for present the political and institutional problems involved.

Contacts with France were, of course, maintained. On 23 November Heath met the French Ambassador, who explained that his President's attitude was that if the United Kingdom wished to join the EEC so much the better. It would be welcome, provided it had the intention to help achieve the objectives of the Treaty of Rome and not frustrate them. It was not mentioned what hostages Britain would have to offer up to demonstrate its sincerity. Two days later the Ambassador was explaining that the Heads of Government meeting on 5 December (which did not take place then because of Adenauer's illness) would discuss the future of political and other relationships consequent upon the coming into being of the EEC. What was sought was a united approach to relations with the United States. De Gaulle's view was that if the United Kingdom wished to join the EEC it could be arranged, but he thought Britain would prefer some form of association [58].

Heath also pursued his explorations in conversations with Prof. Hallstein, President of the European Commission, in November and December. As the instrument of the Six governments the Commission would not be a party to any inter-governmental agreement, but it was in a position to help or hinder and, under the Treaty of Rome, could have been charged with the conduct of negotiations aimed at a purely trade agreement.

Heath's report on the first meeting [67] showed that the Herr Professor was prepared to be frank:-

> He would say that if another Power (say, Britain) wanted to join the Community it would not be sufficient for them to be willing to accept the principle of a common tariff (which was the essential hallmark of any "State" - and he regarded the E.E.C. as a potential "State"), and to be willing to join the institutions of the Six. It would also be necessary that the newcomer should accept the "principle of growth" which, he alleged, the Six countries had accepted, and should not come in with the object of "freezing" the institution at the point at which it had arrived.

Hallstein was also confidently prophetic, arguing that the Commission's objective of some form of Federal State would be sure to win in the end, even if the governments from time to time drew back. He did not see why the creation of two low-tariff clubs in Europe should lead to any division or split and was unimpressed by Heath's invocation of the menace of Communism and the emergence of the nationalistic and self-conscious world of Asia and Africa. At the second meeting he continued to emphasise political integration, though, interestingly, he ruled out military sovereignty for the new State. He envisaged a triple entente of Community, Commonwealth and United States, with their strategic co-operation ensured by NATO and their economic problems adjusted by OECD. This was not a prospect that enthralled Heath, who referred again to the political and strategic dangers and the economic disadvantages of the division. He went on to hint that the United Kingdom might have to reduce its defence contribution if it found itself subject to discrimination, an idea which was presumably making the rounds in government, for Gladwyn had mentioned it earlier in the year[68]. The British government was clearly not going to make any headway along this route [69] and, in Heath's view, Hallstein had formed the conclusion that we shall eventually have to come to terms with the Community and to make most of the concessions in doing so.

Sovereignty

One such concession, in the event of accession to the Treaty of Rome, would be sovereignty. Foreign Office officials had touched on this as early as August [70] with a mild disagreement whether in negotiation a strict attention to the provisions of the Treaty would be the only wise course, i.e. to assume a federalist, supranational outcome, or whether that would be a sterile and unrewarding approach. By December it was felt to be needful to have an authoritative view of the Treaty's provisions and Heath, who was of the opinion that we were over-impressed with the extent of supranationality in the Treaty, wrote, with the Prime Minister's agreement, to Kilmuir (Lord Chancellor) to seek such a view. Because of the importance of this aspect in the later debate, as well as at the time, his reply is given in full [71]:-

My dear Ted

You wrote to me on the 30th November about the constitutional implications of our becoming a party to the Treaty of Rome. I have now had an opportunity of considering what you say in your letter and have studied the memoranda you sent me. I agree with you that there are important constitutional issues involved.

I have no doubt that if we do sign the Treaty, we shall suffer some loss of sovereignty, but before attempting to define or evaluate that loss I wish to make one general observation. At the end of the day, the issue whether or not to join the European Economic Community must be decided on broad political grounds and if it appears from what follows in this letter that I find the constitutional objections serious that does not mean that I consider them conclusive. I do, however, think it important that we should appreciate clearly from the outset exactly what, from the constitutional point of view, is involved if we sign the Treaty, and it is with that consideration in mind that I have addressed myself to the questions you have raised.

Adherence to the Treaty of Rome would, in my opinion, affect our sovereignty in three ways:-

(a) Parliament would be required to surrender some of its functions to the organs of the Community;

(b) The Crown would be called on to transfer part of its treaty-making power to those organs;

(c) Our courts of law would sacrifice some degree of independence by becoming subordinate in certain respects to the European Court of Justice.

(a) The position of Parliament

It is clear from the memorandum prepared by your Legal Advisers that the Council of Ministers could eventually (after the system of qualified majority voting had come into force) make regulations which would be binding on us even against our wishes, and which would in fact become for us part of the law of the land. There are two ways in which this requirement of the Treaty could in practice be implemented:-

(1) Parliament could legislate *ad hoc* on each occasion that the Council make regulations requiring action by us. The difficulty would be that, since Parliament can bind neither itself nor its successors, we could only comply with our obligations under the Treaty if Parliament abandoned its right of passing independent judgment on the legislative proposals put before it. A parallel is the constitutional convention whereby Parliament passes British North America Bills without question at the request of the Parliament of Canada; in this respect Parliament here has in substance, if not in form, abdicated its sovereign position, and it would have *pro tanto*, to do the same for the Community.

(2) It would in theory be possible for Parliament to enact at the outset legislation which would give automatic force of law to any existing or future regulations made by the appropriate organs of the Community. For Parliament to do this would go far beyond the most extensive delegation of powers, even in wartime, that we have ever experienced and I do not think there is any likelihood of this being acceptable to the House of Commons.

Whichever course were adopted, Parliament would retain in theory the liberty to repeal the relevant Act or Acts, but I would agree with you that we must act on the assumption that entry into the Community would be irrevocable; we should have therefore to accept a position where Parliament had no more power to repeal its own enactments than it has in practice to abrogate the Statute of Westminster. In short, Parliament would have to transfer to the Council, or other appropriate organ of the Community, its substantive powers of legislating over the whole of a very important field.

(b) Treaty-making Powers

The proposition that every treaty entered into by the United Kingdom does to some extent fetter our freedom of action is plainly true. Some treaties such as GATT and O.E.E.C., restrict severely our liberty to make agreements with third parties and I should not regard it as detrimental to our sovereignty that, by signing the Treaty of Rome, we undertook not to make tariff or trade agreements without the Council's approval. But to transfer to the Council or the Commission the power to make such treaties on our behalf, and even against our will, is an entirely different proposition. There seems to me to be a clear distinction between the exercise of sovereignty involved in the conscious acceptance by us of obligations under our treaty-making powers and the total or partial surrender of sovereignty involved in our cession of these powers to some other body. To confer a sovereign state's treaty-making powers on an international organisation is the first step on the road which leads by way of confederation to the fully federal state. I do not suggest that what is involved would necessarily carry us very far in this direction, but it would be a most significant step and one for which there is no precedent in our case. Moreover, a further surrender of Parliamentary supremacy would necessarily be involved: as you know, although the treaty-making power is vested in the Crown, Parliamentary sanction is required for any treaty which involves a change in the law or the imposition of taxation (to take only two examples), and we cannot ratify such a treaty unless Parliament consents. But if binding treaties are to be entered into on our behalf, Parliament must surrender this function and either resign itself to becoming a rubber stamp or give the Community, in effect, the power to amend our domestic laws.

(c) Independence of the Courts

There is no precedent for our final appellate tribunal being required to refer questions of law (even in a limited field) to another court and - as I assume to be the implication of "refer"- to accept that court's decision. You will remember that when a similar proposal was considered in connection with the Council of Europe we felt strong objection to it. I have no doubt that the whole of the legal profession in this country would share my dislike for such a proposal which must inevitably detract from the independence and authority of our courts.

Of these three objections, the first two are by far the more important. I must emphasise that in my view the surrenders of sovereignty involved are serious ones and I think that, as a matter of practical politics, it will not be easy to persuade Parliament or the public to accept them. I am sure that it would be a great mistake to under-estimate the force of the objections to them. But these objections ought to be brought out into the open now because, if we attempt to gloss over them at this stage, those who are opposed to the whole idea of our joining the Community will certainly seize on them with more damaging effect later on. Having said this, I would emphasise once again that, although these constitutional considerations must be given their full weight when we come to balance the arguments on either side, I do not for one

moment wish to convey the impression that they must necessarily
tip the scale. In the long run we shall have to decide whether
economic factors require us to make some sacrifices of sovereignty:
my concern is to ensure that we should see exactly what it is that
we are being called on to sacrifice, and how serious our loss would
be.
Yours ever,
David

It is, perhaps, unfortunate that the term 'sovereignty' was
the one deployed in this matter though, as it was first used among
the signatories of the Treaty of Rome, it would have been
difficult to avoid it. It is not a concept easy to grasp, particularly
in a country which can speak of Parliamentary as well as national
sovereignty. With the precedent of the Indian Empire in mind it
might have been better to speak of the transfer of power, but at
least the matter is clear when it is set out as fully as in this letter.
What is apparent is that accession to the Treaty of Rome involved
an unparalleled step for the United Kingdom; to find even a loose
comparison one would have to go back nearly three hundred
years to the Act of Union itself and the transfer of Scottish
parliamentary power to Westminster.

The New American Administration: January 1961
The American elections at the end of 1960 replaced a
Republican with a Democratic president, John Kennedy. Given
the importance they had previously attached to the attitude of the
United States government to the Six-Seven problem, the British
government was naturally concerned to establish what policy the
new administration was likely to follow in the matter. The
Foreign Office accordingly enquired of HM Ambassador in
Washington whether the US government might now be more
supportive of the British case and whether anything could
usefully be done to explain it to them. Caccia welcomed the idea
of a memorandum and went on [72]:-

If we wish to make our policy appear as acceptable as possible
to the Americans we should naturally emphasise two points: first,
that it is essential to bring the two European economic groups
together if the Western world is to present a properly organized and
united front in the cold war; secondly, that our aim is no exclusive

European bloc; on the contrary, we would like to move as rapidly as we can towards an economic system embracing the North American countries as well as the rest of Europe.

A draft was accordingly prepared and Macmillan, while not entirely convinced of its value in advance of his meeting with the new President, consented to it with a few amendments. The first part of the document was historical, but the second shows the British government's view of the problem in January 1961 and how it wished the American government to perceive it [73]:-

But it remains clear that formal negotiations cannot be undertaken with any hope of success unless all the governments concerned are convinced of the political need to bring the existing economic division of Western Europe to an end. In particular, no substantial progress can be made unless President de Gaulle and the French Government can be persuaded that a wider arrangement is not only in the wider political interests of the Free World, but can also be achieved without damage to the essential interests of France and the integrity of the European Economic Community.

The Present Situation

Unfortunately a wider arrangement is not yet in prospect. Meanwhile, the potential dangers arising from the division between the Six and the rest of Western Europe are becoming clear. The Six are becoming accustomed to the idea of consultation and common action amongst themselves and this must be expected to spread to other than economic matters. Although such co-operation could no doubt be valuable, in the United Kingdom view the overriding consideration should be the widest possible degree of unity in the Free World as a whole and in the Atlantic Alliance in particular. In the economic field tariffs among the Six have been reduced by 30% and the first step towards the establishment of the Common External Tariff, involving increases in the tariffs of the Federal Republic of Germany, the Netherlands, Belgium and Luxembourg on imports from countries outside the Community, has now been taken. This problem of discrimination is serious for many European countries. Most EFTA countries are highly dependent on exports: for instance, exports expressed as a proportion of national income amount to 21% in Switzerland. Moreover some EFTA countries send a very large proportion of their exports to EEC countries, in the case of Austria 49%. Investment planning is also obliged to take account of the existence of two separate economic groups leading to wasteful duplication of investment.

The present economic division between the Six and the other countries of Western Europe is unfortunately reflected in Africa. An advantage of a wider arrangement would be that it would inevitably involve the ending of discrimination by Western European countries as between the Associated Overseas Territories of the Six and Commonwealth Territories.

Possible Solutions

So far as its economic aspects are concerned a first requirement of any wider arrangement is that it should be acceptable to the GATT Contracting Parties. Since a free trade area solution appears to be ruled out the arrangement will have to take the form of a custom union or of a compromise between that and a free trade area. It will be a fundamental aim of the United Kingdom to ensure that any wider arrangement is on a liberal basis, thus contributing to an expansion of world trade and enabling the present close relationship between Western Europe and other countries of the Atlantic Community to be developed.   It is the purpose of the informal exchanges which have already taken place or are now in prospect to find the basis for an economic solution on these lines.

At the same time the United Kingdom Government consider, and this has been made clear in the Anglo-German talks and elsewhere, that political factors will also have to be taken into account in any wider arrangement, and that any satisfactory arrangement must involve a political just as much as an economic relationship. No doubt some institutions will be necessary; but the nature of these, and the extent to which different countries should be involved, cannot be prescribed at this stage.

Difficulties

The United Kingdom objective, therefore, is to find a wider arrangement which will promote the closest possible unity between Western European countries without damaging the integrity of the EEC. The United Kingdom must, however, take into account the impact of any such arrangement on their relations with the Commonwealth, whose existence is of great value to the Free World. Trade is of special importance amongst the many factors holding the Commonwealth together, and an important element in Commonwealth trade is the system of free entry or tariff preference for Commonwealth goods entering the United Kingdom.   Any wider arrangement which damaged the essential economic interests of Commonwealth countries would weaken the structure of the Commonwealth as a whole. As an illustration of the importance of this problem it may be mentioned that, if any wider arrangement led to the adoption by the United Kingdom of the Common

External Tariff of the EEC without any modification or special arrangements, the United Kingdom would be obliged, not only to abandon free entry for wheat, but to apply a tariff of 20% against the Commonwealth as well as against the United States and other countries. The United Kingdom must also have in mind the differences between the system of agricultural support in force in the United Kingdom and that envisaged in the common agricultural policy now under discussion by the Six. Finally, any arrangement would have to take account of the interests of the United Kingdom's EFTA partners.

It should be noted that while the document is necessarily guarded on a number of important matters, such as UK agriculture and political institutions, it refrained from insisting on a requirement to maintain Commonwealth free entry.

Attitude of France and others: January to March 1961

It was common form in Whitehall at this time that no progress could be expected with the French unless de Gaulle could be induced into a favourable attitude; French officials would agree to nothing that they had not been instructed to accept by the General. Much was at stake, therefore, when Macmillan met de Gaulle at Rambouillet at the end of January 1961[74]. De Gaulle said that while he would like to reach an arrangement in Europe there were great difficulties at the present time. The United Kingdom rightly did not want to harm the Commonwealth and he could see the problem posed by agriculture. He himself wanted the Common Market for economic reasons, to develop French industry and draw it out of the protectionist shell, but also to hold Germany. The idea of his political initiative was not to upset the United Kingdom and he hoped that it and France could still stay together in world affairs. Any political arrangement would not be directed against the United Kingdom, whose island position and Commonwealth naturally made her look outwards across the oceans. Macmillan expressed the view that it was possible to make a good working arrangement between the Six, the United Kingdom and as many of the EFTA as possible. It was an essential question for the unity of the West because unless it was solved political divisions would inevitably follow economic rivalry. The object of the Western powers should be to have as large a market as possible. Contrary to the view he had expressed at an earlier meeting between the pair about a mere commercial treaty de Gaulle now said he did not see how an arrangement could be made between the Six and the Seven.

Macmillan responded that the United Kingdom felt there might be a method by which they could associate themselves with the Six and accept a common external tariff subject to certain exceptions to allow for the import of Commonwealth raw materials and temperate foodstuffs. It would be necessary to exclude Commonwealth industrial goods from the free area. Thus he made the first overt dent in the principle of Commonwealth free entry.

Recognising the difficulties that it would cause for particular Commonwealth countries he went on to argue that such an arrangement could only be carried forward as part of a large concept for the re-organisation of the West, but de Gaulle continued to argue that he could not see how it was possible for the Commonwealth and the Six to make an economic community without destroying one or the other. When the Common Market had begun he had opposed it because he had thought a Federation was involved, but he had later found a confederation, not integration, was possible. What he did not understand was whether the United Kingdom was afraid of the Six for economic or political reasons. Macmillan replied that from the beginning many British politicians had favoured the European movement but had thought the Common Market would lead to a federation which the United Kingdom would not like. With the advent of de Gaulle it had become clear that federation was not contemplated, only confederation. The United Kingdom was worried about the Six for both political and economic reasons. It threatened economic harm and it made sense to have as large a market as possible so as to have something as big as the United States. Under the present system the United Kingdom might be able to join the various institutions as they evolved. Politically this would still mean France and the United Kingdom could be members of a United Europe and also have together a role in the world outside. De Gaulle entirely agreed that one day, in perhaps three years, there would be great advantage in having one economic system for Europe but he doubted if it was yet possible.

His experts were daunted at the prospect of another negotiation but he agreed that they might take another look at the difficulties in the way of an accommodation between the Six and the Seven. He noted, however, that there were already difficulties about agriculture within the Six.

On the next day de Gaulle said that he saw that the United Kingdom was less disturbed by the idea of the Common Market than she had been. It seemed to him that she was now prepared to take the same path and join something in Europe. He saw that the United Kingdom would nevertheless wish to have close relations with the United States - it was essential - but it might not in the future always be necessary to follow exactly in the wake of America. How long would it be possible for the United Kingdom to pursue both an American and a European policy simultaneously?

These talks have deserved a relatively full account because they contain the first overt, if hesitant, indication that Britain might actually seek to join the Six and might be prepared to pay the price of a common tariff with all that such a step might mean for Commonwealth preference and Commonwealth cohesion. To find de Gaulle playing the Commonwealth card has some amusement value, but his reference to the United States was a serious pointer to a line of thinking on the Continent that would persist. Macmillan may be seen to be probing for some concept that might chime with the Gaullist vision, but the comfort that the two of them found in confederation might have been dissolved had they been inclined to a closer analysis. De Gaulle's final suggestion that the Common Market might not always be limited to the present Six but might expand to other countries in the world as well as the Seven may be either a counter-probe or a *jeu d'esprit*. With these two elderly fencers one should not assume that they always meant what they said or believed that the other did, but their conversations may provide clues for the interpretation of other moves in the game.

Heath's Memorandum - Technical Grounds

On his return Macmillan asked the Cabinet Secretary to draft a paper for the Cabinet [75]. There was a concern that matters should not be taken too far beyond what had been agreed by political colleagues, but the proposal did not find favour with Heath, who submitted a memorandum on 7 February 1961, regarding his conversations with members of the Six and outlining the tactics to be pursued [76]. He began:-

The talks between our own and German officials over the past three months have served four purposes:

(a) They have enabled us to explore thoroughly what the Germans think would be for them and, as far as they could judge, for their partners a reasonable basis of negotiation in the field of trade.

(b) They have given us the opportunity of educating the Germans patiently in the realities of our own problems.

(c) They have provided us with a basis of comparison from which to argue with the other members of the Six.

(d) As a result of the Franco-German talks, they have given us a natural lead into direct talks with the French. This has fortunately coincided with your agreement with General de Gaulle to hold such talks.

Similar talks with Italian officials last week served the same exploratory and educational purposes over a more limited field. The Italians wish to resume these discussions at the end of March.

The discussions have been on the basis authorised by the EQ Committee of the Cabinet the main features of which are:

(a) Discussions to be without commitment.

(b) Agriculture to be excluded.

(c) Commonwealth free entry to be maintained in full.

(d) Consideration to be given to the adoption of the common tariff of the Six on industrial goods outside (c) above.

(e) Institutions to await the formulation of the economic arrangement.

(f) Any arrangement to make provision for our EFTA partners.

Noting that willingness to accept a common external tariff over part of UK imports represented a change in the British position and one which had helped the discussions forward, he expressed the hope that progress would be made in talks with the French, in the sense of testing their position. He added:-

I believe the conditional offer of a limited common tariff is sufficient evidence of our good intentions; we must now make the utmost use of it. Unless we are prepared to change our agricultural support policy, or accept the institutions of the Treaty of Rome, this is the only means of negotiation we have. The more we extend it the more we shall please the Six, but the more we shall come into conflict with the Commonwealth and EFTA.

But his view on the substance was:-

On present form it is difficult to visualise a settlement being reached on the terms in which we are thinking - it will be necessary to bring our colleagues face to face with the realities of the European situation. We may then have to decide either to abandon for some years the search for a satisfactory permanent arrangement between the two economic groupings, or to take a bold step towards a closer economic relationship with Europe. I do not think it is possible to know whether this is necessary until after the Anglo-French talks, nor indeed until after you have met President Kennedy: I would therefore prefer not to raise these matters now.

and he opposed the idea of involving Cabinet colleagues at this stage:-

You mentioned to me that you now intend to bring this before the Cabinet and I have been shown the first draft of the Cabinet paper. I must confess I view this in its present form with serious misgivings.

It would, I am sure, be a mistake to raise before the Anglo-French talks the fundamental questions of foreign policy, national sovereignty and the problem of association with or membership of the Common Market with which the paper begins. It is reminiscent of the July 1960 questionnaire and will, I fear, lead to a resurgence of opposition on the grounds of principle rather than of practice. The detailed technical exposition of the sort of solution we would wish to see will provide much room for argument as to what is, or is not, desirable or possible.

Heath's own expectation of the Anglo-French talks might have led him to believe that the Cabinet could not fail to be faced with these fundamental questions, but as long as it could be suggested that it might not be necessary he preferred to avoid their discussion. If it could be forestalled by getting onto detailed technical ground so much the better.

What the untimely draft paper had said was that agreement should be sought while de Gaulle and Adenauer remained in power. The United Kingdom would have to take a political initiative lest vested interests should have time to develop within the Six. If economic stagnation then set in there it would be more difficult to remove trade barriers and a European Third Force might develop, with closer political consultation. In that event the United States might come to take more account of them than of the United Kingdom. The paper remarked on the tendency for the Community to develop on lines of confederation rather than as a federal state, but added that, even so, to join the Six would involve a greater surrender of our national sovereignty than we had hitherto contemplated. If we were able to get a satisfactory economic settlement and enter the proposed political secretariat - as the Dutch had suggested - it would give as much of what we needed. Political consultations among the Six could do great damage to NATO. Those political consultations were going to take place but if we were to join them we could hope to steer in a direction that would not undermine the alliance.

The United Kingdom could either join the Six, with derogations from the Treaty of Rome, or offer to associate with it. The first would meet UK foreign policy objectives and would be more likely to appeal to de Gaulle. But the Germans had been thinking of an association between the EFTA and the EEC and such an arrangement would find more favour both with the EFTA and with the Commonwealth.

The problem was still the common tariff on manufactures, raw materials, tropical products and temperate foodstuffs. It seemed out of the question that we could accept a common tariff or the other protective devices of the Six for temperate foodstuffs, even from non-Commonwealth sources, because of the impact on the Commonwealth, damage to trading relations with third countries and the consequences on food prices. Temperate foodstuffs would therefore have to be excluded, and we could not then accept the common agriculture policy. We would wish to retain independence in conducting commercial discussions and negotiations with the Commonwealth because of the practical implications and continued cohesion. But that independence would be restricted by acceptance of the common tariff.

It is interesting to see how this line of argument fleshed out the Gaullist observation that the Community and the Commonwealth could not be combined. Heath might well fear that if such a document was put to the Cabinet it might either throw the whole thing out on grounds of principle or settle on conditions that would be impossible to achieve with the French.

Macmillan continued to feel a need for some Ministerial backing and a meeting was accordingly arranged, which was limited to Lloyd, Home and Heath. It took place on 13 February and it was agreed to try to get French representatives to co-operate in working out what arrangements might be appropriate for a settlement if the two governments decided a settlement should be sought. This diplomatic pavane was little more than an ineffective acknowledgement of de Gaulle's lukewarmness towards the expert discussions.

Chancellor Adenauer was in London for talks at the end of February [77]. He informed Macmillan that at his pre-meeting with de Gaulle, in advance of the political discussion which had been postponed from the previous December, he had deprecated the idea of a political secretariat and the General had agreed with him. The meeting itself of the Six had gone badly. In particular, Dr. Luns, the Netherlands Prime Minister, had protested vigorously at the exclusion of Britain from the talks. Adenauer assured Macmillan, in much the same terms as had de Gaulle, that these talks were not directed against Britain; for his part Macmillan asserted Britain's wish to be present.

Sir Frank Lee reported on the informal talks with German, French and Italian officials to the Economic Association Committee on 14 March. For this meeting of the Committee Macmillan had been briefed [78] that the main doubt which must arise was whether any course could be successful, given the present French attitude. All along the French had emphasised as important those points on which they judged the United Kingdom was not prepared to negotiate at the time. Once it was acceptance of the common tariff which was said to be essential. Now that we indicated willingness to consider a common tariff it was significant that the French were saying they would like to discuss agriculture and the miscellaneous provisions of the Treaty - another range of problems on which they expected we should have difficulties. In fact recent reports confirmed the view that the French were opposed to UK membership of the Six, or an association with the Six, because it would weaken French leadership within the Common Market on which her international position now largely depended.

If so, there had to be the greatest doubt whether any concessions we were prepared to consider in the economic field would lead the French to agree to UK association with the Six. The position still seemed to be that they could be moved only in the context of some major political initiative.

The Prime Minister was advised that if Ministers agreed that officials should undertake the proposed study it would be desirable for this to be reported to Cabinet. Otherwise Ministers not members of the Committee might hear of the study for the first time from their officials and the whole purpose of the study might be misunderstood.

Sir Frank Lee's report [79] was very much in line with Heath's prediction in his minute of the previous month.

SIR FRANK LEE said that the informal talks with the Germans and Italians had been reasonably encouraging but that the United Kingdom and French positions were still very far apart. M. Wormser, the chief French representative in the talks, had however said that the situation would be radically changed if the United Kingdom were willing to accede to the Treaty of Rome. The United Kingdom was already committed to a further round of official talks with the French, Germans and Italians, and these were unlikely to be completed before the middle of May. But it was doubtful whether the talks would have any worthwhile result if we continued to adhere to our present line of retaining free entry for all Commonwealth imports into the United Kingdom together with a separate United Kingdom market for agricultural products.

The French could, if it suited them, keep the talks going for a long time without making any effective progress, and in the meantime the Six might reach decisions of great concern to the United Kingdom without our having had any opportunity of influencing what those decisions should be. It would however be dangerous to indicate in these informal talks that we were willing to make concessions since they would be taken by the French as the point of departure for further concessions in any subsequent negotiations.

Lee therefore suggested that officials be authorised to study the implications of indicating willingness to sign the Treaty of Rome. It will be recalled that some officials had formed the views during 1960 that this was the only course that offered any hope of progress and Lord Gladwyn had continued to urge it on the Foreign Secretary [80]. Given the shift in attitude that had been

displayed by the Prime Minister at Rambouillet   and   the
blocking   of the rather more restrained paper that had been
prepared for the Cabinet, it is probable at the least that Lee was
aware of high-level political support for this radical line.
Certainly the Prime Minister, who was not at this meeting, had
been briefed about the proposed study.

Agriculture and the Commonwealth

Members of the Committee, on the other hand, continued to
stress the importance of making satisfactory arrangements for
agriculture and Commonwealth trade; they recalled that at the
Commonwealth Economic Consultative Council the United
Kingdom had said that Commonwealth free entry would be
maintained even if a common tariff was adopted. They did not
agree, therefore, to the inclusion of agriculture and
Commonwealth trade in the study, although it was accepted that a
settlement with the Community was very likely to require some
modification in the government's policies in these areas. There
was no mention of informing the full Cabinet.

The outcome thus presaged, though not yet adopted, was a
full reversal. Instead of refusing to accede to the Treaty of Rome
because of the Commonwealth and UK agriculture the
government was now preparing to contemplate accession if
suitable special arrangements could be found. This was a crucial
change of direction but one for which the ground had been
prepared many months earlier and signalled by the Cabinet
changes. First a European free trade area and then an association
between the EFTA and the EEC had been sought to remove the
threat of growing trade barriers within Europe and at every turn
the road had been blocked by France. De Gaulle himself had
more than once suggested British membership as a solution, as
has already been seen, but one must suppose that it was being put
forward by his representative as a suggestion that expected a
negative answer.

On 17 March there was a meeting, chaired by Lloyd, with
the Prime Ministers of Australia and New Zealand and the
Finance Minister of Ceylon [78]. Heath reported on the position in
rather general terms and said he found the current atmosphere

with the Six rather more favourable to agreement, while US sympathies were no longer wholly on the side of the Six. In answer to Holyoake he affirmed that free entry of agricultural products from the Commonwealth should be maintained. Menzies remarked that any arrangement for settlement between the Six and the Seven would have an important effect on the Commonwealth. He felt that discussions between Australia and the United Kingdom should be held before the latter entered into any agreement in principle or was even partly committed. The Commonwealth should not be put in the position of having to press the United Kingdom to withdraw. The timetable should allow for these discussions before negotiations with the Six began, since afterwards it would be too late. To which Lloyd responded by promising categorically that before the beginning of actual negotiations there would be full consultation with Commonwealth governments.

Canada was not represented here but its government was known to be hostile, as explained in a Commonwealth Relations Office briefing of 29 March [78]. They feared heavy damage to their exports to the United Kingdom and were opposed on doctrinal grounds to the creation of a discriminatory regional bloc. They felt it would be better to work with the United States in the GATT to reduce the tariffs of the Six. They, like others, questioned whether the division represented by two trading groups were so deep as at one time might have been feared and whether the gulf was so wide as to endanger the stability of Europe and the strength of the free world.

Calling in the New World: February to May 1961

It has been seen that the attitude of the new American administration was a matter of some concern to the British government. Its predecessor had been felt to be unhelpful, attached as it was to the development of the Six, and if Britain was to find some accommodation in Europe it would, at the very least, need the benevolent neutrality of the US government and, if possible, their active support [81]. Sir Frank Lee, who was in Washington in February, reported [82] that the tenor of his talks, which were principally on other subjects, were indicative of a good practical relationship and mutual support. He found, however, that the position on the two European trading groups was the same as that of the previous administration. This view was somewhat at odds with a briefing prepared for the Prime Minister from January onwards by the Cabinet Office and departments. It said at one point [83]:-

> The attitude of the new Administration in the United States will be important. Mr. Kennedy may lose patience with the division between the Six and the Seven and throw his weight into finding a solution in the interests of Western unity. There are two points here:
>
> (i) There are signs that some of Mr. Kennedy's new advisors may see greater political advantages in a wider European association, including the United Kingdom, and be less inclined than the Eisenhower Administration to back the Six. But, if we made no move ourselves and relied on the United States to influence the Six in our favour, the latter might be less likely to respond.
>
> (ii) An accommodation between the Six and the Seven must lead to increased discrimination against exports from the United States, and this will be particularly unwelcome to the Americans at a time when they are concerned about their balance of payments. If we wish to win their support, we must persuade them to subordinate their economic to their political interests. From this point of view the lower the tariffs of the European group, the better.

What it was referring to was the development of an Atlantic Community based on a much greater degree of free trade in Europe and North America, which an American as well-placed as Dean Acheson had been reported as believing could come about quite rapidly. He was said to feel that if Congress was handled sensibly and shrewdly there was no reason why the United States could not accept sufficient surrender of sovereign rights to make some such scheme workable. Such a concept had its obvious attractions for the British, and it was worked out in some detail, particularly with regard to its effect on other countries and world trading relationships generally. As the briefing paper said:-

> For the United Kingdom, with its world-wide trading and political interests, could not afford to throw in its lot with an inward-looking European association, regardless of those wider interests and especially its close relations with the Commonwealth and the United States. Our special role is to act as a bridge between

Europe and North America. We have a special interest in fostering and developing the concept of an Atlantic Community.

Other reports [78] suggested that while the new administration was thinking seriously about an Atlantic Community they did not really want an accommodation between the Six and the Seven lest it prejudice the wider project. When Heath and Sir Frank Lee met George Ball (Under Secretary of State for Economic Affairs) on 30 March they were told that the kind of solution then envisaged by HMG would not be acceptable to the United States. The latter would like to see the United Kingdom join the Community. There might have to be derogations, which would have to be considered on their merits. Lee commented that UK public opinion had developed and it was now possible to go a long way towards the Community. There was a strong body of opinion which held that any weakening of Commonwealth links would be more than balanced by the advantages of membership or close association. In reply to Ball's comment that in the American view the ultimate goal of the Community was some form of federation Lee said that he thought the move towards federation might have been checked for a while but it would continue. Ball thought France would not be opposed if British derogations were not too extensive. Association would erode the political content of the Community.

It was not, of course, supposed that a comment by Dean Acheson constituted US policy, but it was thought that if the idea of an Atlantic Community could be introduced carefully to Kennedy it might win his support. But it should not be allowed to hold up the development of European economic unity.

The meeting between President and Prime Minister took place in Washington in early April [83]. When Kennedy referred to the problem of Sixes and Sevens Macmillan responded with the Atlantic concept, saying that his own dream was that the Six and the Seven should form part of a wider Atlantic Union. Otherwise the Six could develop into a Third Force. The United Kingdom and some, at any rate, of the Seven had to find some form of association with the Six. De Gaulle was the obstacle now but the leadership would later pass to Germany and it was therefore to the advantage of the Western world to associate the United

Kingdom and the Six; the United Kingdom could provide both a stabilising element and a bridge to the United States and for those reasons he sought United States support. While Kennedy expressed some agreement with these ideas he showed no inclination to develop them. Home remarked at this point that Britain had been slow to come to the conclusion that it should join the Six because of its desire not to harm the interests of the Commonwealth countries, but it was now beginning to see how to deal with the problem without undue detriment to itself and members of the Commonwealth. Ball was more forthcoming than his President. He said that the United States saw the political advantages of a united Europe, which was why the creation of the EFTA had caused it concern. A purely economic association between the Six and the Seven would weaken the political value and potential of the Six and make the commercial problems more difficult for the United States. If the United Kingdom became a member of the EEC she would provide an element of stability and confirm even more closely the special relationship of confidence between the US and UK governments.

The position taken by the United States was confirmed in an aide-mémoire [84] and a letter from Kennedy to Macmillan on 22 May [85]. The President noted the growing political coherence in Western Europe as the only way to a stable solution to the place of Germany. He was prepared to face some economic disadvantage for the United States if the United Kingdom went into the EEC. But neither of these documents picked up the idea of an Atlantic free trade area or Community.

Macmillan thus got what he had sought from Washington, a degree of support for the more adventurous solution to which he had been moving, though the US administration was careful to make it clear that it did not wish to appear to gang up with the United Kingdom in relation to the Six. Despite Ball's attitude it could not be said that the Administration was actively pressing Britain towards the EEC - indeed the British were anxious beforehand that they might not receive any support in Washington and were ready to settle for benevolent neutrality - except insofar as American hostility towards a purely economic association which would raise further barriers to imports from the

United States without 'contributing to the cohesion of Europe and the Western world' can be regarded as a negative impulse.

The US government also made clear its opposition to substantial derogations from the principles of the Treaty of Rome to accommodate third countries, i.e. the continuation in some form of Commonwealth preference, towards which the Americans felt an atavistic hostility. It was not any more sympathetic to the EFTA, which they regarded as a problem the British had created for themselves, and a minor furore was caused by some of Ball's comments in his aide-mémoire. But it would appear from these documents that the Americans would have been content with the *status quo* and it was only later that they sought positively to have the United Kingdom included in the EEC. They were never impressed by the British government's arguments about the perils of a split between the Six and the Seven but came away from the talks with the clear, and probably correct, impression that Britain had actually resolved to apply.

The Cabinet Contemplates Accession: April to June 1961

Macmillan's report to the Cabinet towards the end of April on this aspect of the talks, however, seems to have come as something of a surprise to them, although he was more guarded there than he had apparently been with the Americans, especially when the Cabinet was compelled to take a second bite at its task. It had been envisaged at the Ministerial Meeting of 13 February that the Cabinet would consider policy towards Europe on a substantive basis before the Washington talks, but this had not come about. On this occasion it was not possible to conclude the discussion at the regular Cabinet meeting and a further special session had to be arranged. The full texts appear in Appendix D.

The discussion was begun in the broadest political terms of Cold War rivalry and the need to take precautions against domination in Western Europe. To meet these goals, it was suggested, it might be necessary to pay an economic price, though there were also those Ministers who saw it as a matter of taking political action to secure an economic objective. These differences of emphasis would not matter as long as Cabinet members could agree that an application should be made, but it was not to be as easy as that.   Ministers rehearsed the Commonwealth and agricultural difficulties, together with those of surrendering sovereignty. Butler, in particular, reminded them that they had previously felt the difficulties were insuperable. What struck some of them most forcibly was the problem of presentation, of how to carry people and Parliament with them if it was decided to make the dramatic change towards which Macmillan was evidently steering them. It is not easy to see why he thought he could carry his colleagues with him simply on the basis of a favourable report from his discussions in Washington, but there was no difficulty for him in simply ignoring a suggestion to seek improved trading arrangements with Canada.

It is apparent that there was still a considerable degree of disquiet. Heath proposed that discussions with the French should be continued, in which the British government could be more forthcoming than it had been hitherto, but without indicating willingness to accede to the Treaty, for purely tactical reasons. His suggestion was in line with the disclaimer Macmillan felt obliged to make, that there was no need for an immediate decision. The Prime Minister continued to emphasize the global context of the matter and expressed the hope that Kennedy might be able to move de Gaulle into a more receptive attitude. On that condition the Cabinet was induced to agree to further negotiations looking to some form of association.

What the Cabinet was now contemplating, however decked out as a wider political and economic association, was accession to the Treaty of Rome. The Commonwealth, UK agriculture, sovereignty, which had previously been markers defining the country's course were now being shifted into the position of obstacles that needed to be overcome. These were the narrow technical grounds that Heath preferred; the envisaged statement showing the balance of advantage and disadvantage was never provided, presumably because the Government was driven to submit its application without being able to determine beforehand whether satisfactory terms were likely to be negotiable, or even whether the application would be genuinely welcomed. This was to deprive it of the room for manoeuvre on which Heath himself was insisting.

Between the two Cabinet discussions three Ministers made interesting submissions to Macmillan. In the case of Lord Mills (Paymaster General), who was a member of the Economic Association Committee of the Cabinet, this was because he was unable to attend the adjourned meeting. He said [78] that he thought the agricultural position was satisfactory, though the Party might lose some agricultural seats and the support of the consuming public. Some industries would be adversely affected, though some would be able to expand. His greatest concern was over relations with the Commonwealth. His constant aim was expansion of trade with the Commonwealth; he was convinced of the future ability of the Commonwealth to continue to expand; we should only move forward in harmony with them. He asked whether it was not possible to consider the close association of Commonwealth countries with any plan for joining the Common Market.

The other two Ministers, Watkinson and Eccles (respectively Defence and Education) seem to have felt that the points they wished to make could not be got over in the full Cabinet. The former looked forward to Britain leading Europe in the context of a wider Free World grouping, including the United States, that would be able to match the unified leadership of the Communist world. He seems to have expected that Britain could continue to lead the Commonwealth. The latter came to a somewhat similar conclusion by a different route. After rehearsing the obstacles that had been revealed to the Cabinet he expressed the view that a rigorous examination of the political difficulties would show that unless the Americans and the Commonwealth (other than Asian members) themselves all but joined the Six there would be no sure hope of carrying the British people into Europe. The tremendous new turn in British policy would have to be presented as a stage on the way to some larger, more universal destiny. He noted that the opening of North American markets would be a quicker and more effective route to free world expansion than the contrivance of superior methods for Europe to take in its own washing.

These comments, and the Cabinet discussion itself, continue to contain a powerful dose of wishful thinking. The Americans had not been enticed by the prospect of an Atlantic Community, though they ignored it rather than opposed it, while the French were hostile both to an association with the Commonwealth and links with the United States. The President of France was hardly likely to be induced by the President of the United States to risk French leadership of the Community to bring about a wider unity in the free world. On the other hand, the difficulty of redirecting public opinion turned out to be exaggerated.

Heath reported to the Cabinet on 4 May [87] that Anglo-French official discussions on the two previous days about the possibility of forming a wider economic and political association in Europe had been more encouraging. He said that the French had seemed ready to recognise that any settlement must be acceptable to the EFTA and they had shown special interest in the possibility of an agreement on agricultural policy. In fact matters at that time were well beyond such anodynes.

Officials had continued to study the implications of the Treaty of Rome, excluding the problems of the Commonwealth and agriculture, in accordance with the instructions given by the European Economic Association Committee [88]. Their paperwork was completed in time for consideration by Ministers on 9 and 17 May. The topics covered included Sovereignty, Commercial Policy, Economic Policy and Balance of Payments, Associated Overseas Territories and the Future of EFTA. The crucial statement by the Treaty of Rome Working Group [89] ran:-

> We do not think that any of these difficulties are of a kind which would be overriding if Ministers felt it was in our wider interests to accede to the Treaty of Rome.

Among other points made in the working papers officials noted that we should have to recognise that the ultimate aim of the founders and many of those most closely concerned with the implementation of the Treaty was a closer political relationship, though its form was an open question. This relationship would be based on the Franco-German rapprochement and the need to tie Germany as closely as possible to the West. UK influence in Europe would decrease if we remained outside and the United States would pay more attention to the Six. The United Kingdom would thus also lose influence in the Commonwealth and among the uncommitted countries and would not be able to exercise any claim to be a world power. The Treaty was quite unlike anything since the Act of Union; much of individuality would be absorbed and though we should gain advantages we should also have to surrender rights we now had and valued. We should gradually cease to have a special relationship with the United States and have to work to replace it with a special European relationship with the United States. The status and relationships of the Commonwealth would be bound to change. The Commonwealth would be much disturbed and regard it as turning away from them. But no institutional clash need arise in the early years. It was not impossible to harmonise the political development of the Commonwealth and Europe. On the other hand economic relations with the Commonwealth would be more difficult; UK freedom of action would be reduced and direct commercial relations curbed, if not ended. They thought that if we did not apply the United States might put us under pressure to do so.

Heath reported in writing on the current attitude among the Six. The Germans and Italians very much hoped that the United Kingdom would accede to the Treaty of Rome, while even the French had been much more forthcoming. Wormser (in charge of economic affairs at the Quai d'Orsay) said that if the United Kingdom was prepared to accede subject to certain broad conditions the French response would be one of "unreserved welcome".

The Prime Minister opened the discussion by saying:-

That assuming the Commonwealth and agricultural difficulties could be settled satisfactorily, there were two general questions which deserved consideration. The first was that if we were to sign the Treaty of Rome we should have to accept its underlying political objectives and although we should be able to influence the political outcome we did not know what this would be. But there would be political advantages to be gained from joining the European Economic Community (EEC), which if it succeeded, would become the dominating influence in Europe, and our accession would strengthen Europe as a political entity. There would be corresponding dangers to us if we stayed outside. The second general question was whether the Commonwealth countries would consider that by joining the Common Market we were turning away from them and what effect this would have on the Commonwealth relationship. There were also several special problems discussed in the papers EQ(61) 5 to 11.

In discussion of the considerations set out in EQ(61) 4, the general view was that the case for accession to the Treaty of Rome would have to be based on the broadest political arguments, involving a judgment of how the world political scene would develop over the next twenty or thirty years. Would the Six develop into a major political entity comparable with the USA and Russia? And what would be the role of the United Kingdom as a part of Europe compared with our role if we remained outside? It was suggested that the influence of the United Kingdom would decrease if we did not join the Community, but as a member we would be able to influence its policies and might exercise leadership. On the other hand, it was argued that the political future of the Six was obscure and there was a real possibility that it might fall apart after the departure of President de Gaulle and Dr. Adenauer. There might therefore be advantage in delaying any decision until the outlook was clearer. Against this, it was possible that after General de Gaulle and Dr. Adenauer had gone, and if we were not there to influence it, there would be a movement towards federation in Europe which might destroy all chances of our associating with Europe.

The Commonwealth reaction to a decision to join the Common Market would be important but could not be fully assessed at present because it was impossible to separate the political from the economic considerations. If we were able to secure suitable derogations which would safeguard the trading position of Commonwealth countries, it was unlikely that the strain on the Commonwealth would be insupportable, provided that we showed that we wanted to maintain the political links. If, on the other hand, we were unable to get such safeguards, then other Commonwealth countries would consider that we were losing interest in the Commonwealth and it might not survive the shock of our joining the Community. But the strain might be less if our accession could be shown to be part of a wider objective in which the whole Western world was involved. Commonwealth countries might be influenced also by the argument that if we remained outside the Common Market our ability to help them would decline, while if we became members we might hope to influence its policies and to give more support to Commonwealth countries. Nevertheless, it would be unwise to seek the views of the Commonwealth about our accession to the Treaty of Rome until we were quite clear what it was likely to involve for Commonwealth trading arrangements.

One argument for entering the Common Market was that the need to compete on equal terms with Europe would provide a stimulus to British industry. It was, indeed, one of the few ways in which the Government could bring pressure to bear on industry to make it more competitive. It would at the same time create difficult problems of adjustment for industry and the trade unions. Paragraph 8 of EQ(61) 4 stated that the Six would not think that we had made a genuine offer to accede to the Treaty of Rome "unless we were to accept, <u>at least as long-term aims,</u> the objectives of the Community as set out in Articles 2 and 3, though there would be room for give and take about the means of reaching the objectives and <u>about the transitional arrangements</u>".   This should not, however, be taken to imply that the derogations we should seek in respect of our main difficulties, e.g. Commonwealth free entry, would be only temporary. There were sound arguments, based on the importance of the economic strength of the Commonwealth to the survival of the Western world, for claiming that these derogations should be a permanent feature of our accession to the Treaty. Nor did it appear to be the intention of European countries that any derogations which we might secure for the Commonwealth would be temporary. To the extent that we needed permanent derogations, e.g. from the common tariff, we would not therefore be accepting the objectives of the Treaty of Rome, even as a long-term aim. That was why officials had suggested that the number of derogations should be kept to a minimum.

Although the objectives of the Treaty of Rome were expressed in general terms and in many cases little progress had been made towards achieving them, a decision to accede to the Treaty of Rome would raise great presentational difficulties. On the one hand, it would be necessary to convince the Six that we genuinely accepted the purposes of the Treaty; on the other hand, we did not want to give the Commonwealth the impression that we were entering into a political relationship with Europe which would adversely affect their interests, and we should have to satisfy public opinion in this country that the implementation of the objectives of the Treaty would not require unacceptable social and other adjustments. The problems of public relations would be considerable.

Summing up, the Prime Minister said:-

That, apart from the major Commonwealth and agriculture problems, there was a third group of difficulties which had been disclosed by the reports by officials. Officials had expressed the view that no one of the difficulties in this third group was likely to be such as to prevent our acceding to the Treaty of Rome if it were decided that it would be in our wider interests to do so. They had also recommended that we should, on seeking to accede, make as few reservations as possible, and be prepared genuinely to accept the basic objectives of the Treaty. Nevertheless, it would be necessary to decide what our attitude to the difficulties in this third group should be, and to what extent and how we should reveal our attitude if and when we applied to accede to the Treaty. The choice seemed to lie between relying on the possibility of negotiating our way out of those difficulties as far as possible, subsequent to declaring our willingness to accede to the Treaty; and stating at the outset that (in addition to the derogations which we should no doubt decide were essential in respect of the much greater problems arising in respect of our agriculture and commonwealth policies) we wanted derogations in respect of a limited number of the Common Market obligations which gave rise to the most important of these difficulties in the third group. These latter were probably matters affecting the social services and social conditions, insofar as we should be under pressure, and particularly early pressure to conform to the obligations of the Common Market.

At the next meeting Ministers were particularly concerned with presentation.

It was pointed out that public opinion at home was unprepared for, and was insufficiently informed about, the likely consequences of a decision to accede. Similarly, Commonwealth countries were as yet unprepared for a settlement which involved them in losing any of their present rights of free entry. However, until the Government had reached a provisional decision to accede to the Treaty of Rome, and had a clearer view of the kind of settlement likely to be achieved, little could be done to mould opinion. More thought needed to be given to the advantages to be gained from entering the Common Market. It tended to be overlooked that, if we entered it, we might be the most powerful member and be able to exercise a strong and sometimes a decisive influence upon its policies. On the economic side, the main prize would be free access to a large and rapidly expanding market for our manufactured goods. But perhaps the strongest argument for joining the Six was based on the potential dangers of staying outside; as the Six consolidated, we would inevitably enter into a period of relative decline in which not only our industry and agriculture would suffer, but also our political influence with the Commonwealth and the world generally would diminish. This, however, was a difficult argument to present publicly.

The difficulty of the task of carrying opinion at home and in the Commonwealth would depend largely on how far we were likely to be able in negotiation to safeguard essential interests. And this in turn would depend to a large extent on the political will of the French. If they wanted the United Kingdom to become part of the Common Market, and if they accepted that it was in the broad interests of the West for the Commonwealth relationship to be unimpaired, reasonable negotiations should be possible.

Another problem was how to handle the consultations with the Six and the Commonwealth. It would be unprofitable to discuss with the Commonwealth the question of United Kingdom accession without having a more precise idea of what it was likely to involve for Commonwealth trading arrangements. This could probably not be known with any certainty until we had opened negotiations with the Six. But we were fully committed to consultations with the Commonwealth before entering negotiations with the Six. The way out would probably be to have continuing discussions with both the Commonwealth and the Six; these would be carried on almost simultaneously, and at each stage we should get a clearer picture of the likely outcome, and nearer to the point of final decision. On this basis, the need for important political consultations with the Commonwealth might come comparatively soon.

The present phase of exploratory talks with the Six could not go on much longer. A decision to enter into negotiations with the Six would have to be reached before the end of the year.

It was thus taken for granted that the United Kingdom could not submit to a federation. Although it would have to support the underlying political objectives of the Community, it was evidently assumed by Ministers that the United Kingdom would be able to block the known federalist impulses on the Continent and in this they would have the support of de Gaulle, for as long as he lasted. There was a good deal of confidence that valuable derogations could be negotiated and the stated interest of the United States in this area was disregarded. Similar optimism was expressed about the powerful, potentially leading position of the United Kingdom within the Community, which might be thought not quite to square with the picture of the same country outside the Community falling into a decline. It was unfortunate for the Government's position, or, rather, the one it was rapidly moving to adopt, that the argument that was perhaps its most compelling was not something that could be mentioned in public. Finally, one should note the appearance of an argument that was to have a long run, that the only way to discover if acceptable terms could be procured was to apply for membership. Nothing was said of the embarrassments that might arise if it was decided to withdraw the application.

Rather more strikingly, nothing is recorded as having been said about sovereignty, given the importance this topic inevitably assumed in later debate, the introduction to the officials' paper (below) and the references made to it at the April Cabinet.

In the past, the loss of National sovereignty has been the most potent argument against United Kingdom participation in supranational institutions. It was to a large extent responsible for our decision, in 1950, not to join the European Coal and Steel Community and, in 1955, to withdraw from the discussions which led eventually to the drafting of the Treaty of Rome. Although the Treaty of Rome does not express this explicitly, it has underlying political objectives which are to be brought about by a gradual surrender of sovereignty. Continental opinion would not think that we were in earnest in establishing a new relationship with the Six unless we were prepared to abandon a significant degree of sovereignty.

The body of the sovereignty paper covered much the same ground as had the Lord Chancellor at the end of 1960 and only a few extracts need be given here. On majority voting it was noted:-

The United Kingdom would, in acceding to the Treaty of Rome, be committing itself to a range of <u>indefinite</u> obligations over a wide field of action within the economic and social sphere which might subsequently be translated into <u>specific</u> obligations within the same field by means of a decision, regulation or directive adopted by the Council with which we would not necessary agree. This is a commitment of a kind different from the obligations restricting freedom of action which we have accepted under other treaties. These are either definite and specific in nature (e.g. the commitments under WEU, GATT, and EMA) or, as in the case of OEEC, where power has been vested in the Council to take decisions binding on member States, it is clearly provided that the Council should act by unanimity (a State may abstain, but in that event, the decision is not binding on the abstaining state).

On withdrawal:-

The absence of a withdrawal provision is inherent in the future of the Treaty; it is a permanent union and its aims and objects are to consolidate that union. Nevertheless we should retain, as do the other members of the Community, effective national institutions having at their disposal the power, as a matter of practical politics, to withdraw from the Community if continued membership became intolerable, although to do so would be bound to cause a major disruption in Europe.

They also provided some comfort:-

> It is also important to note that the fields covered by the Rome Treaty are strictly limited. For example legislation affecting public health and public order is specifically excluded, as are all matters connected in any way with defence. The Treaty-making powers which are transferred to the institutions of the Community are limited to the narrow, albeit important, field of tariff and commercial matters.

Ministers must be assumed to have accepted the final argument:-

> The delegation of national sovereignty involved in joining the Treaty of Rome, moreover, is something which other major powers - France and Germany - have been prepared to accept in their own wider interests. In fact, in the context of merging our economic identity with that of the Community and aligning ourselves politically with the other members, the partial surrender of sovereignty involved would be a necessary element and it is arguable that it would be of less significance than the broad political and economic factors.

Nobody sought to suggest that the United Kingdom might be in a different position from France and Germany, or that the transfer of some powers might provide a plausible basis for the transfer of more.

The same meeting considered[90] a memorandum on agriculture from Soames, the responsible Minister. He noted that in the Common Market the consumer would be called upon increasingly to provide the bulk of support for agriculture but he felt the outlook for the cost of food was by no means as threatening as was sometimes supposed. The extra cost was calculated at about £225m., i.e. some 4½% of the household food bill and 1½% of the cost of living. There would be considerable savings and additional revenue to the Exchequer. The rise in the cost of food imports was not expected to be serious and would have to be set against other factors that would influence the balance of payments as a whole.

For the agricultural industry he felt an agreement should be negotiable which would mean little adverse effect during the transitional period; in the longer term there would be both losses and gains. Hostility was to be expected because under the Common Agricultural Policy of the Common Market the position of the National Farmers' Union would be greatly limited. He envisaged a safety net for farm income and there would be a need to seek the maintenance during the transitional period of some features of the present system of support and a longer transitional period for the United Kingdom than was envisaged for themselves by the Six. He felt the major food exporting interests of the Commonwealth could be safeguarded. In any case, the country would not be able to sustain in the long run its policies of a free market and purely Exchequer-supported agriculture in the face of the protection, support and subsidy provided elsewhere in the world.

The *desiderata* thus outlined would be subject to the negotiations and further detailed work was required.

The Prime Minister's briefing[91] for these Cabinet Committee meetings continued to assume that a full memorandum would go to the Cabinet. Macmillan had himself encouraged this on his return from Rambouillet earlier in the year, while even Heath had envisaged a paper that would face them with the fundamental question. In the April Cabinet discussion reference was made to a paper setting out advantages and disadvantages, narrower grounds than those of principle which had perturbed Heath, but even this, as has been noted, failed to appear. What happened was an *ad hoc* meeting of a number of Ministers at Chequers on 18 June. The recorded discussion [92] was confined to Commonwealth access to the UK market and the safeguarding of British agriculture. These were, of course, the subjects excluded from the officials' recent study.

On the first issue the meeting agreed that arrangements should be sought which:-

(i) in the transitional period, would permit exports to the United Kingdom of Commonwealth goods of major significance (with the possible exception of manufactured goods from the developed countries of the Commonwealth) to be maintained at substantially the same level as at present;

(ii) in the Common Market period, would continue unchanged except to the extent that it could be shown that changes (a) were necessary in order not to frustrate the purposes of the Community, and (b) would not damage the essential interests of Commonwealth countries.

On agriculture the meeting agreed that:-

> in any negotiation to accede to the Treaty of Rome, the United Kingdom should seek to retain the right to continue to give some Exchequer support to farmers for so long as the United Kingdom Government considered it necessary.

Commonwealth Consultation: June to July 1961

An initial consideration then took place of the nature of the approach to be made to Commonwealth Governments. On Sandys' advice the meeting agreed that it would be fatal to seek agreement from these governments on what they would be prepared to accept.

> If we were to expose now what we thought we might reasonably secure in the negotiations, we should run the risk of seriously weakening our bargaining position. Moreover, if we tried to get the Commonwealth to agree to accept what we now thought might eventually be negotiated, we should risk doing serious damage to Commonwealth relations while there was still no assurance that we might negotiate satisfactory arrangements with the Six.

On the 22nd, therefore, what the full Cabinet had put before it was a memorandum by the Prime Minister [93] setting out the line to be taken by the Ministers who were to visit the Commonwealth countries for consultations.

Nevertheless, some disquiet continued to be expressed at the change in tactics. The previous position had been that there should be no application unless there was a reasonable chance of British, Commonwealth and EFTA requirements being secured. It was pointed out that it was not clear why this attitude should be radically changed and that if the different approach was put to Commonwealth governments it would be taken to mean that there had been a definite decision to apply. It was also remarked that the proposed subscription to the basic principles of the Treaty of Rome could not be made consistent with the retention of Commonwealth free entry. But the objections were not pressed and discussion turned to the Commonwealth tours.

Sandys was to go to New Zealand, Australia and Canada, Thorneycroft to India, Pakistan, Ceylon and Malaya, Hare to Sierra Leone, Ghana, Nigeria and the Central African Federation, Perth to the West Indies and Heath to Cyprus. A Commonwealth conference, which might have found the other members uniting against the British aspiration to join the Community was thus avoided [94]. The main point to be made to the Commonwealth countries was that it was not possible to make an assessment of the conditions which would meet the requirements of the United Kingdom and the Commonwealth, conditions which would need to be secured if the United Kingdom was to accede to the Treaty of Rome, without entering into negotiations with the EEC. Only after consultation with the Commonwealth and EFTA countries would the Cabinet decide whether or not to open negotiations with the Six. The purpose of these visits was to explain that the broad political consideration was that the most effective way of securing our political objectives in the world and averting continued division in Europe lay in full UK membership. The touring Ministers would explain that the United Kingdom would be prepared to accept the basic principles and objectives of the Treaty of Rome and that Commonwealth free entry could not therefore, be maintained for all time. The Commonwealth governments were not asked to agree to the United Kingdom joining the Six but to discuss what were their essential interests. At the end of the negotiations the British government would finally decide on the package as a whole. There might at that time be a Commonwealth Conference, but an earlier one was to be discouraged.

The Cabinet discussion [95] necessitated some revision of the Ministers' instructions, which were issued on the 27th without attracting any further objection.

The line thus taken was essentially negative in tone, containing no hint that any initiative from the Commonwealth might be accepted, let alone welcomed. It was expected that the greatest difficulties would arise in Sandys' discussions with the Prime Ministers of Canada and Australia. Accordingly, on 3 July, Macmillan wrote to both Diefenbaker and Menzies making the points which had been discussed in Cabinet and which Sandys was to make again[96]. Although he spoke of the decision to enter negotiations as still hypothetical the repetition of the argument that only in negotiations would it be possible to ascertain what special conditions the Six would be prepared to accept made it clear that in practice the decision had already been taken. The accompanying memorandum, which rehearsed briefly the history of UK - European relations since 1955, stated, in effect, that in order to avoid the risk of economic and political division in Europe the UK government was prepared to accept the obligations of membership of the Community, provided only that some special protection be found for the economic interests of Commonwealth countries and UK agriculture. Macmillan was, of course, aware, though he did not say, that the obligations were political as well as economic.

The reports from the tours were first considered in the Economic Association Committee on 14 July [97]. A Foreign Office brief for this meeting [98] was able, unsurprisingly, to say that there was:-

nothing to prevent the UK government from going ahead and saying that they wished to negotiate with the Six.

All the officials concerned felt there was grave danger in what might look like a half-hearted approach to the Six. The government should say that it accepted the main principles of the Treaty and wished to enter negotiations to see how these could be reconciled with UK commitments to the Commonwealth, the EFTA and its farmers. A half-hearted and grudging approach would not command the support which we hoped to win in five of the six countries, some sections of French opinion and the United States. The Commonwealth would do nothing to provide an alternative; Australia had been cutting its preference to the United Kingdom, Canada had refused a free trade area in 1957, and no Commonwealth government had suggested to the touring Ministers that if the United Kingdom stayed out of the Community there would be any *quid pro quo*. There was no alternative Commonwealth dynamic. This judgement seems both superficial and harsh. Many things had changed since 1957, not least the whole British stance. Objections raised by Commonwealth governments during the tour had afforded Ministers the opportunity to explore the possibility of greater Commonwealth cohesion had their instructions allowed for it. What is more surprising is that officials should have thought it necessary to play back a number of points that Ministers had already made and of which one would suppose they were fully seized. One must conclude that there was some apprehension that at the political level continued opposition would succeed in limiting the approach to be made.

On the positive side it was suggested that investment in the Commonwealth, which was precluded by British balance of payments difficulties, could in future come from the EEC. Britain could not on its own continue to maintain sterling as an international currency but if we were inside the Community others would have to help and sterling might become the European common currency. These arguments were scarcely very realistic and have the air of being produced *ad hominem*, to counter objections rather than having much substance of their own.

But there were no problems at the Committee and two days later memoranda[99] containing the Ministers' reports were considered in Cabinet [100]. From Asia it was reported that no government was actually opposed but they felt that consultation during the negotiations would be important. The Indian government had felt that the conception would divide the Commonwealth and had formed a political dislike for it. In fact, Thorneycroft had reported separately to the Prime Minister [101] on 13 July that Nehru had questioned whether the United Kingdom would gain any influence by joining the Six, to which he had rejoined by emphasising influence on the Six.

Sandys reported some apprehension, e.g. on the part of Menzies, that a closer economic union would lead to a political union and weaken the Commonwealth. Canada might be sucked into the economic orbit of the United States. He had said that we had no thought of allowing our political identity to be submerged in a European superstate and would be more likely to favour an Atlantic Union than a purely continental system.

The African countries were principally concerned lest there be neo-colonial implications in the Associated Oversea Territory status that had been devised by the Community for the former French colonies.

Macmillan summed up by saying that there was general agreement that the right course was to enter negotiations and to announce it at once, rather than to say the government was considering these important issues and would make its decision after the recess. The government would be in a stronger position if it had negotiated and found out whether the interests of the Commonwealth and the Community could be reconciled than if it announced that informal soundings had led to the conclusion that negotiations could not be successful.

The Cabinet's main concern was about presentation to a variety of audiences. On the one hand it should be emphasised that there was no commitment until other Commonwealth governments and Parliament had had an opportunity to discuss the results of negotiations. On the other the government must embark on the negotiations in good faith with the intention of making them succeed. The prospect of membership might be held out as a step towards the larger concept of a union of the Free World. From inside the Community we might hope to transform it into an outward-looking group of nations mindful of its responsibilities to the world as a whole. The decision to negotiate was different from the later and much more critical decision to join. Since the question never arose it is hardly possible to judge what weight to put on this argument (though the issue had already been moved onto more technical ground) but we can surely put none on the Free World union. Kennedy had ignored the suggestion and it conflicted with the protectionist and anti-American attitudes displayed on the Continent. Officials had dismissed it a year earlier [102].

Telegrams were despatched to Commonwealth governments to inform them of the decision, which could hardly have come as a surprise [103]. The text of these messages, however, maintained the charade that the Cabinet had weighed the reports of Commonwealth consultation before coming to a conclusion.

Presentation of the Decision: July 1961

At their next meeting the Cabinet considered the draft of the public statement and amended it to head off a motion tabled the previous day in the Commons opposing any material derogation of British sovereignty or any endangerment of the future expansion of trade with the Commonwealth and the EFTA [104]. A specific undertaking was included to consult Parliament before entering into an agreement. However, as Camps has noted [105], once the House had approved the Government's motion it would be extremely difficult for it to oppose entry unless the terms were clearly unsatisfactory. By the use of the argument that they were seeking approval only of the search for terms the Government got the House onto the narrow technical ground. It was a technique that would re-appear.

There was some talk of issuing a White Paper for the better information of MP's and the public. The idea appears to have originated with the 1922 Committee of Conservative bankbenchers and a draft was prepared containing a Summary of the Treaty of Rome. An *ad hoc* meeting of Ministers [106] on 10 July agreed that publication would provide material for attacks on the proposal to apply. This was in line with Macmillan's own view, which was elsewhere [107] expressed as being that it would only be possible to set out the positive aspects of the Treaty, all of which would be more or less unpopular. It would not be possible to explain the view that in fact many of the paper provisions would prove in practice to be less onerous than they were in theory. Nor could the case in favour of joining be frankly argued, which does, of course, imply that government speakers would be less than frank. Macmillan put this to the House by saying that it, presumably the frank case and not the summary of the Treaty, would give away the British negotiating position if published in a White Paper. An official of the Cabinet Office noted at the time that the real reason for going in was based on apprehension of what the country's political and economic position would be in ten years' time. Clearly the public expression of this sort of pessimism would not merely have surrendered a negotiating position; it would have made it impossible to secure the support of Parliament. In the event actual copies of the Treaty were made available to Members and only one Conservative backbencher, Anthony Fell, attacked Macmillan in the House.

The debates themselves have been adequately covered by Camps, but there is an interesting anonymous report of the reaction of Wormser, the senior French official, to the impending announcement [103]. He was said to have judged that there were three possibilities: 1) HMG was playing for time for internal political reasons; 2) the British were looking to join only on British terms and there would be tough bargaining from the start; 3) the British would be willing to sign the Treaty on terms set by the Six, which he totally discounted. He felt it was not really in the interests of the United Kingdom to join at this time, unless it was willing to forsake the Commonwealth.

Negotiations with the Europeans: October to November 1961

The major opening move in the negotiations was Heath's statement to the member Governments of the Community on 10 October. Much of the material was detailed and technical but his approach was fulsome, to say the least. Two paragraphs will suffice to make this point:-

I am deeply conscious of the importance of this occasion and of the work on which we are embarking together. There can be no doubt that the success or failure of these discussions will determine the future shape of Europe. They will affect profoundly the way of life, the political thought and even the character of each one of our peoples. Her Majesty's Government in the United Kingdom have asked me to set before you today, in clear and comprehensive terms, the view they take of this enterprise and to emphasise the importance which they attach to its success.

The British Government and the British people have been through a searching debate during the last few years on the subject of their relations with Europe. The result of the debate has been our present application. It was a decision arrived at, not on any narrow or short-term grounds, but as a result of a thorough assessment over a considerable period of the needs of our own country, of Europe and of the Free World, as a whole. We recognise it is a great decision, a turning point in our history, and we take it in all seriousness. In saying that we wish to join the EEC, we mean that we desire to become full, wholehearted and active members of the European Community in its widest sense and to go forward with you in the building of a new Europe. [107]

The documentation of Heath's statement has a curious history. Although copies were provided for member Governments of the Community the Commonwealth Governments were sent only those portions which the United Kingdom considered to be their concern; nor *a fortiori* was the text provided to Parliament and the public. Heath, who had been worried that his words to the Western European Union shortly before had been too effusive [103], remained sensitive, and when William van Straubenzee MP said in a speech that the statement to the Community indicated agreement to federation he hastened to track down the source. [108]

Disconcertingly, the origin of this interpretation turned out to be Prof. Hallstein, President of the European Commission. As Heath has since come out of the closet as a federalist it may be that his own views had become apparent to Hallstein in unofficial conversation and had coloured the latter's interpretation.

Pressure for release continued and towards the end of November the statement was released on a confidential basis to governments of the Commonwealth [109]. On the 27th a Private Notice Question put down by Hugh Gaitskell, Leader of the Opposition, made it clear that the text had got to the Press and the statement was rapidly published. There is no sign that the publication had any untoward effects in Britain and Macmillan's argument [110] that it was resisted lest it set a precedent for the negotiations that were to follow is too skimpy a smokescreen to be worth pursuit.

Heath's sensitivity is evidenced elsewhere. On October 26, Sandys had said in Brussels that the United Kingdom government recognised that the Treaty of Rome was not simply an economic agreement but also had an important political content [111]. This might be thought to underplay the government's political appreciation and intentions, as has been seen, but it was too much for Heath. He set officials urgently to work to check what Ministers had been saying in public and a line was developed of arguing that the Treaty contained no political obligations, only implications. The United Kingdom would not regard itself as committed to any particular development or extension of obligations merely by virtue of EEC membership. But the difficulty of implying one attitude to members of the Community and another for domestic and Commonwealth consumption was never going to go away [112]. How it would have appeared if negotiations had proceeded to a conclusion, it is fruitless to speculate but the difficulty was abolished (for the time being) by the Gaullist veto of early 1963.

This narrative does not go so far but it is worth recalling de Gaulle's visit to Macmillan at Birch Grove on 24 and 25 November 1961. The full record of these talks will be found at Appendix E.

It is always difficult to know what to take at face value in recorded conversations of this kind. Certainly de Gaulle's welcome of the UK application was disingenuous, to judge by his later veto, though his insistence on the value of delay may be regarded as coherent with his position at the end of the decade in the Soames affair. Macmillan's urgency is more curious; there was nothing in the domestic situation to suggest that this was a last chance and his forecasts of a collapse of NATO and threats of troop withdrawals were both implausible and unfulfilled. On the other hand, a European Community set in its ways after a number of years and lacking de Gaulle's hostility to federalism did offer a prospect of being even less palatable to the British. No doubt much of what he said was selected to appeal to de Gaulle's temperament, though references to Charlemagne and Russian accommodation might be regarded as frank by the standards of summit diplomacy. The menace to European civilisation presented by New Zealand might be explicable as no more than an appeal to the President's taste for the grandiose (which does not explain Macmillan's willingness to circulate this philosophy within government, even with a top security classification) were it not for the fact that he reveals his source, in the opening pages of the last volume of his autobiography [114], as Arnold Toynbee. Futurology of this kind is normally soon forgotten by all, including its authors, though the fragments that appear to cohere with later events may be exhumed. In any case it is not normally allowed to serve as the guide for action which it purports to be in this case; if Macmillan had produced it in public as a fundamental reason for accession to the Treaty of Rome it would have had short shrift, and so would he.

For all the warmth of the words these conversations foreshadow the veto that followed after little more than a year of negotiation.

Chapter Two

An Intellectual Journey

Over a period of some eighteen months at the beginning of the decade the British government thus moved from decrying entry as unthinkable, to thinking about the unthinkable and, finally, to enthusing about it. Its movement may best be described as being pushed backwards, as it tried to reconcile its apprehensions about living in a world that also held the Common Market with the political fundamentals with which Ministers had grown up. The power behind the push was France. From early in the process it was clear to the government that it should settle with France first if it was to make any progress. Even before the resurrection of de Gaulle the French had stalled the negotiations for a free trade area, had then broken their undertaking to conclude an agreement and, in the Six-Seven discussions, had continually emphasised as important those issues on which they thought British would have to refuse to negotiate, whatever fitted that requirement at the time. In response the British government steadily adjusted their position because they felt it to be risky to just stand there - things might be worse later on. Even the minor tactical point of concealing from the French their eventual willingness to accede until after derogations had been negotiated had to be abandoned. From one angle this shift could be described as the French hooking their fish, playing it and bringing it to shore. The trouble was that they never really wanted it; when it refused to wriggle away de Gaulle had publicly to throw it back into the water and put up with any consequent difficulties with his partners.

Sources for the reasoning process that accompanied the government's reversal have been set out in the preceding section. It has to be said that they look compelling but it must be remembered that is in the nature of things. The records of an institution or an individual provide much more evidence for the causes they espoused than for the opposite case, the support for which must be found in some other way. Disagreements with the way things were proceeding were occasionally expressed, and in the summer of 1960 created something of a blockage, but the government machinery was in the hands of those who were determined to reach an accommodation with the Six because they were convinced of its high importance. That is why the documents were written in the way they were. But the reasoning they contain calls for analysis, the more so because it was destined to become the establishment orthodoxy, enabling those who clung to the positions embraced by the government only a short time before to be dismissed as witless cranks. That there was something oddly uncertain about the process is indicated by the fact that nearly twenty years later, and seven years after Britain's actual entry, a group of academic specialists in the subject could find themselves unable to identify what Britain's objectives in the Community were. [142]

To conduct this analysis it is necessary to separate a number of themes, and these will be examined in the following pages. Obviously in practice they are interwoven and there is no question, for example, of having to decide whether politics or economics was predominant. That would be of concern only if the reasoning developed in opposite directions, which was not the case, though it has to be said that proponents of entry on finding difficulty with one set of arguments would seek retreat in emphasising the importance of the other.

In judging the quality of the reasoning it is important always to bear in mind the massive scale of the change it was employed to support. It is not simply that the government reversed completely its own earlier views, for they might have been in some sense mistaken, or strongly dependent on external circumstances that had changed. In fact there was no change in external circumstances, other than the fact of the Community itself, and those earlier judgements had not been based on an assumption that the Community would not see the light of day.

What is important is that the earlier view was entirely in line with British history and with longstanding British policy, which was why Eden had been able in 1952 to appeal to the instinct of the nation in saying "the United Kingdom could not join a federation on the continent of Europe; this is something which we know in our bones we cannot do." Such automatic rejection remained the established view for the rest of the decade and was expressed, in relation to a Customs Union, by Macmillan in the House in 1956. Even within government as the change of approach was being worked through some proponents of entry were inclined to minimise its significance, though the Prime Minister was willing to tell Cabinet just how dramatic it all was in much the same way as he told posterity in his diary.

In public it was in the government's interest to play down the magnitude of the decision (a sort of housemaid's baby argument), just as it was for opponents of entry, such as Sir Derek Walker-Smith and Lord Hinchingbrooke, to emphasise it. Their judgement, though not their conclusion, was supported by Lord Chandos, who brushed aside in the House of Lords the reassurance emanating from the government and its supporters, such as Lord Gladwyn, and said that we might be taking a step of far greater importance in the national life than any of which he could readily think, even the repeal of the Corn Laws. He was, however, convinced that we should be stronger, richer and happier, which was, at any rate, a testable assertion. Perhaps the fairest assessment came from the spectators across the Atlantic, where the administration saw it as an astonishing reversal and the Sub Committee on Foreign Economic Policy in reporting to Congress [143] remarked on the significance of the United Kingdom turning away from the Commonwealth and the special relationship. Surely when Gaitskell at the Labour Party Conference in 1962 spoke of the end of a thousand years of history he had got the right perspective, even if his oratory was somewhat excessive, and he was entitled to a more substantial rejoinder than Butler's sixth-form repartee asserting his party's claim to the future.

This fundamental change of direction needed to be justified by the most powerful of reasoning.

Economics

The origin of British concern about the development of the EEC lay in economics. However significant the political aspect came to appear, even with the designation of the Foreign Office as lead department in place of the Board of Trade the titles of file series and committees bear witness to that origin.

In the first place the Community was a trading threat. The most extreme version of that threat was expressed in the December 1959 Treasury memorandum [23], which posited that if the EEC swung away from the ideas of multilateral world trade they might push the balance over to a different kind of trading system. What this meant was that the EEC might move so heavily in the direction of protectionism that all other trading countries in the world would be obliged to follow suit. It is understandable that officials who were obliged to cover all the ground should express some horror at the possibility of a re-run of Thirties trade wars but it was never very likely that the Community would go quite so far nor, given that much of its members' trade was with each other, that its activities would be capable of nullifying the GATT. When the issue reached the Cabinet the end of multilateralism was not perceived as very likely, nor was more apprehension aroused by the rather more plausible thesis that the greater weight of the Community in GATT negotiations might induce the United States to concoct deals with it at the expense, for example, of the United Kingdom and the Commonwealth. It was, after all, well understood that US trade policy was liberal and that it would press the Six in the direction of reducing its common tariff.

Potentially more serious was the challenge of rapid economic development on the Continent. The Community of the Six would match the United States in size and both as importers and exporters would challenge UK trade around the world. This view was expressed most forcibly by Maudling in the early spring of 1960 and, no doubt jaundiced by his experience of negotiations, he asserted that the French and Germans were

determined to exclude Britain. It was not so much a matter of
exclusion by tariffs from some part of a market which constituted
only 14% of UK exports, nor even lack of access to a home
market that afforded substantial economies of scale, though these
were the points of which much was made in public discussion; it
was that if the economies of scale and the greater bargaining
power came to pass Britain's trading position with the rest of the
world would be weakened. What was more, EEC success posed
a risk to the survival of the EFTA, a number of whose members
were very dependent on their trade with the Six.

This argument, which may be called the Maudling thesis,
was the core of the commercial case for entry to the Common
Market. It is essentially negative and has to be set alongside the
positive arguments, but before this can be done it will be
necessary to examine the general economic position of the United
Kingdom as it had developed over the years.

By 1961 it was apparent that the United Kingdom was
suffering a relative economic decline. Its rate of growth of output
and productivity was lower than that of its competitors around the
world and had been so for a number of years [115]. There are those
who would say it had been going on for much longer. [116] At all
events, British governments that were dependent on the goodwill
of the electorate for survival and shared a determination never to
repeat the horrors of the prewar slump, were inevitably alarmed
at their inability to get a grip on the country's economy. A major
indicator of difficulty, which was at the same time a major
constraint on growth, was the balance of payments. Indeed, one
of the worries about accession to the Treaty was the possible loss
of power to act independently in the face of a sterling crisis. The
current position in the summer of 1961 was bought to the
attention of the Cabinet, though apparently as background rather
than for detailed discussion, in a report [117] entitled *Balance of
Payments Trends* by Sir T. Padmore, Acting Chairman of the
Economic Steering (General) Committee. He reported that
domestic demand exceeded productive capacity and needed to be
checked. The visibles account had deteriorated over some years
and as a percentage of GDP imports had grown more than
exports. There was nothing to suggest that in the next few years

the visible trade deficit which had existed in almost every year since the beginning of the century would be greatly changed. The net balance on invisibles had almost disappeared since 1952; net earnings on the private account were being absorbed by government expenditure and this situation was not likely to change. Overall a major turn-round in the course of foreign, i.e. visible, trade was needed, since invisible earnings were soaked up and the long-term capital outflow was likely to increase. In the short term sterling difficulties were expected, affecting the reserves, requiring early and drastic action to restore confidence. He noted that much of the decline in the UK share of world exports was but a reflection of the very great expansion of Japanese and German exports from their low post-war level. The traditional major markets in the sterling Commonwealth had been expanding less rapidly than in the more industrialised countries, which had hitherto been less important in the UK trading pattern. Much of the favoured trading pattern in these Commonwealth markets had disappeared with shrinking tariff preferences, the removal of export restrictions on competitors' goods and the falling away of commercial connexions as independence was gained. Not much could be done to alter the external conditions affecting sales abroad; we had therefore to adjust our economy to them in order to establish a viable balance of trade and of payments.

He offered three possible explanations of these failures: (i) that we have not succeeded in producing enough of the sorts of good most in demand at home and abroad; (ii) our costs of production for the goods for which we compete with foreign producers for customers, both at home and abroad, are too high; (iii) our producers do not strive sufficiently energetically to win business in competition with foreign producers. These were not so much explanations as directions for possibly finding solutions. Padmore suggested that it was necessary to look at investment, competition, the pressure of demand and wages and the pressure of demand and resources. He saw the principal remedies as disinflation and control over costs, together with a continuing lower level of home demand. What is interesting, given the current climate of opinion in Whitehall, is the absence of any direct reference in this analysis to the EEC. Indeed, Padmore went so far as to remark that the examples of Switzerland and Holland showed that export success is possible without the support of a large home market. This may well be seen as the last kick of a previously established Treasury view. A few days later the Cabinet approved a number of proposals from the Chancellor to convince opinion that excessive pressures on the economy would be brought under control.

There was no serious suggestion in official circles at this time, whatever may have been the case in later years, that the superior performance of the Six countries was due to the establishment of the Community. In public opinion, on the other hand, such a connexion was adumbrated, to the extent that one authority, Lamfalussy, found it necessary to controvert it [118]. He not only found no causal relationship, he suggested that it was the high rate of growth of Continental Europe which stimulated trade between members of the EEC and made it possible to set up the Common Market. This example of the general proposition that the time to introduce drastic changes is when things are going well seems not to have occurred to those in government.

Whether or no location in the larger home market might reasonably be expected to improve the economic balance of the United Kingdom there was certainly a concern that a unified economic control of the Six could by its sheer weight affect the management of the UK economy. In this regard the Treasury memorandum of 1959 [23] cited above appositely noted that this was already the position in respect of the United States. It would hardly be possible to judge, and no attempt was made, whether two heavyweight economies would produce balanced or cumulative effects on the United Kingdom.   But the memorandum did point out that there was no reason to expect the rate of economic expansion over a long period to be faster in an economic unit of 160 million people than in a unit of 50 million.

The argument for a larger home market was undoubtedly of great weight in governmental discussions and this positive approach was more attractive, particularly for public consumption, than the negative aspects of the Maudling thesis. A major element in the case that was made was economy of scale in manufacturing, although it was recognised that the United Kingdom's peripheral position could be disadvantageous in distribution. The superior growth performance of the Six was seen as likely to accelerate under the stimulus of greater internal competition, which would produce its own dynamic and from which the United Kingdom would be cut off if we were "out", even if the common external tariff was low. Increased competition would stimulate British industry, while the research and development needed to match the United States in world markets would be possible only for the large units brought into existence by the creation of a large home market.

Home [119] felt that entry would be Britain's economic salvation. Only that sort of market unity could get and mobilize wealth for research on the scale the Americans could command. Other remedies for Britain's economic malaise having failed she should be exposed to the astringent of competition.

It was seen, of course, that there were risks, even if they did not receive as much attention as the advantages. These advantages were no more than potentialities and could be achieved only by being fully competitive with the Six, which Britain needed to be in any case and which required appropriate economic policies at home. What seems not to have been assessed with any rigour was the likelihood of British trade becoming competitive, given its record, the relative merits of stimulus *via* GATT liberalisation and accession to the Treaty of Rome and the possibility that access to the British market would afford the superior economies of the Six more advantage than Britain was capable of reaping on the Continent of Europe. If things went well they might go very well; they might also go very badly indeed.

One particular feature that gave cause for concern was investment and capital movement. It was seen that the Six might attract inward investment, particularly from the United States, away from Britain; on the other hand to counter this by accession would lead, in due course, to complete liberalisation of capital movements, with worrying possible sequences for the balance of payments. Yet outside the Six there would be pressure from

British industrialists for freedom to invest on the other side of the tariff barrier.

It was an age in which investment abroad was seen as less desirable than it has since come to appear. On the other hand, inward investment was to be attracted and the foreign ownership that it carried with it was not seen in this context as the bugbear it has been on other occasions. All in all it would appear that the exchange control to which Britain had become used would be eroded whatever happened about accession and it would be necessary to adapt. At any rate the Treaty would permit some protective action in the event of severe difficulties with the balance of payments.

A good deal was made of pressure from British businessmen for access to the continental market, though it was cited more often than evidenced in the government's records. In May 1960 it was reported that there was great unease among leading industrialists at the prospect of being cut off from the markets of the Six and in Cabinet a year later that many of the leaders of British industry were in favour of joining the Six. Such comments may well have been based on contacts that have not left a mark on the records but such evidence as there is points in a different direction. Moon[120] notes that Sir William McFadzean, President of the Federation of British Industry (FBI), was able to write to the Chancellor of the Exchequer in January 1961 (when the government was well down the road) about the problems of British industry and the economy without even mentioning entry to the Common Market as a solution.

Just before the July announcement the FBI produced a statement [121] which emphasised the importance of the Commonwealth and the EFTA. It noted that a Europe-wide multilateral trading system had always been their desire and, they believed, that of the great bulk of industry in Europe. Nevertheless, a large majority was of the opinion that it was not right to become committed to formal negotiations with the Six until existing differences over the problems had so far been narrowed as to offer the prospect of a satisfactory outcome. When a meeting was held with FBI representatives on 17 July Sir W Palmer remarked that as it seemed more likely that we should negotiate the opposition to this course seemed to be hardening, while others emphasised the importance of and the risks to the Commonwealth market.

Foreign Office officials expressed themselves in a hurt tone when minuting and suggested that the statement contrasted sharply with indications of more favourable views, for example of Sir William McFadzean (despite what he had not written in January) and the overwhelming majority of the Association of British Chambers of Commerce who had, at any rate, favoured exploring the possibilities. Presumably if they had been able to cite anything more impressive they would have done so, but they were able to take some pleasure in the opinion of the *Economist*, which had said the FBI views had sounded very like those of the Board of Trade. Which makes it clear that not everybody was sanguine about prospects in the EEC. The Board of Trade also reported [122] at this time that British businessmen were limited in their enthusiasm and could be described as cautious. While there were no doubt those who favoured entry for reasons of profit, just as there were those who opposed it (in the Commonwealth Industries Association) for the same reason, there is no evidence that commercial pressure could be advanced as a solid reason for entry.

In sum, it may be seen that the economic case for accession was by no means as compelling as enthusiasm could make it appear. Economic benefit from entry was only a potential, as was recognised, and there were potential risks as well. Even if the aim were no more than to provide a defence against the threats envisaged in the Maudling thesis it could not be effective unless it produced an improvement in British economic performance, and it needed a degree of optimism to foresee that. Of course, some of the risks involved were implicit also in the European free trade area proposal but the price demanded was now much higher. On the economic front alone the imposition of the common external tariff against the Commonwealth would deprive the United Kingdom of preferences that covered 20% of its export trade, while the loss of access to the competitive world food market would raise wage costs throughout industry. Observations that pointed to a different conclusion were not totally lacking from the discussion, although they did tend to become swamped as it proceeded. In 1959 [23], for example, the Treasury argued that an economically expanding EEC would draw its neighbours along with it in any case (and could also pull them down if it declined), while the Chancellor emphasised the relative merits of the EFTA despite its smaller population. Voices continued to be raised as late as the summer of 1961 in favour of Commonwealth trade expansion and seeking to open the North American market.

There was thus something of a gamble in the judgment that other measures having failed to improve the country's economic performance a high price should be paid for accession to the Community. As the price was driven higher by successive failures to negotiate alternative arrangements it became necessary to vaunt the prospects. As the price was increasingly seen to be political it is not surprising that emphasis began to be placed on a political vision.

Politics

That there were political aspects to the Treaty of Rome and, consequently, to any attempt by the United Kingdom to accede to it was understood from the very beginning. However, it is necessary to disentangle them before proceeding to consider the development of the attitudes of the UK government towards them.

In the first place there were the institutions of the Community, namely the Council of Ministers, the Commission and the Court. The fact that they had supranational powers and could override national authorities was, rightly, seen as a political fact, however limited the areas in which those powers could be exercised.

Then there was the evident political purpose of the Community, which was seeking to arrive at a political end by an economic route. The exact form of the "ever closer union" adumbrated in the preamble to the Treaty was not fixed but, at the very least, it was intended to enable the Community to make a political impact on the world and it was this impact that Macmillan sought as early on October 1959 [20] to turn into harmless channels. Equally, it was this political purpose that Ministers were advised it was necessary to adopt if a success was to be made of British membership.

Again, to join together as members of a Community was seen to be a political action in itself, most frequently evidenced by the assertion that for the success of any of the various attempts made by the United Kingdom to come to an arrangement with the Six there had to be the political will on their part, especially that of France. This will had to be political in the sense of overriding, because more fundamental than, differences in commercial interests.

Finally, there were the political objectives of the British government, which took on a greater importance as negotiations progressed, or failed to progress. More will be said of them later.

The political aspects faced Ministers with a difficulty that has been typical of the European debate in Britain. They could not deny them, in plain defiance of the facts, nor could they belittle them without offence to their prospective partners. On the other hand they were capable of arousing great concern in the country. Thorneycroft in speaking [123] to representatives of the Yorkshire and Northern Areas of the Conservative Party in September 1961 contrived to go both ways. He described the problem as political more than economic and then denied that there was any intention anywhere of pooling sovereignty. There would be a sacrifice of sovereignty but Federal Europe was a long way off and not to be taken into account. The political decision was about how to organise the West in the face of danger. His listeners may well have been bemused. The following month Sandys said in Brussels that the Treaty was not simply an economic agreement but had a political content. This loose formulation, which officials had regularly used to Ministers, was, unsurprisingly, too advanced for Heath [124]. He set his officials to work to establish what Ministers had been saying in public, which turned out to be fairly limited, and to produce a formula for future use. This emphasised that the obligations of the Treaty applied only in the limited areas of trade and some social matters, though they could be expected to have political implications and results.   If we joined we would not regard ourselves as thereby committed to any particular development.

It has been seen that Ministers were warned, particularly by Sir Roderick Barclay writing from Brussels, of the risks involved if British commitment to political Europe came to be thought not to be genuine. Lee's paper of May 1960 had pointed out that the relegation of the federal objective under the influence of de Gaulle might be only temporary and it was impossible to say to what extent accession would commit Britain to accept that objective. At the Cabinet in July the more optimistic line was expressed that there was no need to become alarmed about political integration because UK membership of the Community would enable her to throw her weight on the side of those who preferred confederation, and this was the thought that underlay much of the reassurance that was given in public. Nevertheless, public warnings were also given, notably in Parliament by Lord Strang and Sir Derek Walker-Smith. The former, after defending the existing British policy towards Europe, said it would be dishonest to join the Community unless we were ready for political integration, while the latter prophesied that unless the government was prepared to go the full way with the Six the last state of relations with Europe could be worse than the first.

Inside government there were, occasionally, equally radical observations, particularly on sovereignty. Kilmuir, having noted that what was demanded by the Treaty of Rome was quite different in character from GATT and NATO obligations, explicitly balanced some sacrifice of sovereignty against economic factors and urged that the matter should be brought into the open. Officials went even further and warned that continental opinion actually required Britain to abandon a significant degree of sovereignty to demonstrate the earnestness of its attachment to the Community. Observations such as these formed no part of the government's case in public, when it was more inclined to point to similarities with NATO and GATT. What was missing from these arguments was any exploration of the possible evolution of this sacrifice of sovereignty. It was understood that the Treaty contained no time limit nor arrangements for withdrawal, but some comfort was drawn from the legal pronouncement [125] of the inherent right of a sovereign country to withdraw from an international agreement in certain circumstances. More frequently, the unlikelihood of Continental countries, some of which were substantial and some of which were monarchies, being willing to give up significant sovereignty, was asserted as a kind of proof that little was being demanded of Britain. This was reinforced by emphasising the limitations of the Treaty to economic matters and the veto that a United Kingdom inside the Community would have on any extension. This was to ignore both the very clear exposition of the political objectives of the Six that had been presented to government on many occasions and the extent to which the willingness of the Continental countries to submit themselves to a higher authority was founded upon a sense of humiliation (Macmillan's term) at national failure. If they could have seen the Community as a consolation club for the conquered the attitude of British Ministers might have been different.

But most of all, there was no apprehension of the possibility that this surrender could lead to pressure for further surrender, pressure that a British government might find impossible to resist, or even that it might provide the basis for the involvement of Community institutions in areas of national behaviour far beyond what was envisaged of a straightforward commercial treaty. Nor was there any sense of a ratchet process at work, by which the authority of the Community could only be extended, never retracted, although the ambitions of the Commission were perfectly clear to those who wished to understand.

It would not be surprising if the tone of discussion within the United Kingdom that was engendered by such a lack of radical analysis encouraged some elements of Continental opinion to believe that the United Kingdom as a member of the Community would seek to arrest its development.

But if there was one thing that British government was clear about it was that it would have no truck with federalism; consequently, it was obliged to be quite confident that if federalism should have the temerity to re-appear on the scene it could be quickly routed. Naturally, this was not how it appeared to everybody. Lee commented to George Ball that the move towards federalism, though checked, would continue and Hallstein expressed himself similarly to Heath. But these were comments that could easily be depreciated by pointing to the circumstances in which they were made and the general attitude in government could be summarised as the argument that now the threat of federalism had been removed it would be possible for Britain to sign up for this adventure. This was curiously prospective of the Wilson government's argument that now the threat of economic and monetary union had been removed it would be safe to vote 'Yes'.

The reason for all this optimism was, of course, de Gaulle, who explained to Macmillan his own conversion to support for the Treaty by pointing to his recognition of the possibility of confederation instead of federation. What this might mean in practice appears not to have been explored in any detail. It seems to have been understood that the powers to be transferred to the centre under such an arrangement would be strictly and permanently limited, so that there would be simply, in de Gaulle's phrase, co-operation among sovereign states. Nobody pointed out that the powers which might normally be thought appropriate to the centre of a confederation would be those related to its dealings with the external world, namely foreign policy and defence, which were precisely those which de Gaulle's sovereign states were insistent on retaining in their own hands. Furthermore, amid all the enthusiasm with which the British took to the Gaullist path, nobody paused to ask exactly how the Community might focus all the political influence that was predicted of it unless it moved in a federal direction, i.e. in some way obliged all its members to act as one. De Gaulle's idea of a political committee served by a secretariat might have provided the opportunity for member countries to take a common line, if it had come into existence, but that is not the same thing.

In government circles it was, of course, understood that things might be different after the departure of de Gaulle, specifically that there might then be a move towards federation. It was assumed that such a move would be fatal to British chances of accession to the Treaty, meaning, presumably, that it would be impossible to sell it to the country. The lesson drawn from this, however, was not that it would be wise to form some judgement of the likely weight behind such a move; on the contrary, it was urged that advantage should be taken of de Gaulle's presence and known views to press forward with an application.

In all the circumstances it was undoubtedly shrewd of Heath to avoid any reference to federalism when speaking in the House of Commons in the debate that followed the announcement of the decision to apply.

What took the place of an analysis of the meaning of federalism was an insistence in official discussions, of the importance of influence. It was this that formed the basis for the assertion that there were strong reasons of foreign policy for joining the Six. It was first the expected influence of the Community that made the running in debate, for it was argued that as its political integration developed it would acquire international influence at the expense of the United Kingdom, particularly within NATO and in relation to the United States. At the same time as it was perceived that the exercise of such influence beyond commercial negotiations was related to political integration it was being argued, by some, that the impetus towards such integration had largely disappeared. What is more, it was argued that the United Kingdom could somehow enhance its international influence by being inside a European bloc and at the same time continue to speak on its own account. But it could equally be argued, and was, that bloc membership could dilute the international impact achieved by members who needed to agree a common line and that the United Kingdom's influence would actually benefit by being outside. All arguments of this order came down to matters of judgement, but judgement can be improved by clarification of a kind that was not really present here.

Given the degree of contradiction between the influence of the Community and the influence of individual members that suggested itself some thought could have been given to the ways in which this might be resolved in practice, how lines of responsibility might be drawn or areas demarcated. How, for example, would the evident absence of any ambition for military power at the Community level affect the thesis that the Community was on the path to becoming a great Power? In the absence of some kind of analytical framework it was not possible for fundamental questions to pose themselves. What were the basic political interests of the United Kingdom? Previously one would have supposed them to include national independence, but this was no longer self-evident. Might it be the case that members of the Community were set, even unwittingly, on a course of trading in their international influence for internal influence within the Community? Might membership actually change a country's perception of its own interests? Obviously, these are all very difficult questions but it would have been better to make some organised attempt to answer them rather than simply to assume that membership would somehow gear up British political influence while leaving it completely independent. Of course, if membership produced riches they could be deployed to serve national interests but that is a separate argument and not of much effect if it had to be argued at the same time that political considerations should override possible economic difficulties. Assertions such as Home's, that membership was the road back to power, or George Brown's, that Britain's role was to lead Europe, whatever else they were, were not the result of sustained clear thinking in the circles of government.

Other aspects of influence were not ignored. Clearly Britain could expect to exercise influence on the internal affairs of the Community in proportion to her weight, though no case was set out for asserting that this might amount to leadership, beyond referring to the potential for holding the balance between the ambitions of France and Germany. Such influence would have relevance in favour of accession, however, only to the extent that the internal activities of the Community would affect the United Kingdom even if she were not a member. They might indeed, particularly in commercial matters, but on that sort of argument any country might argue that it should become a member or the United Kingdom might seek to join any grouping that was available.

Other arguments, relating to the possible effect of Britain on the Community, were more coherent. Now that it existed it was important, in Cold War terms, that it should not come apart and thereby afford the Soviet Union a toehold in Western Europe. One might certainly put some weight on that but, given that Britain would have been content, not many years earlier, to see the whole thing collapse one must doubt whether it could ever be a major plank. Then there was the possibility that the Community might hold together but move off in an undesirable direction. When this was explored, rather inconclusively, by officials some sort of neutrality was thought to be the greatest risk, despite the fact that in de Gaulle's view the Anglo-Americans themselves were likely to be soft on the Soviets. All this sort of thing was seen to be very speculative, though some running was made with the notion that British membership could keep the Community oriented to the Western Alliance, with even a possible evolution to an Atlantic Community, again despite de Gaulle's known views. The exploration of all these possibilities was not sufficiently rigorous to weigh the alternative view that the best way for Britain to meet the challenge of a neutralist Western Europe was not to become too close to it.

So far there is nothing particularly compelling about the argument from influence, but it has another aspect. It was said that outside the Community Britain's position and power would decline. It had certainly declined already, both economically and militarily, even without any rivalry from a new participant in the game. This was not, it was recognised, the sort of argument that could be deployed in public, but might we find here reasons of a force that would measure up to the scale of the policy reversal that the British government came to contemplate?

There is another thread that should be picked up first. It was regularly argued, both internally and externally, in support of the demand for an arrangement between the EEC and EFTA, whatever form of it was proposed at the time, that the economic division was bound to lead to a political division. This was the problem of Sixes and Sevens. The difficulty is that this danger was never spelt out in detail. One can imagine that Community members, as they became used to their obligation to arrive at agreements in trade matters, could easily fall into the habit first of consulting each other on other questions and then of seeking, if at all possible, to arrive at agreed positions.   Even without de Gaulle's plans for overt political co-operation.   But there appears no particular reason to suppose that policies thus reached would be adverse to the other countries of Western Europe, particularly in view of the overlapping membership of other organisations, above all of NATO.   It has to be said that the argument based on the threat of a split made no impression at all on a number of those who were exposed to it.   Hallstein did not see why the creation of two low-tariff clubs should lead to a split.   The Canadian government questioned whether the division was really so deep and dangerous.   No headway was made with the Eisenhower administration, which also did not see why the existence of the EEC should create a political split in Europe.   It can be argued that all these responses arose directly from the interests of the respondents, each of whom had their own agenda. But the same might be said of the British government, except that it is not obvious what was the agenda that drove them to harp on the dangers of political division.   The clue may be found in remarks made by the Prime Minister in Washington in March 1960, remarks that were leaked and caused a minor fuss, particularly in France.   Frustrated at inability to come to an agreement with the Six he was said to have evoked the shades of Napoleon and the Russian alliance, which was taken at the newspaper level as a threat.   When he met de Gaulle the following month at Buckingham Palace he felt obliged to offer the explanation [30] that he had in fact been arguing his thesis that the economic plans under discussion might cause a further division of Western Europe.   What he did threaten, however delicately, was to withdraw British troops from Germany to ease the balance of payments deficit.   On neither issue did de Gaulle appear to be perturbed.

Nor was this Macmillan's only appeal to history.   On the same visit to Washington [29] he referred to the situation of 1940 (a hostile Western Europe) as a danger, that might be repeated and noted in his diary shortly afterwards [126]:-

Shall we be caught between a hostile (or at least less and less friendly) America and a, boastful, powerful Empire of Charlemagne - now under French but later bound to come under German control? Is this the real reason for 'joining' the Common Market (if we are acceptable) and for abandoning (a) the Seven (b) British agriculture and (c) the Commonwealth? It's a grim choice.

It was certainly a grim choice and one can see why every government speaker strained to deny that this was what was at issue. Even Macmillan could later see that it was all somewhat exaggerated, but it does become clear that what might be called the 'Charlemagne thesis' actually was the 'real reason' and that assertion of the dangers of a political split in Western Europe was a coded expression of fear of a power hostile to Britain dominating the Continent. To this traditional British fear there was a traditional British response, the formation of an alliance with a power on the further flank. Hence Napoleon, 1940 and Russia.

The questions that had to be answered at the time were how realistic is the Continental threat to Britain? and what are the appropriate measures to circumvent it? The delicacy of the matter can hardly be overstated. Not only was it impossible to advance any such argument in public, it would have been risky to be explicit even in official documents. Even the suggestions of historical analogies could cause trouble (as it had done as early as 1957 for Eccles), but it would be safe to talk vaguely of a split, as long as the concept was not too closely questioned. The possibility that a 'Third Force' might be actively hostile was not among those canvassed in the Prime Minister's Questions of 1960, but from such material as is there it does not appear that it would have been regarded very seriously. In terms of power politics it was said that the value of the Community lay in tying Germany down, or keeping her in; on the Charlemagne thesis British membership would be aimed at doing the same to the Community.

One must concede that there might have been a long-term risk of Continental hostility to the United Kingdom, and that it might have coincided with American indifference and the impossibility of seeking any counterbalance in the East. The combination is so remote as to afford very little ground for action, especially drastic action, but the evidence, as we have seen, is that it formed part of the Prime Minister's reasoning, even a decisive part. This was the real objective of the search to exercise influence in the inner councils of Europe, since a Britain in decline would have no other means of averting the threat.

Overall, therefore, the political part of the case for switching policy to entry to the EEC was muddled in public and muddled in private. Federalism was abhorred on all sides but as a threat it was discounted by virtually everyone involved. Sovereignty would be affected in some minor way, which was not completely understood. In a variety of ways Community membership involved politics, in some sense, but the risk that the British interpretation of such involvement might be at odds with that of the Six was disregarded. There was a consciousness of the decline of British power, which somehow might be rectified by entry. If not that, at any rate the anger of a hostile Western Europe would be nullified. It was said at the time that the members of EFTA were united by a common funk; it might equally have been said that a large part of the impetus for British entry was also funk. But it could not be said that fear of continental domination induced a conscious pre-emptive surrender; those involved were completely confident that Britain would always be able to control the situation.

The Commonwealth

The importance of the Commonwealth connexion and the necessity to maintain it is a thread that runs throughout the debate. When in the summer of 1960 the possibility of a closer approach to the Six was brought to the Cabinet it was asserted that the political importance of maintaining the connexion could be demonstrated to Britain's prospective partners. The difficulty was seen to lie on the economic front where neither the complete abandonment of free entry to the United Kingdom for Commonwealth products nor its retention in full could be envisaged as acceptable. Yet the political relationship was also seen to be dependent in large part upon the economic relationship and if that was seriously disturbed the value of the

Commonwealth as a stabilising factor in the free world could be lost. In its initial approach to the American government the following year the British government continued to insist on the great value of the Commonwealth; in fact at no time did the government, even initially, appear to question the principle or attempt to balance losses in the area against gains elsewhere. Officials on the other hand, particularly Sir Frank Lee, were from time to time critical of the orthodoxy, but it was left to the French to put the knife in. Both Wormser and de Gaulle were perfectly clear that British entry meant forsaking the Commonwealth; for them it was part of the price they expected to get.

This was not something the British government was prepared to admit in public, indeed it ferociously denied that it was faced with the choice between Commonwealth and Europe, even though Macmillan could confide to his diary at an early stage that abandonment was what was in contemplation. The evolution of thinking about free entry is the clearest marker of the way in which the government was forced back into a position of salvaging what pieces it could of its original policy. The earlier free trade area proposals had sought to find a way in which Commonwealth goods could continue to be freely imported into the United Kingdom, without their re-export to the continent breaching the common external tariff of the Six. After that had failed it was at first supposed that some free entry could be preserved, though the existing form of preference, which included the preferences in Commonwealth markets, could not be expected to survive. Further, it was perceived that unless special arrangements could be negotiated joining the Common Market would actually reverse the preference given Commonwealth goods in the United Kingdom by giving Europe preferences against them. It was supposed that, apart from agriculture, Commonwealth countries might be able to secure some preferences for themselves in Europe but their governments would have, would indeed wish, to negotiate that for themselves.

Despite what was being written within government circles no hint was given externally of any withdrawal from free entry until Macmillan met de Gaulle at Rambouillet in early 1961. He proceeded cautiously, in the context of only an association with the Six, and indicated his acceptance that industrial goods from the Commonwealth would have to be subject to the common external tariff. The memorandum prepared for the new US administration mentioned free entry but tactfully avoided any commitment to its retention. The Americans could be relied upon to be hostile. At that time, negotiations at official level were still being conducted on the basis of the full retention of free entry, including industrial goods, while at Cabinet Committee shortly afterwards Ministers recalled that at the Commonwealth Economic Consultative Council the United Kingdom had said that free entry would be maintained. But only a little later still the New Zealand Prime Minister was told merely that free entry of agricultural products should be preserved.

By the summer the exclusion of industrial goods could be aggressively defended on the ground that Britain could not be expected to go on indefinitely providing an open market for them; the contrary argument that in that case an open market for British industrial exports might have been sought in those Commonwealth countries in which it was not available seems not to have occurred to anybody.

At all events, as has been seen, the principle of free entry had been exchanged for a search for any special treatment that might ease the economic pain for some Commonwealth countries, even if only for a time. The damage to the economic interests of the United Kingdom that would be sustained by the abandonment of the preference was ignored, treated as one part of the price that it was seen to be necessary to pay. The importance of the Commonwealth to the stability of the free world was no longer a part of government doctrine, but the old beliefs had not simply disappeared in all quarters. That was why special arguments had to be prepared, for example about getting investment for Commonwealth countries out of Europe, and why it had to be asserted that ways had been perceived in which Britain could proceed without undue detriment to itself and members of the Commonwealth, a remark which has virtually no substantive content.

Nor was the need to pay overt heed to Commonwealth interests a consequence of the sentimentality of an uninformed general public. It has been seen that Lord Mills, who had been a member of the Cabinet Committee on Europe, felt it necessary to assert to the Prime Minister his own robust belief in the future of the Commonwealth.   When the announcement was made Macmillan's Solicitor-General (Sir Jocelyn Simon) was worried enough to write to him to seek alternative Commonwealth arrangements. The reply was that were no indications from the Commonwealth that they would like such an idea.   This was disingenuous even by Macmillan's standards. He went on to say that if Commonwealth countries found themselves faced with gradual supersession in the UK market there might be some change of heart and if negotiations were to fail we should have to look again at the possibility of closer Commonwealth ties. By the time this undertaking might have been put to the test the government had more pressing problems but it is interesting that Gaitskell's mind was also proceeding along these lines. At the time of his death and before the Gaullist veto he was actually planning a tour for this purpose [127].

The effect of a closer association with Europe on Britain's relations, in the widest sense, with the rest of the Commonwealth was therefore always a matter of concern to the British government, though this concern steadily diminished in practice. At an early stage it was noted that there would be serious misgiving in the Commonwealth if it was thought that the United Kingdom was prepared to become part of a political federation or if European free trade extended to agricultural as well as industrial goods. Since the government was perfectly confident of its ability to overcome the former threat it was not surprising that it felt able to disregard more pessimistic views on the part of Commonwealth members, even while it acknowledged the theoretical difficulty that would be presented to the maintenance of Commonwealth relationships. As for the second it would have to wait and see what could be negotiated; it was understood that if the terms did turn out to damage particular Commonwealth countries there would be political consequences that might go so far as to endanger the existence of the Commonwealth, but simply to rebut this point it was argued that a Britain in economic decline would be of reduced value to its Commonwealth partners.

This was to ignore the admitted fact that Europe offered no more than a potential for improving the country's economic position by the stimulus of competition; if this potential was not realised there would be Commonwealth as well as economic disbenefits.

The British government was ready to assert an intention to preserve the fundamental Commonwealth trading interests, and continued to do so even after its application was in. It is not surprising that both Canadians and Australians complained of their difficulty in getting any position out of the United Kingdom[128]. Since the government had decided to apply first and negotiate afterwards and had, in addition, set its face against seeking an agreement with the Commonwealth countries on the terms that might be acceptable to them, it chose in effect, to put the preservation of its negotiating position with the Six before its need to allay Commonwealth disquiet. This was bound to impair Commonwealth relations despite the government's own assertions of the importance of the Commonwealth for the stability of the free world and for its contribution to the international influence of the United Kingdom itself. Whatever happened in the negotiations such impairment was a fact. In reality, therefore, when Sandys said that if Britain was forced to choose between Europe and the Commonwealth it would choose the Commonwealth this was the exact opposite of the truth.

Agriculture

There were two aspects of the problem presented under the label of agriculture to the closer association of the United Kingdom with the Six. The first was the system of support that had been developed for British farmers, which was quite different from what was envisaged on the continent, and the second was the supply of foodstuffs to British consumers at the lowest world prices, particularly from the Commonwealth. These two policies were closely bound up with each other in practice, since the deficiency payments system of support was designed to enable British producers to survive the challenge of cheap food in the home market. They were also combined as responsibilities of the Minister of Agriculture.

Agriculture had been excluded in the British proposals for a free trade area in Europe precisely because of these difficulties; no doubt the exclusion was a significant element in the failure of those negotiations. When in 1960 proposals for joining the Six were brought to Cabinet it was recognised that while British farmers might not suffer on the whole they would need to be convinced that they would not be disadvantaged by a radically different policy. After all, they had been given a pledge that the current support system would be maintained during the lifetime of Parliament. Consumers would have to pay more for food, perhaps 7½% more, but the savings to the Exchequer from abandoning the support system could be used to lower taxation.

The Minister of Agriculture, then John Hare, was not impressed. He felt there was little chance of a settlement that would be fair to Commonwealth countries and acceptable to UK farmers, while the complexities of renegotiating trade agreements and instituting new systems in the country would be formidable.

It needed a change of Minister to produce a more favourable line. When the question came again to the Cabinet in the following April, Soames argued that the Six would build up agricultural surpluses to which the United Kingdom would be exposed if free entry of food was retained, thereby increasing the support from the Exchequer necessary to maintain British farmers. This is an argument which sits oddly with the claim that British farmers had little to fear because they were capable of greater efficiency than their continental rivals. He was prepared to see both the net income of British agriculture and Commonwealth trade reduced but hoped to shift some of the burden to third countries. To put it baldly this was now a proposal to abandon a cheap food policy which had lasted for more than a hundred years (and was directly opposed to the Continental attachment to autarky and protectionism) in the hope of reducing Exchequer expenditure that would then have to be counterbalanced by tax reductions. He could equally have argued that if the burden on the Exchequer became intolerable because world food prices were driven down by surpluses then the net income of British agriculture should be reduced - since he was prepared to contemplate this in any case. This, however, was not the angle of attack chosen in Cabinet, where the main concern was to avoid the appearance of pledge-breaking. Nothing had yet been proposed to protect the interests of horticulturists, pig-farmers and egg producers.

In response Soames made a crucial point. He fully accepted the importance of the pledges but said that the Six would require the abandonment of the cheap food policy because it kept down wages. He was thus advocating that the United Kingdom should enter into an arrangement that was intended by its prospective partners to make it less competitive. This does not sit well with the argument that entry was essential to combat competition.

When Soames returned to the charge the following month in the European Economic Association Committee of the Cabinet he now estimated the addition to the food bill at 4½%. He attributed the hostility of the National Farmers' Union to the limitation of their role that would follow the adoption of the Common Agricultural Policy but expressed confidence that arrangements could be made that would in the long term preserve the agricultural industry overall.

In the broadest sense this was not an unreasonable expectation. The Six were clearly bent on a policy of support for agriculture and, in the event of entry, that would have to include British agriculture. But this support would be at the expense of consumers and Commonwealth producers and what was not calculated was that, given the greater scale of agriculture in the Continental economies, a common policy, as opposed to national support policies, would be likely to transfer resources from Britain to the continent. Of course, in 1961, the government could be excused for not foreseeing the enormity of the eventual financing of the Common Agricultural Policy - only a manic depressive could have done that - but it was surely remiss in not considering the point. On the strictly agricultural balance the only benefit was a dubious gain to the Exchequer, and even that had to be set against the aim of the Six to reduce British competitiveness while increasing the market for their own production. Clearly agriculture was an obstacle to be overcome for the sake of benefits elsewhere.

The United States

The attitude of the United States to Britain's relations with Europe developed in a manner that was curiously parallel to the evolution of British government thinking, even though they were at times at odds. Keeping the American connexion in good order was a virtually permanent priority for British governments and neglect of it at the time of Suez seemed only to emphasise how crucial it was. While it was not pressure from the United States that led to Britain first to hold back from the developing union on the Continent and then to seek to be embraced by it, the implications for the relationship with the United States were never far from British thinking.

The fundamental characteristic of American policy towards the EEC was a belief in its value as a bastion of the Cold War. Its economic development might cause problems for a United States then beginning to see the end of its absolute domination in the free world but it was a price readily paid for the creation of a political unit in Western Europe capable of resisting the encroachment and the blandishments of the Soviet Union. After all, there were countries on the Continent in which the assumption of power by the Communist Party was far from inconceivable. American reaction to any proposed arrangement between Britain and the Six depended on what was thought to be the likely effect on the programme of political integration. It seems to have been supposed in Washington that the success of the federal cause in that country offered a sensible and practical example to Europe, while there was no evident apprehension of the potential for anti-American policies on the part of the Community. Yet all the countries involved had either been rescued or defeated (or both) by the United States, which might have given some pause for thought.

Under the Eisenhower administration there was no wish to see an agreement between the Six and the Seven. Apart from increasing discrimination against US exports such a development was liable to dilute the political content of the Community [129], i.e. progress towards a United Europe. If that desirable result came about its trading relations with the rest of Europe and the world could be negotiated within OEEC and GATT. Nor, given the

North Atlantic Alliance, should it lead to a political split. What did concern the Americans was to press the Six towards a liberal trade policy that would reduce the economic damage to them. Sir Frank Lee was probably right to argue in the spring of 1960 that the Americans were more likely to be swayed by a political case than by Macmillan's concern over the acceleration of tariff reductions; the trouble was that there was no political case at the time other than the threatened split, which was either a discredited or a dangerous card to play.

Lee was to contend a little later that if a Six-Seven agreement could be obtained by paying a sufficiently high price - the terms he laid out amounted to accession - the United States would be obliged to accept the *fait accompli* with a good grace. By the time the matter went to the full Cabinet it was being suggested they would probably welcome it.

It is not at all clear that any of these prognostications in the first half of 1960 were based on any detailed discussions with the US administration. Since the last of them depended on a substantial shift in British policy which the government had not yet made that is unsurprising. What is important about these points is that the British had previously argued to themselves that the maintenance of the special relationship, among other things, prohibited too tight an entanglement with European developments. This argument was now beginning to be turned on its head by those who were working for entry. The Cabinet memorandum went on to suggest that the growing power of the Community would increase its influence on the United States at the expense of the United Kingdom and, as a corollary, that British influence on America would be increased if it was associated with the Six and could serve as an intermediary. This is a difficult concept which was not fully explored. The role of broker, to which de Gaulle thought Britain naturally gravitated, is conceivable for a third party not wholly committed to either of the others, but a United Kingdom which had become a member of the Community would be obliged to adopt the Community's stance in trans-Atlantic relations; the most it could do would be to soften them, but it would hardly be acceptable to its partners for Britain to act as a channel or filter. It was partly the apprehension of such an attempt that led to the Gaullist rebuff. A rather more realistic scenario that came to be deployed was that Britain's special relationship would be transmuted into a European special relationship - but what would happen if this turned sour?

Since the British government had experienced from the United States at best a lack of support and at worst hostility in its efforts to resolve what it saw as the European problem some excitement was inevitable following the Democratic victory in the 1960 election.

A fairly cautious document was fired off to Washington; George Ball's response when he met Heath and Sir Frank Lee at the end of March was to say that the kind of solution at present envisaged would not be satisfactory to the United States, which would like to see the United Kingdom join the EEC. This was a position well in advance of the attitude Lee had found in Washington only the previous month or that displayed by the President a little later, but Ball was both an associate of Jean Monnet, founding father of the Community, and, in Macmillan's eyes hostile to British policy in Europe. According to Ball [130] it was the British who were now talking about entry. What all this confusion probably covers is that this turned out to be a meeting of fairly like-minded enthusiasts who were in no position to commit their governments, but at least there were signs of possible development in the attitude of the United States, though always within their traditional policy of pressing for European political integration.

Enough groundwork had been done to make possible an advance in the crucial Washington discussions of 1961. Macmillan and Home went there to seek American support for the policy of accession on which they had determined and naturally tried to make it look as attractive to their hosts as they could. There were two reasons for this. The first was to disarm those potential critics at home who clung to the older idea that to draw closer to the Europeans was also to draw away from the Americans, an idea that was shared by no less an authority that the French President. The second was to induce the US

Administration to press the Six, particularly France, to admit the United Kingdom.

What was offered the Americans to prevent them from reverting to their earlier hostility to a British involvement with the Six was the idea that this could be the start of something big, an Atlantic Community that would prevent the development of the European Community into a Third Force. It would enable the United States, with the United Kingdom as a partner, to continue to exercise influence in Europe and keep the new political unit on track. But Kennedy did not pick up any of this at the time and his own ideas, when they emerged, were to be significantly different. However, Macmillan secured the American support he wanted and was emboldened to tell his Cabinet that the main US concern was to prevent the Six from developing as a separate political force. But there is no sign of any such anxiety in the record; if anything, the Americans continued to insist on their old policy of expediting the further political integration of the Community and hostility towards EFTA.

On the American side the talks were seen as introducing an extraordinary reversal [131]. The British Prime Minister had come to announce his government's resolution to apply for membership of the European Community. For this there were two grounds, the economic hope of a competitive stimulus and the political hope that in the twilight of empire Britain could find a new role of leadership in Europe. The second was the more attractive in Washington since it offered the prospect of greater political stability, of a greater likelihood of low tariffs and the basis for a true political federation of Europe. There is some support for this view of Schlesinger's in the record of the talks but it is attributed to Ball, not Kennedy, and what the Administration made clear it was officially concerned about was not appearing to exert pressure on the United Kingdom.

When Kennedy visited de Gaulle in June [132] he attempted to persuade the latter of the virtues of British membership, not omitting to point to the economic problems that the United States was prepared to face for the sake of European political and economic unity. De Gaulle's response was on lines that for him had become traditional and this discussion was not unlike that which he had had with Macmillan earlier in the year, though he tactfully omitted his poser about the United Kingdom becoming less inclined to follow the United States, offering instead for Britain a choice between Commonwealth and Common Market. The door to membership was open but he doubted whether Britain really wanted it. The President of the United States cannot be said to have had a success with the President of France on this issue and this failure should have led to some reconsideration in Britain, where the Cabinet had previously agreed that a favourable response from de Gaulle was a precondition of further negotiations. But the government acted otherwise and put in their application first and negotiated afterwards.

It is worth noting the United States policy as it developed in the following year. While it became enthusiastic and forceful about British membership it remained hostile to special arrangements for EFTA and the Commonwealth. The Kennedy Grand Design foresaw an economically and politically integrated Western Europe joined to North America by policies and institutions in common pursuit of economic expansion and military defence. To adapt a phrase they would be equal but separate; there was no place here for Britain as a bridge or intermediary with a foot in each camp - it would enjoy a relationship with the United States only by virtue of being a member of the Community.

By the end of the year the failure of Skybolt could be seen in Washington as a grand opportunity to terminate the special relationship and force Britain into Europe [132]. But at this date who was it that needed to be forced?

The American connexion thus progressed from hostility through support and enthusiasm to pressure. It never took much heed of what Britain saw as its pre-existing obligations except to oppose them. But it did not provide the original impetus for Britain's application and its own unchanged aim of the creation of a powerful political unit in continental Europe on Cold War grounds was quite at odds with the fears that induced the British government into performing a somersault.

The Officials

A brief mention of the role played by the civil service in these developments would be in place. Officials were careful not to undertake tasks, particularly in official level committees of the Cabinet, without securing Ministerial approval in advance. On the other hand, they quite properly felt free to put up suggestions for bold demolition of the limits imposed on them, for example in the spring of 1960, when a serious re-assessment of the whole problem was on the cards [26].

The traditional service role of providing warnings was not neglected and may be best exemplified by Sir Roderick Barclay's insistence on the need to accept the Community's goal of political union and the advice to the government, as it approached the point of applying to be allowed into the club, not to do so in any half-hearted way.

But the operation of these normal procedures was itself subject to the general climate of opinion in Whitehall which, not unnaturally, moved in the same general direction as that of the politicians, though it was sometimes in advance. During 1960 support for accession changed from being a decidedly minority cause to a stock establishment view, at least in some departments. Moon [134] gives evidence of this, as well as of the growing importance attached to the political aspects of the question.

At the middle levels of the bureaucracy, in the Treasury and the European Organisations Department of the Foreign Office, there was a willingness to express radical views about pulling up roots and full membership being the only logical outcome. This sort of attitude was understandable among those engaged full time in the area, but the position of officials at senior levels was potentially more significant.   Lord Gladwyn in the Paris Embassy was a longstanding advocate of accession. Although his seat in the Lords enabled him to address the Foreign Secretary as an equal [135], it may be doubted whether his influence was particularly strong - Eccles referred scornfully to the economic pundits, the enthusiasts and the Lord Gladwyns of European integration [78] - but it was enough to make him one of the recipients of Sir Frank Lee's trial balloon in May 1960.

The transfer of Lee to the Treasury at the beginning of 1960 must be regarded as one of the most significant points in the development of Britain's attitude to the Common Market. On his arrival the Cabinet Committee of officials that dealt with the subject was re-organised, though this seems to have been no more than an administrative tidying. He was translated from the Permanent Secretaryship of the Board of Trade with only a limited time to serve before retirement and his pro-accession views must have been known to the Prime Minister, who would normally be involved in appointments at this level. At some time, then, in the second half of 1959, the year in which the Conservatives had scorned at the General Election Liberal advocacy of the European solution and the year in which the British government had entered into the EFTA treaty, thereby re-affirming the country's refusal to join the Common Market, Macmillan chose to place an enthusiast for the Community at the heart of government planning. It can only be concluded that he had already decided on the goal towards which he was to manoeuvre over the next two years.

Conclusion

The reasoning process that accompanied the great reversal may be summarised in the following way. Clear advantage might be obtainable, on conventional free trade grounds, if an agreement could be reached with the Community to extend its internal free trade arrangements to the United Kingdom. When this proved impossible what was perceived was a competitive threat to Britain's international trade from a Community not only advancing rapidly on the basis of its very large internal market but also containing elements of hostility to the British. This threat could be met only by improving British economic performance, which had long been in decline, and access to the Common Market offered the potential for this via the stimulus that would be imposed on British industry and commerce. This could not be certain; what was certain was that the Common Agricultural Policy would increase British wage costs (unless taxation could be reduced) and that for better access to a market which then accounted for 14% of British exports preferences would have to be given up in Commonwealth markets that then accounted for 20% of British exports. It is, perhaps, not surprising that within government the emphasis began to turn towards the politics of the issue.

The political grounds on which entry had been opposed were the immediate transfer of some sovereign powers to the Community, the threat of further transfer posed by the federalist impulses present on the continent and the detriment caused thereby to the intimate relations of the United Kingdom with the other members of the Commonwealth and with the United States. In the case of the former there was also the damage arising from the reversal of trade preferences. These factors came to seem less important as the argument from influence and split were developed. The loss of sovereignty was confined to limited areas, the federal threat could be indefinitely contained and the value of the Commonwealth was played down. Damage to the special relationship with the United States seemed less significant when the Americans became enthusiastic about British entry, though there was also the somewhat wistful thought that the Community could develop a special relationship of its own with the Americans.

In place of links with United States and Commonwealth, two of Churchill's interlocking circles, all the emphasis was now transferred to influence in and through the third. This was not analysed as closely as it might have been. British influence inside the Community was thought to be an insurance against the risk of the Community heading off in a non-Atlantic neutralist direction and, more positively, as a means of creating some sort of Atlantic Community, with Britain in an intermediary role. Britain's influence in the world, in some fashion not clearly set out, might actually be enhanced rather than reduced by becoming one among the members of the Community. The reason that dared not speak its name and could not, therefore, be openly analysed was to nullify the risk of a politically hostile Western Europe. It is really not possible to assess how realistic such apprehensions were or what alternative political plans might have been laid to deal with them. But it is not easy to believe that dramatic and irrevocable steps were appropriate in 1961 to deal with this kind of cloud on the horizon.

Thinking was not simply shallow; it was also wishful. The prime example of infirmity of judgement is the dismissal of Britain's application by the President of France. This was not only a massive disabuse of the belief, which existed in the face of all the evidence of French hostility and intransigence, that even de Gaulle would not be capable of going against all his partners as well as Britain on some minor technicality arising from the negotiations; it was mercilessly rapid and complete. It had long been argued that the key was the political will of France and that, accordingly, negotiations should not be commenced until goodwill on the part of France had been ensured. When this was clearly not available the British government reversed its position, only to find, humiliatingly, that it had been right the first time.

The government never really faced up to the threat to the Commonwealth inherent in its move towards Europe but continued to tell itself of the organisation's value, to convince itself of its ability to persuade its prospective partners of that value and to assume that Britain would continue to lead the Commonwealth from a position of strength inside the Community. All this despite the political and economic blows to its fellow members that it was prepared to inflict as it moved steadily towards compliance with Continental requirements and despite the evident hostility of some of their governments.

It has to be said that over the period other Community governments than the French exhibited some willingness to recognise the United Kingdom's obligations to the Commonwealth (and to EFTA) but that offers only a limited excuse for British optimism, given the evident determination of France, and the United States so far as she was involved, to weaken the Commonwealth ties of a Britain inside the Community.

Nor was there much substance in British aspirations to build an Atlantic Union by bringing the United States and the Community together. Insofar as they could be pushed together by the Soviet threat they were already together in NATO and there was no conceivable leverage that Britain could exploit to pull a Community still dominated by France down an economic route to a closer association with the United States. It was precisely that the Gaullist fear of such an outcome, already evident in our period, that help to impel his rejection of Britain in early 1963.

The idea that Britain could exercise leadership in Europe is something of a magical reversal of the Charlemagne thesis. It is not advanced very often in the sources but seems to be particularly associated with, though not unique to, Macmillan. Not only was it ascribed to him in the American version of his meeting with Kennedy, at the same period he confided to his diary the thought that Europe and Britain acting in a harmonious leadership would be the equal of the USA and USSR. It was not an idea that could have been much explored.

There were other ideas that would take more time to expose. The government was utterly confident that it could control the internal development of the Community, that is prevent any aspirations of a federal kind from having effect. This was not inherently as unlikely as some of its fancies, though it was aware that it was undertaking some degree of commitment to a political union of some sort.

Finally, there was an assumption that does not appear very often but must have underlain all the government's actions. This was that it and its successors could go on indefinitely performing a balancing act in convincing the other members of Britain's full-hearted consent to their aspirations for the Community while simultaneously playing down the significance of the application in order to reassure the Conservative Party, the Commonwealth and EFTA [136]. In the first instance this turned out to be much less difficult than had been expected and to this extent was not an instance of wishful thinking at all. What was not taken into account, and it might have been, was that this presentational problem would not go away, that British governments inside the Community might regularly find themselves obliged to say one thing to their fellow-members and something else to everybody else. What was wishful thinking was to suppose that the problem could occur only once.

To get Britain to the point of asking for admission to the European club a good deal of manoeuvring was inevitable. We have seen how the key Cabinet places were filled by known enthusiasts for entry and how, in early 1961, a balanced draft memorandum was held back from the Cabinet on Heath's intercession. He wished then to avoid a discussion of principle but it continued to be envisaged that at some point a memorandum balancing advantages and disadvantages would be produced. This point never came. The factors that had previously been held to militate against entry were transmuted into obstacles to be overcome, or disregarded, while even the tactical stance advocated by Heath as late as April, of securing adequate derogations by negotiations in advance of expressing willingness to accede to the Treaty, was simply dropped two months later and reminders of it equally simply disregarded. This gives it the air of having been produced only to fend off disquiet. A spurious consultation of Commonwealth governments was conducted to smother other objections. The Cabinet was thus moved towards the crucial decision to apply subject only to commercial negotiations, a decision which was truly one of principle and one from which the government was not in practice likely to be in a position to resile [137]. There could have been no truly balanced memorandum at the conclusion of negotiations.

The control of intra-governmental debate was accompanied by restraint on public discussion. The proposal for a White Paper was dismissed precisely because it would give rise to attacks. The attempt to suppress Heath's speech to the governments of the Six was due to its trumpeting of the scale of readjustment that was being demanded of Britain; it was accompanied by his anxious attempts to play down references to the political aspects of accession. Presentation was always perceived to be both essential to overcome opposition in the country and the party and extremely difficult to carry off successfully; in the event the ovine tendency of the Conservative party and the nearly universal support of the Press made all their worries otiose.

How was it that the Prime Minister and his allies came to satisfy themselves that reasoning of the calibre that has been set out justified them in pushing the government and the country into the change of attitude and direction represented by accession to the Treaty? How was it that the political classes came to accept it as readily as they did? The answers to these questions lie in the heart rather than the mind, in motives as opposed to reasons. They are really outside the scope of this work and will be touched on only briefly. Kitzinger [138] identified five milestones on the road to Damascus. Two of them are economic reasons and are dealt with elsewhere; the other three are Suez, the abandonment of Blue Streak and the collapse of the Paris Summit in the spring of 1960. They stand as motivation because the Community was not designed to restore to Western Europe the capacity for independent military adventure, particularly in the case of the British, who clung to the American Alliance and American armaments, nor could it be represented as an alternative route to superpower reconciliation and the unfreezing of the Cold War. What they point to is a profound discomfort over the decline of power, a state of demoralisation.

Macmillan himself has been represented as reaching his decision because of the collapse of the Summit in April 1960, on the evidence of his Private Secretary, Philip de Zulueta, confirmed by Leo Pliatzky [139]. He had long been thought of as one of the "European" members of the Cabinet but had disappointed those of like mind by his failure to push towards the continent after becoming Prime Minister. We have seen there is reason to suppose the decision was made earlier than April 1960; what is interesting is Pliatzky's description of the Prime Minister sitting with his foreign policy in ruins about him and wondering what he was going to do for a foreign policy. One might well ask what he was doing with a personal foreign policy, since Britain's policy after the Summit was clearly going to be to soldier on in NATO as it had done before. Pliatzky's own answer was that Macmillan was attempting to secure a niche in history, which is confirmed by Horne [140]. This is probably the right answer and a demeaning one. The temptation for ageing politicians to push themselves into action for the sake of leaving a mark is a commonplace but it is not the less reprehensible for that. Whenever Macmillan may have made the decision to pick up his

European credentials there is certainly a feeling of haste about him in 1960 and 1961.

If Macmillan was demoralised on account of his own ambitions there was a wider mood of defeatism over British decline. A Cabinet that could produce and leave unchallenged an assertion that Soviet industrial output per worker was far greater than that of the United Kingdom was in a mood to convince itself of anything. Evidence of this spirit and that it continued for years has been assembled by Peter Jenkins [141], though as a backcloth for the Thatcherite upheaval rather than Macmillan's. It is as though informed opinion had cultivated a sense of defeatism, rather in the way that Wilhelmine Germany had convinced itself that it was surrounded by enemies, and had thereby become susceptible to anything that might relieve the pain. They were looking for a man on a white horse.

Chapter Three

The Results

To test the British government's reasoning by the results of accession to the Treaty of Rome it is necessary to look at them from the point of view of British interests. The British government, quite properly, did not introduce into its arguments the visionary aim of bringing into existence a Power capable of protecting and giving full play to the European talents, whose superiority was attested by their achievements in the world. This is not to say that there were not members of the government for whom such a vision was the fundamental motivation. This seems to have been the case with Heath and there is a trace of it, to say the least, in Macmillan's Toynbean argument. But it is all at a different level from the case based on British interests; in working to an end of the visionary kind national interests might have to be disregarded as not significant except insofar as they hindered the necessary developments. Within such a policy, which could be summed up as *Europa über alles*, national interests might be expected eventually to wither away.

So that we have to concern ourselves with is whether, in Chandos' terms the United Kingdom and its people are stronger, richer and happier as a result of accession. This cannot be a counterfactual exercise, in which we attempt to work out what might have happened had other decisions been made, as they might easily have been, but some use can be made of comparison between the period from the failed attempt up to eventual entry to the Common Market and the period that has followed. For convenience the economic and political spheres are treated separately, as they were in the previous section.

The Economy

In the period since Macmillan's application there have been three major financial crises for the United Kingdom, the 1967 devaluation, the 1976 recourse to the International Monetary Fund and the 1992 retreat from the Community's Exchange Rate Mechanism. The last of these is evidently bound up with Community membership but it is not possible to discern any substantial relationship between the first two and the country's non-membership or membership.

It has been suggested [144], however, that the Labour government's decision in 1967 to renew its predecessor's application for membership was a factor tending to increase market pressure on sterling. It was feared that the balance of payments costs of entry would lead to devaluation, but market sentiment of this kind was short-term in character and relatively insignificant. Indeed, it could not have existed had there not been much more fundamental reasons for devaluation. The combination of continuing deficits on the balance of payments (to which government expenditure made a considerable contribution), leading to heavy calls on the reserves, with fiscal deficits resulting from the government's reflationary policy were the major factors, helped along by the Six-Day War and closure of the Suez Canal. At no time has it been suggested that Britain would have avoided devaluation had it been enjoying the benefits of the large home market of Western Europe or even that it would have received sufficient support for that purpose from its partners. The leader in the failed last-minute attempts to put together a support package was the United States.

In 1976 the obligation to maintain a fixed parity had gone, thanks to the floating of the pound, while the long-term economic prospects should have been improved, in market eyes at least, by attachment to the European growth engine. To what extent the excesses of its predecessor were responsible for the difficulties the Labour government ran into will no doubt be as matter of debate for many years but it is not our present concern. After a referendum had confirmed Britain's membership of the Market the ending of uncertainty, at any rate, should have assisted business confidence. It will suffice to note the major elements that marked the crisis, without any assertion as to the links between them. Public expenditure rose even more rapidly in 1975 than in 1974 and was accompanied by both a large Public Sector Borrowing Requirement (11% of GDP) and a sizeable balance of payments deficit. By the end of the year output had fallen 2% below that of the previous year, while unemployment worsened. The government adopted a disinflationary policy during 1975 by increasing the Minimum Lending Rate, instituting a pay freeze, announcing a money supply target and, in 1976, by heavily cutting public expenditure. But sterling continued to fall against the dollar while the current deficit rose. In September the government announced its intention to borrow £2300m from the International Monetary Fund. Despite what had been said in Labour's White Paper there is no evidence that help was sought from Community countries (if it was it was refused), although in 1977 the Bank for International Settlements provided a standby credit of £1765m and the government later negotiated a loan of £873m from UK, German and American banks.

The ignominious and expensive exit from the ERM would not, of course, have been possible without Community membership. Whether Britain joined because of Chancellor Lawson's conversion to exchange rate monetarism or because of a more general aspiration to demonstrate European credentials is not of consequence for present purposes. Nor is it necessary to consider here the argument that earlier entry to the system would have avoided the problem, though one might note in passing that the Deutschmark was being shadowed for some years before formal entry. In terms of results Britain's experience in the ERM was part of its European adventure, extremely costly - to the extent of some billions - in cash and highly damaging to the government's credibility and authority. If some of the blame is attributable to the government's eagerness to take a risk of this magnitude some of it must also be assigned to the Community membership that made the temptation available.

One of the minor themes in the body of argument that eventually took Britain into "Europe" was the belief that it alone offered the prospect of carrying out research and development on the scale necessary to compete with the United States. This, for some reason, was an aspect that was particularly attractive to Home [145], who exemplified what he meant by the Concorde agreement with France. It seems to have escaped his notice that the two governments signed that agreement in November 1962, shortly before de Gaulle delivered his mercy blow. The French President was evidently not of the same mind about the necessary connexion between joint development and Community partnership [146]. Nor was this the only case of joint ventures outside the Six. Earlier in the same year twelve countries set up the European Space Research Organisation, while in September 1967 the United Kingdom joined France and West Germany in the Airbus project. This was followed, after a very brief interval, by de Gaulle's second veto. He seems not to have let business interfere with pleasure, or vice-versa. A year later the United Kingdom formed a science and technology association with the Community.

No doubt there have been arrangements for joint research and development, perhaps particularly at the level of individual firms, that have been fostered by the Community, but the argument depended for what force it had on there being no alternative route; the results show this to have been an error.

In some ways the most portentous economic event was one in which Britain did not participate directly. This was the final settlement of the financing of the Community's Common Agricultural Policy in December 1969, the same month in which it was agreed to recommence negotiations on British entry. The two were avowedly connected; the French were willing to consider British accession only after they had locked in an adequate tribute from their partners in the Community, which they might not have gained if the United Kingdom had been involved in the negotiations.

The British system of deficiency payments, about whose continuation Soames had been pessimistic in 1961, was unchanged in principle during the period of exclusion. It

combined access to cheap food at world prices for British
consumers with the maintenance and development of British
agriculture by making up the difference between the world price
and a national price negotiated annually. The objectives were
strategic, social and to save foreign exchange [147], and the cost to
the taxpayer was not challenged at this time, though there were
concerns over the effectiveness of the system in meeting its
goals.

It is quite mistaken to suggest that if the British, with this
background, had entered the Community in 1961, or even in
1957, and so participated in the negotiations, the Common
Agricultural Policy would not have taken the form it did. The
French saw agricultural protection as a *sine qua non*, without
which they would not have signed on [148]. Protectionism was the
essence of the Policy and the basic principles had already been
very painfully evolved by 1961, although much remained to be
fought over in the rest of the decade. The complexity of the
system is horrendous and has been fully discussed elsewhere[149,150],
so that only the essentials need to be rehearsed here. They are
high prices to Community consumers, maintained by intervention
buying of surpluses, export subsidies and import levies (which
pass into the Community's budget as own resources), and
common financing of the whole system. As a net importer of
food the United Kingdom is obliged to be a net contributor to this
part of Community expenditure. Since it amounts to some two-
thirds of the whole Britain is a permanent net contributor to the
Community. The prospect of changing this position is negligible.

That this would be the case was apparent when the second
and third attempts were made to enter the Community . There
was no more talk of savings to the Exchequer from the change in
the system of agricultural support, leading to tax reductions.
They would instead be accompanied by a net reduction of
government revenue through payments to Community funds [151].
The rise in the cost of living was estimated at 4% or 5%, while
the country's contribution to the Agricultural Fund was expected
to be between 15% of it and 20%, or £270-350m in 1977 [152]. The
White Paper of 1971 [153] put the figure somewhat lower. Figures
for the total outturn will be found below; what was not fully

perceived at the time was that a system of protection and subsidy based on the highest cost producers was bound to give rise to massive overproduction, which would not only require to be supported by increased levies on European consumers and tax payers but would distort world food markets by the subsidy of exports. What is more it would bring into being an array of vested interests that would render the system virtually impervious to reform.

Nevertheless, the nature of the risk was apparent to some. Richard Crossman wrote * :-

But by far the most damning effects on our national interest would follow from the provisions of the budgetary and financial system which the Six adopted only last year, and which at the insistence of France cannot now be changed.   ... to finance the costly agricultural price support and farm reconstruction policies of the Six we must pay over to the Community the yield of three separate taxes ... the effect is knowingly disproportionate as between this country and the rest.

The response of both the Wilson and Heath governments to this formidable difficulty was to assert that the known impact cost would be more than counterbalanced by the dynamic of Community membership, a formula inherited from 1961. That this had been qualified at the beginning of the decade as only a potential was lost to sight as the benefits to follow from accession were trumpeted. By 1980 it was possible to see that the dynamic benefits were going to others [154].

Before moving on to deal with other aspects of trade some detail should be given of the cost of the Common Agricultural Policy and the effect of that cost. It is much greater than the scale of the British net contribution to Community funds, which is discussed below. The combined cost to consumers and taxpayers has been estimated at £1000 per family per year, [155, 156], taking account of world prices for food which are lower than those paid within the Community. On a conservative calculation the annual loss to the United Kingdom is £10bn. The higher wage costs brought about by these prices are not, of course, uncompetitive within the Community but they add to Britain's competitive burden in the rest of the world. Because Britain is a net importer

* I am indebted to J.A. Obdam for this quotation.

of food the higher prices are a burden on the balance of payments; because of the greater importance of food in the budgets of the poor they operate as regressive taxation; and they are an inefficient method of supporting the farming community.

The 1970 White Paper recited the general trade and GNP statistics for the Community and the United Kingdom and asserted that it was highly probable that the Community itself had generated a higher rate of growth for its members, but it shrewdly forswore any numerical predictions of the benefits that would flow from entry. The arguments for these benefits rested on the same general grounds as those previously used.

It was seen that the question was whether the cost to the balance of payments (the impact cost), which might be anything from £100m to £1100m, would be outweighed by an improved rate of growth of GNP arising from membership of the Community (the dynamic effect). Since it was envisaged that membership would give British insurers access to the continental market it cannot be said that the research was exhaustive. The White Paper did at least contemplate the possibility that the total burden on the balance of payments might become excessive; in that case it felt that the Community might be drawn into giving help to the United Kingdom on account of the common interest.

While the theoretical economic arguments of specialisation and competition were perfectly sound it was thus recognised, however haltingly, that there was a risk that the benefits would not accrue to Britain. The costs were certain, if not amenable to close calculation; the immediate negative effect on the visible balance of trade for example, excluding food, was thought to lie in the range £125m - £275m. The benefits, however, were dependent on the country's own economic performance. In the previous decade this had been turned out to be adequate, as will be seen, though the rate of growth had not been as good as in the Six. Since this had also been the case before the Common Market came into full operation the argument based on growth statistics has an air of sympathetic magic about it; what is interesting is the extent to which UK trade with the Community while it was not a member had grown, which bore out an old argument from the Treasury.

The 1971 White Paper, which followed the Conservative victory in the election, told the same tale but omitted many of the figures, although it did remark on the Community's surplus on current account over the previous decade and expressed its confidence that the effect of membership on the UK balance of trade would be positive and substantial. Which was even more sympathetic.

The actual results for the balance of payments are shown in Appendix (F), Figures 1-7, based on the Central Statistical Office publications *United Kingdom Balance of Payments* and *Economic Trends*. Since the concern here is with commercial activity all government transactions, which are of appreciable magnitude, and private transfers, which are not, have been excluded from the calculations. The subsequent totals are shown as percentages in relation to Gross Domestic Product, which avoids the distortion of inflation. Invisibles are unconventionally described as imports and exports, as they amount to the same thing in the end.

The surprising thing about the overall position (Figure 1) is that the balance is positive for almost all the period, with falls from grace only just after accession (not necessarily *post hoc, propter hoc*) and in the last years. There is an acceleration in external trade beginning in the late sixties, self-evidently not brought about by accession. What it does represent is the growing importance of foreign trade in the UK economy and the general growth in international trade during the period (subject to a qualification on invisibles discussed below). Evidence of the effects of Community membership has to be sought in a more detailed breakdown of these figures.

Visible trade (Figure 2) is in deficit over almost all the period and if there is a trend it is downwards. The improvement during the eighties can largely be attributed to North Sea oil, whose positive balance peaked at £8bn in 1985, just as the fall in the seventies can be associated with the greatly increased price of oil. One the invisibles side (Figure 3) the balance is uniformly positive and, as we have seen, generally large enough to offset the unsatisfactory performance of visibles. What is striking is the much greater share taken by invisibles in the growth of trade and though it does appear to grow a little faster after accession than it did beforehand this is due to a change in the way in which the gross figures were recorded up to and including 1971. The net balances were unaffected by this change but it should be noted that the gross totals shown in Figure 1 also reflect it.

The impact of the European Economic Community on Britain's foreign trade is shown in Figures 4 and 5. It must be noted that the number of countries covered by these figures grows from 6 in 1960 to 11 by 1979, which accounts for some of the growth, and that the regional division is not available for invisibles before 1973. Up to 1972 the balance on visible trade (in Figure 4) is fairly even and it can be assumed that it would be pushed in a positive direction if the invisibles balance could be brought into play to produce an overall picture. After accession there is a very noticeable acceleration on both sides of the account, but the balance is substantially negative, except during the oil years, and at the end of the period, when there was a large reduction in imports. The growth is what might have been expected when to the advantage of proximity has been added the reduction of tariff and other barriers, combined with the exhortation of the government and the rest of the establishment to look to Europe. It would appear that the process described by Wilson in his days of hostility to membership as selling each other washing machines has been financially unfavourable to the United Kingdom; there is certainly a dynamic but not in the direction of offsetting the impact costs. The analogy that springs to mind is of a company in pursuit of turnover at the expense of profits. Not that the story is wholly bad; free trade in visibles has enabled UK consumers to get better value for their money than they were getting from the products of an over-protected home industry.

Growth in invisible trade, which is more affected by non-tariff barriers, has not been pronounced, though it is certainly worthwhile. The generally positive balance has been insufficient to offset the visible deficit and the decline at the end of the period offers little assurance that if negotiations within the Community produce an increased volume of invisible transactions it would lead to an overall improvement.

These outcomes need to be set against the United Kingdom's trade performance with the rest of the world. Figure 6 shows that in contrast with its European trade its world trade in visibles has grown only in line with GDP. This steady performance is very creditable when to the advantages of European trade noted above one must add the reversal of preferences previously received from and given to other countries, particularly in the Commonwealth. On the other hand it has to be said that towards the end of the period the proportionate volume shows signs of decline. The balance is negative, though less so than with the other members of the Community. When we turn to the invisibles, however, the picture is much brighter. The volume has grown, the volume is much higher than with European trade (whereas the visibles are roughly on a par) and, most importantly, the balance is positive and large. Insofar as the United Kingdom has kept its trading head above water all these years, particularly the more recent years, it has been by virtue of its invisible earnings outside the Community. The most significant of these have been the returns on foreign investment, which the inhabitants of these islands continue to prefer to make elsewhere in the world than within the Community. This is a factor that deserves a closer analysis, the place for which is not here. On a balance of trade basis (which is not the whole of the story) the benefits hopefully awaited from accession - and confidently vaunted - have simply not arrived. On this section of the mark sheet we must inscribe it as a grievous mistake.

When the Labour government pursued Britain's second application to be permitted to join the European club it was recognised that the way the Community was organising its finances meant that Britain would be required to make a net budgetary contribution. This was another element in the impact costs which it was hoped that dynamic of membership would more than counterbalance. The governmental estimates were given above; the actual results are as follows.

Table 1

PAYMENTS AND RECEIPTS FROM EC

£m

	Payments	Receipts	Balance
1973	187	83	- 104
1974	186	153	- 33
1975	350	400	+ 50
1976	474	299	- 175
1977	750	376	- 374
1978	1364	533	- 831
1979	1606	658	- 948
1980	1767	1062	- 705
1981	2174	1777	- 397
1982	2862	2259	- 603
1983	2976	2328	- 648
1984	3201	2545	- 656
1985	3759	1914	-1845
1986	2792	2216	- 576
1987	4049	2345	-1704
1988	3525	2183	-1342
1989	4431	2116	-2315
1990	4658	2183	-2475
1991	3309 *	2766	- 543

* Reflects substantial abatements and adjustments in respect of previous years.

If these contributions are totalled they amount to upwards of £21bn in 1990 prices. Since they are net of receipts from the Community and also reflect the sums recovered by Mrs Thatcher's negotiations they are not strictly comparable with the Labour White Paper's estimate of contributions to the Agricultural Fund. Even so, after adjustment for inflation they are somewhat above the top of the range then estimated. What they do constitute is a constant drain from the UK economy and, far from being counterbalanced by dynamic effects perceptible in the trade balance, they must be added to its deficit.

In another sense, however, what matters fundamentally is the growth of domestic production, consumption and investment. In 1960 the Gross Domestic Product was £23011m. It rose to £56610m by 1972, the last year before entry, to £173235m in 1979 and £495647m by 1991. When these figures are adjusted for inflation they reveal an annual growth of 3.6% p.a. before entry and 2.25% thereafter. By far the greater part of this last figure was achieved in the years from 1980 onwards, when the annual rate recovered to almost the same level as before entry, whereas from 1973 to 1979 it was only 0.27%. A similar general picture has been produced by Crafts [157] in terms of real GDP per head. It has been remarked that by unfortunate coincidence 1973 marked not only Britain's accession to the EEC but also the end of the world's long post-war boom, while it has been noted above that the decade also saw a major financial crisis. But the 1967 devaluation was a comparable blow and while entry could not be expected to shield the United Kingdom from world events it was predicted that it would be enabled to match Community growth. But Burkitt et al [158] have shown that the annual rate of growth for Italy, France and Germany has been 3.2%, 3.16% and 2.54% respectively, compared with Britain's 2.12% for the same period. What all this indicates is that, setting aside events on a world scale, what really makes a difference in economic performance is the domestic policies pursued by the government. And even those can have only a very slow influence on real long-term factors as those which Britain's relative decline is a symptom.

The fact that despite this relative weakness in growth the United Kingdom has contributed substantially to Community funds, second only to Germany, has been a constant grievance to the British government. The rebates that Mrs Thatcher secured by a display of intransigence that distressed the right-thinking in Britain, while valuable, have not produced an equitable distribution of the Community's costs. Can it then be said that we are richer on account of membership? Gross Domestic product has grown, somewhat spasmodically, but it has also grown in countries outside the Community. Trade with Europe has grown appreciably, affording British consumers more choice, but it has brought large deficits with it. When to these one added the direct costs of the contribution and the indirect costs of lost access to cheap food, money that might have been invested more effectively at home, it would take a bold man to assert that Chandos was right. As in the eighteenth century Great Britain has laid out treasure on the continent, but in those days it was clear what we were to get for our money and the tap could always be closed.

Politics

If we have paid an economic price have we secured a political benefit?

Although the period from 1963 to 1973 was one of non-membership it was marked not only by the fact that a British government had shown itself prepared to reverse the policy of centuries but also by a succession of further attempts by both Labour and Conservative administrations to push the country into the Community. It is not the intention here to rehearse the events of this period, which have been thoroughly covered by Kitzinger, or of the period of membership, except insofar as they afford a test of the arguments deployed in 1960 and 1961.

Kitzinger argues [159] that the Wilson application, a reversal of his previously critical stance towards entry, was made on overriding political grounds [160]. This was to adopt the position, as we have seen, developed by the Macmillan government, though publicly an enormous amount of effort was put into compilation and calculation, particularly in the 1970 White Paper discussed above. While one cannot point to any fresh setbacks for British policy in the world to account for this no doubt the same feeling of malaise and impotence was present in government circles as before; certainly the same kind of groundless optimism persisted, as evidenced by George Brown's unfounded and undiplomatic claim of a leadership role for Britain in Europe. This second attempt was met by a second Gaullist veto but British aspirations remained in place; this led to the curious affair of Soames.

The tale has been narrated, and evaluated, by Kitzinger [161], Jay [162] and Sked [163]. It is unlikely that anything can be added until official records are released and possibly not even then. What is of interest for present purposes is the light it throws on the British government's grip of its own objectives. Soames, whom we have met as Minister of Agriculture and a convinced European in Macmillan's government, was appointed H.M. Ambassador in Paris towards the end of 1968. Britain was continuing to try to find a way in. With the willing help of Michel Debré, French Foreign Minister, he secured an invitation from de Gaulle for lunch and discussion on 4 February 1969. It appears the President was keen to see if a reconciliation between Great Britain and France could be brought about and proposed bilateral negotiations between them. What he envisaged was that the arrival of the United Kingdom, with her partners, would transform the Common Market, loosening it into a free trade area. What de Gaulle sought from this process was an unspecified political association between France, the United Kingdom, West Germany and Italy, which would thus form an inner council. He expected the American-dominated NATO, of which France was no longer a member, to fade away but did not set this as a precondition. What is interesting about this formulation is how closely it approaches the fundamental British requirements as worked out at the beginning of the decade. A free trade area instead of a supranationally controlled single commercial policy, together with a forum for the co-ordination of foreign policy, would have provided both the larger home market and the political influence in Europe that Macmillan had sought. There was no price demanded in sovereignty and no risk of commitment to an eventual political union. The negotiations might, of course, not have succeeded but this should have been seen as an attractive opportunity for a British government to grasp. What they did was to destroy it. De Gaulle had made his proposal in confidence; the British, that is Wilson, on the advice of the Foreign Secretary (Stewart) and the Foreign Office promptly revealed it to the German Chancellor. At the same time a version of Soames' report to London was provided to the other Community governments. The French were predictably outraged, their Press even more so, and the opportunity was lost. It was claimed in the Foreign Office that it was necessary to take precautions against the probability of a French trap; it has also been suggested that Stewart was determined on the Community and nothing but the Community and could not respond favourably to a proposal that might suggest something less. At all events, the professed masters of the diplomatic art had contrived an international debacle by substituting for a clear-headed grasp of British interests an obsession with acceding to the Treaty of Rome. Whether this was cock-up or conspiracy may never be finally determined.

Heath came to power in 1970 determined above all to reverse his failure of seven years earlier. De Gaulle had gone, the ground had been laid by the Labour government's persistence with its application; all that needed to be done was to negotiate out of existence any gap that might lie between the terms the French would demand and what Parliament could be induced to accept. The principle of accession to the Treaty of Rome had long been yielded, though what this might mean over the years was far from certain, perhaps particularly in respect of Britain's contribution to the Community budget, and the transitional terms that would lessen the shock for British agriculture and Commonwealth countries remained an issue. For the French the key was whether Britain as a member of the Community would be truly European in the sense in which the French understood that term. In May 1971 Heath was able to convince de Gaulle's successor, Pompidou, that the United Kingdom's focus of attention would in future be in Europe or, more specifically, in the Community rather than across the Atlantic or on the countries of the Commonwealth. It has been seen that Heath's White Paper eschewed the arithmetic that had been a feature of Wilson's and it deployed much the same broad brush arguments as had been worked up at the time of the first application. There is no need for present purposes to rehearse them and there is little to remark on by way of points derived from the experience of the intervening years. One of these was the Luxembourg compromise, of which a good deal was made and of which more will be said below; another was the strong balance of payments position of the Community as a whole. They were not to know this would not endure. Much of the weight, if not bulk, of the paper was applied to allaying fears about the long-term political and constitutional effects of accession, which time had done nothing to lessen; this included the now notorious statement that there was no question of any erosion of essential national sovereignty. For the Commonwealth countries all that had been secured was safeguards for New Zealand exports of dairy produce and lamb (which that government described as the best in the circumstances), together with sugar from the Caribbean. This was much what had been arrived at in 1962, though Rippon, the UK negotiator, had said he would not have taken the job if he had thought it meant undermining the Commonwealth.

In Opposition the Labour Party had swung against entry though, given their previous stance, their objections could reasonably be based only on the narrow technical grounds of whether the right terms had been achieved. When it came to implementing the Treaty of Accession that had been signed in Brussels by the United Kingdom, together with Denmark, Ireland and Norway, on 22 January 1972 legislation in the UK Parliament was required. With the help of Labour rebels Heath got his Second Reading through by eight votes in February. How that came about is a story that has been adequately told before, particularly by Kitzinger, and need take up no space here.

These later applications and their eventual achievements can in themselves form no part in testing the adequacy of the original decision. They are included here principally to complete the picture. The published accounts do not take the original reasoning any further, though the willingness to continue to seek entry when further evidence was in of the immediate financial costs of membership testifies to the extent to which the more nebulous benefits had secured a grip on the political imagination of the UK establishment.

When the Labour Party returned to power in 1974 it thus found that the country was committed by Treaty to an arrangement which it had opposed only two years earlier. It therefore set out to renegotiate the terms and, having secured some trivial amendment, resolved to heal its own fissures by conducting a referendum in 1975. The government now recommended to the electorate staying in the Common Market and voters therefore received two pamphlets to one for that course; unsurprisingly, they voted in this proportion. The referendum debate produced no fresh reasoning.

This *résumé* of the development of relations between Britain and the Community, at the most general level, clears the ground for an examination of the political benefits gained from accession. It will be recalled that these were expected to take the form of influence, first a share in the international influence of the Community, which would somehow enhance or gear up Britain's independent influence; secondly, influence on the internal policies of the Community; finally, influence on the external policies of the Community, either by inhibiting any tendency to develop a Third Force role, or by preventing it from behaving in a manner seriously hostile to the United Kingdom. An official formulation of Britain's political interests has been cited by Wallace and Pinder [164] in the course of their examination of this question. These are the external security of the United Kingdom, the promotion of economic and social well-being, honouring existing commitments and obligations, and working for a peaceful and just world. Rather more loosely the Heath White Paper argued that the geographical, military, political, economic and social circumstances of the Community and the Kingdom were so similar and their objectives so much in common that it made sense to combine forces. This, of course, was an argument that had weight insofar as the interests and objectives were not shared with third parties, and even more weight if third parties were actually hostile to them.

The principal mechanism for external security was, of course, NATO, and the contribution of a Community some of whose members were not in NATO, one of whom in fact left it resoundingly, cannot have been great. Wallace and Pinder make something of the Community contribution to the Conference on Security and Co-operation in Europe, but they do not claim it as substantial. Indeed, until comparatively recently the Community adhered to the Hallstein doctrine of avoiding a military role.

The economic aspects have been discussed above and need no repetition. As far as commercial policy is concerned the Community as a whole has had more difficulty in proceeding towards liberal trade through GATT negotiations than Britain's own interests would have required.

It is not surprising that it is difficult to point to instances in which the Community has been induced to support specifically British obligations and needs in a way in which they would not otherwise have done; while the attractions of Community membership might have had some influence in drawing Greece, Portugal and Spain into democracy, which was certainly in conformity with British views, these developments can hardly be regarded as a substantial British interest. Wallace and Pinder do their best with the case up to 1979 but it cannot be said to amount to a great deal, nor has some of their optimism been justified.

It has to be said that a search for examples of the international influence of the Community, outside the field of trade, within which it might be possible to discern a gearing up of specifically British influence is hampered by the inability of the member countries to put together a common line in the face of the world events. Quite possibly in the constant to and fro of diplomatic negotiations over a myriad of lesser issues there might be found instances of the sort of influence that is claimed, but if they cannot be found on the large scale can they be worth the price of membership?

In the really major matters Community countries have tended, by and large, to go their own way. When de Gaulle, in 1966, saw it as in French interests to leave NATO it was an undoubted blow to the other members of that organisation which those who were also members of the Community were unable to prevent. Britain was not, at the time, one of them but it can hardly be supposed that it would have made any difference as a partner in the Community when Germany could not. Similarly, when the United Kingdom has been directly involved support from its fellows in the Community has been limited, uncertain and hard to find. When Argentina invaded the Falklands valuable, if discreet, aid towards the military operation was provided by the United States; the Community agreed to impose economic sanctions but these were never likely to produce the satisfactory result gained by armed force, while had Spain then been a member it is doubtful whether an agreed Community position could have been reached.

When Mrs Thatcher's government provided facilities in 1986 for the U.S. raid on Libya even those other Community members who were also in NATO refused their support and, to some extent, the story was repeated four years later in the Gulf. Although Britain responded at once to the American initiative to repel Iraq's invasion of Kuwait, she was unable to carry some other Community countries with her. Germany was evasive, France duplicitous and Belgium actually hostile.

The one instance in which a *communautaire* foreign policy might be seen to have been attempted was that of Yugoslavia. It is not possible to say at this stage whether the Community's actions, such as the recognition of Slovenia, Croatia and Bosnia were well chosen, or to identify the influence to be attributed to British diplomacy. What is clear, unfortunately, is that the Community's actions have not been effective in bringing an end to the fighting; that the deployment of troops from the Community and other countries for humanitarian purposes has needed a United Nations umbrella and that there are, in any case, no specifically British interests in the area to offer a test of the argument from influence.

The only conclusion that can be drawn from this necessarily limited survey is that the Community has, at this stage, little foreign policy influence and that rather than being geared up by it British policy risks being diluted.

Even in a case in which the interests of the Community, as such, were directly affected it has not been in a position to pursue them against the determination of a single member. The other countries, even if they had wanted to, could have done nothing to prevent the reunification of Germany; what is more the point they did not prevent the former East Germany from being brought within the Community on monetary terms that were very damaging to them. If one is looking for an example of one country's influence on the Community it is surely to be found in Germany's ability to export the costs of reunification.

In dealing with the extent and value of Britain's influence on the internal development of the Community one needs to remind oneself that it is generally irrelevant to the issue here under consideration, that of the reasons for entering the Market in the first place. For non-members the flood of regulations and directives has no direct application. No doubt some of them amount to non-tariff barriers against imports from non-members, who are not in a position to influence their formulation; the benefits of British membership in this regard may be assumed to appear in the economic bottom line, which has been discussed earlier. On the political side there was a good deal of confidence in Britain's ability to manage developments from the inside, particularly in smothering any federalist impulses that might re-appear. Home was able to assert in 1961 that he saw no sign of any Common Market country sacrificing any significant amount of sovereignty, though this view did not quite chime with what the Foreign Office was telling him. In the same vein he said in 1969 that none of the machinery established had been, or looked like being, federal. He thought the Council of Ministers would retain the ultimate say as far ahead as one could see and so failed to reckon with the role of the European Court of Justice in interpreting what Ministers thought they had agreed and with the growing pressure for European Parliamentary power. Yet it was perfectly visible to others, such as Neil Marten; it cannot be argued that developments have been unpredictable.

At the same period a good deal was made of the Luxembourg Agreement, enabling a country to protect what it perceived as a vital interest against the wishes of its Community partners. De Gaulle had secured this compromise in 1966 by temporarily withdrawing France from the Community, but it was not observed that to invoke Luxembourg one needed to have the backbone of a de Gaulle. At all events, despite all the developments in the Community over twenty years, no British government has been prepared to say the country's vital interests were threatened, although Mrs Thatcher appears to have come close to it, much to the disgust of the Foreign Office.

This is not to suggest that the United Kingdom never succeeds in having its way in all the haggling that goes on in Brussels. For example, the imposition of worker-directors on the boards of companies in the Continental fashion has been successfully resisted, though the demand for it continues. This highlights one of the problems of the way the Community is run, namely that rejected proposals and the battles over them can constantly be renewed, but once they are accepted there is practically no way of reversing them.

While it would be wrong to suggest that the United Kingdom is always in a singleton minority - for example, in 1978, it was at one with France in refusing to tolerate any extension of the powers of the directly elected European Parliament - it does seem to occur with some regularity. The country is clearly regarded by some among its partners as obstructive of Community developments and there is even some feeling that if it cannot change its attitude it should depart. That there should be regular occasion for hostility is not surprising, given the imbalance between British and continental interests that was predicted by Crossman and remarked upon in 1980 by Wallace [165]. In 1977 British Ministers were accused of pursuing national interests during their turn at the Presidency. It must be doubtful whether such pursuit was any more blatant than that of their colleagues; the complaint is more likely to be the result of some more regular hostility.

The general impression one gains of British influence on the Community is one of a constant fight against proposals which it sees as unsound, but which it may only ever be able to delay, and no success in securing major changes such as reform of the Common Agricultural Policy or expansion of membership. No British government, not even Heath's, has ever accepted the "federal" goal of a European Union as a full-blooded international entity yet none of them has been able to put a stop to the remorseless accumulation of additional authority by the Community's institutions, an expansion which is overtly directed at a goal whose existence British governments routinely deny at home. Given the early confidence on this very issue, which was no doubt sincerely felt and expressed by those responsible for managing British accession to the Treaty of Rome, one must conclude that British influence on Community developments has not been such as to justify them.

What is more they failed to predict that the Continental zeal for harmonisation, of which French demands in respect of social legislation had been a harbinger as early as 1957, would result in a campaign of interference in domestic issues without much regard for their importance in transborder trade and complete disregard of their painful impact on businessmen, farmers and consumers. It may be that British Ministers and officials secure their share of benefits in the bargaining that goes on but that is an argument that misses the point; the accretion of authority to the Community institutions that is involved in the process of constantly legislating to control activities within the United Kingdom is contrary to what was originally seen as a strategic British interest.

What then of the Charlemagne thesis, the argument that British accession was essential to prevent the emergence of a hostile Power on the Continent of Europe? It need hardly be said that no such Power has yet appeared, though there are those with ambitions to create a Great Power, ambitions that British governments have been unable to check. They have chosen instead to acquiesce in the extension of Community competence and authority rather than become isolated, as it is expressed, though it is never made clear what form such isolation might take. Like 'split' it has become a code word to conceal what cannot be spelt out. The danger from a power hostile to the United Kingdom, one must suppose, was that the country might fall to be dominated by it; rather than run this risk British governments have, in effect, opted for progressive pre-emptive submission. Effective hostility appears no more likely, thirty-odd years on, than it did in 1961, though the hostile mood of our partners has, if anything, been exacerbated by the bickerings associated with membership. Truly, those who warned that if entry was not accompanied by a full willingness to work towards the political goal it might turn out to be the worst of all worlds had wisdom on their side. The belief that it would be possible to limit the Community to questions of international trade, with political matters handled on a strictly intergovernmental basis, proved to be hopelessly misjudged.

One would be hard put to it, after looking at influence from these various points of view, to argue that membership has passed the Chandos test of making Great Britain more powerful.

Summary

In sum, therefore, while the price of entry has been paid, not merely in cash but in the erosion of Commonwealth intimacy (despite all the promises) and the transfer of power beyond the realm, it would be difficult to argue that the desired results have been delivered. What was to come to pass has not come; what was not to come to pass has come; on any normal reckoning this would be called an error but on the scale of these events it can only be called a disaster.

APPENDIX A

THE CABINET 1960 - 61

Prime Minister	- H Macmillan
Home Secretary	- R A Butler
Lord Chancellor	- Lord Kilmuir
Foreign Secretary	- S Lloyd (to 27 June 1960)
	- Lord Home (from 27 June 1960)
Chancellor of Exchequer	- D Heathcoat Amory (to 27 June 1960)
	- S Lloyd (from 27 June 1960)
Secretary of State for Commonwealth Relations	- Lord Home (to 27 June 1960)
	- D Sandys (from 27 June 1960)
Lord President	- Lord Home (to 27 June 1960)
	- Lord Hailsham (from 27 June 1960)
Lord Privy Seal	- Lord Hailsham (to 27 June 1960)
	- E Heath (from 27 June 1960)
Secretary of State for Scotland	- J Maclay
Minister of Aviation	- D Sandys (to 27 June 1960)
	- P Thorneycroft (from 27 June 1960)
Secretary of State for Colonies	- I Macleod
Minister of Defence	- H Watkinson
Minister of Housing & Local Government	- H Brooke
Minister of Education	- D Eccles
Paymaster General	- Lord Mills
President of Board of Trade	- R Maudling
Minister of Agriculture	- J Hare (to 27 June 1960)
	- C Soames (from 27 June 1960)
Minister of Labour	- E Heath (to 27 June 1960)
	- J Hare (from 27 June 1960)
Chancellor of Duchy of Lancaster	- C Hill
Minister of Transport	- E Marples

APPENDIX B

The Six and the Seven: Long Term Arrangements [37]

I

THE IMMEDIATE OUTLOOK

1.   The negotiations in 1957 and 1958 for a European Free Trade
Area foundered largely because of a lack of political will on the part of
some Governments of the Six (especially the French) to see the
European Economic Community supplemented by a wider economic
grouping.

2.   The recent initiative of the Governments of the Six to resume
negotiations with the Governments of the Seven in the Paris Trade
Committee looks, on the face of it, more like a renewed offer of a
"Commission de Contract" in a modified form than a genuine offer to
move now towards a single European market.*   It is possible that the
failure of the Summit may bring about a radical change of attitude in
the months ahead.   But at the moment it is not possible to say with
confidence that that will happen.

3.   It therefore still seems likely that after the 1st July next the Six
and the Seven will go their separate ways at least for the time being.
Each will discriminate against the other and against the rest of the
world. The immediate discrimination may be increased at the end of the
year if either or both groups decide to accelerate then the tariff
reductions between themselves.

4.   This division in Europe will be disliked and deplored by all the
countries of the Seven and by important elements in the Six. But unless
the political situation is transformed as a result of the failure of the
Summit, the division may well continue for a considerable time - say
eighteen months or two years at least.

II

IMPLICATIONS FOR THE UNITED KINGDOM

5.   The economic division of Europe will confront the United
Kingdom with a most serious situation.   There are significant political
dangers which Ministers have emphasised in recent months - the fear
that, despite the manifest advantage of the rapprochement between
France and Germany, economic divisions may weaken the political
cohesion of the West at a time when a common Western front is more

* The phrase a "single European Market" is used in this paper to mean
some form of association between the Six and the Seven. The position
of the peripherals is not here taken into account and will require
separate consideration.   It seemed better to use some neutral phrase
rather than technical terms like "free trade area" or "customs union".

than every necessary. If, as seems to be the intention, the policy of the Six is to press forward with economic integration, impetus will be given to political integration.

The Community may well emerge as a Power comparable in size and influence to the United States and the USSR. The pull of this new power bloc would be bound to dilute our influence with the rest of the world, including the Commonwealth. We should find ourselves replaced as the second member of the North Atlantic Alliance and our relative influence with the United States in all fields would diminish. All this would add to the strains on EFTA. The independence which we have sought to preserve by remaining aloof from European integration would be of doubtful value, since our diminished status would suggest only a minor role for us in international affairs.

6. From the economic standpoint the immediate and overt effects will not be disastrous (only 14 per cent of our exports go to the countries of the Six, and it is reasonable to hope that a substantial part of this trade will continue despite tariff discrimination against us). But even in the short term the fact that our exports will be increasingly at a disadvantage in the markets of the Six (where the rate of economic growth has been high and is likely to continue so) will be a serious matter at a time when our balance of payments position once more gives cause for concern.

7. In the longer term, if we have to assume a situation in which the Six are a group continuing to discriminate in each other's favour against us (and the rest of the world) and constituting a bloc with a high rate of economic growth, the situation will still be more serious, for the following reasons:-

(a) So far as direct trade is concerned, much may depend on the levels of the common external tariffs of the Six. If these are relatively low, the United Kingdom should be able to continue to export freely to the Six (as we do now to the USA) notwithstanding the tariff barrier. But, a great part of the success of the Six will derive from the dynamic of the new large common market and the scale on which their industries can think and plan. To share in that dynamic requires us to be "in". To be "out", even with a low tariff, is to be cut off from it. In addition, given the strength which will come from their large internal market, the industries of the Six may well develop into most formidable competitors in third markets. If the external tariffs of the Six are high, it will be more difficult for the United Kingdom to export there, but the competition of the Six in third markets may be less severe because of the higher cost of their imports.

(b) The Seven is not a despicable grouping in economic terms. The Scandinavian countries and Switzerland together form a market nearly as large as Canada (larger than Australia); and between the United Kingdom and the Scandinavian countries there are close and enduring ties. But it is doubtful whether a heterogeneous and scattered grouping - brought together by "ties of common funk" rather by any deeper purpose or by geographical contiguity - can develop a real cohesion or even continuity. In any event, the basic factors of population and economic resources must mean that the Seven is bound to be a weaker economic group than the Six. This is likely to have a profound psychological effect on United Kingdom industry. We have already been warned privately that although the FBI have been active and loyal in their support of Government policies in regard to the Seven, there is great uneasiness, amounting almost to dismay, among leading industrialists at the prospect of our finding ourselves yoked indefinitely with the Seven and "cut off" by a tariff barrier from the markets of the Six. The prospect is seen of three powerful economic groupings - the USA, the USSR, the Six - able to develop internal markets of scale and therefore strong and competitive industries based on such markets - whereas the United Kingdom will have a preferential position only in the Seven and in Commonwealth markets (where we face tariff barriers in any event and where our position is likely to weaken rather than grow stronger).

(c)   "Nothing succeeds like success". There is already a belief that the Six are going to come out on top in Europe. This will almost certainly lead to a diversion of United States investment - which otherwise might have come to this country - to the Six (it has already happened in one or two instances), and to a move by United Kingdom industrialists themselves to invest in the countries of the Six. And the psychological feeling that the United Kingdom is bound to "lose out" in the countries of the Six can have a serious effect on the efforts of our exporters to hold their position in these markets - e.g. in keeping the goodwill and interest of agents.

(d)   In these circumstances it is doubtful if we could hold EFTA together. Some members - notably Austria and Switzerland - depend so heavily on their trade with the Six that it is doubtful whether, if they could no longer see the prospect of a Single European Market, they could avoid making an accommodation with the Six on the best terms they could negotiate unilaterally.

8.   The conclusion is inescapable - that it cannot be compatible with either our political or our economical interests to let the situation drift on indefinitely on the basis of a divided Europe, with the United Kingdom linked to the weaker group. We must therefore seek a wider economic grouping which should at least comprise a single European market, assuming that any still wider grouping - e.g. an Atlantic Free Trade Area - is not a practicable objective - at any rate at this time, - and we must be prepared to examine what this is likely to mean in the way of positive "contributions" on the part of the United Kingdom Itself.

III

SOME CRITICAL FACTORS

Timing

9.   As regards timing, the essential need will be the existence of a political will to see a European settlement on the basis of a single market. At the time when this paper is being written, it is impossible to tell whether the failure of the Summit will change the situation

materially. Until the events of the last two weeks, it seemed that there was no prospect whatever of the early emergence of the political will for a comprehensive settlement. Indeed it seemed likely that any proposal by the Seven at the present time to resume negotiations for a single market would only have been regarded as one more piece of evidence that the real objective was to delay or prevent the formation of the Six as a separate entity: and that may still prove to be the position. It is possible, indeed, that a successful move towards the achievement of a single European market could not be undertaken until the Six had completed, or almost completed, their Customs Union and thus had no longer any fear of frustration in that purpose. But this is probably too pessimistic a view. The political situation in Europe is obviously not static and the forces in the Six opposed to economic division may well get stronger as time passes and their trade suffers in the countries of the Seven.

10. But these uncertainties about timing should not deter us from deciding (a) what our broad objective is, (b) the form in which it is most likely to be achieved, and (c) the sort of concessions we are likely to have to make. This will be all the more important as, whatever the objective or means of achieving it we adopt, we shall have to make new efforts to carry with us both other countries (the Seven: the Commonwealth: the USA) and important sections of opinion in this country.

The Seven

11. In anything we seek to do we must try to carry the Seven with us. Otherwise we shall run the risk of being left without a friend in Europe. From one standpoint it is certainly an advantage to have the Seven negotiating as a group. But we must recognise the fact that we are now partners in EFTA - and particularly, perhaps, the inclusion in it of "neutrals" like Switzerland, Austria and Sweden - may limit our freedom of manoeuvre in certain important respects.

The Commonwealth

12. Obviously the attitude of Commonwealth countries will be affected by the form which the ultimate solution takes. If it were thought that the United Kingdom was prepared to become politically part of a federal European State, or if European free trade arrangements extended to agriculture as well as to industrial goods, the initial reaction would be one of serious misgiving on political and economic grounds.

But basically the strength of the Commonwealth depends on the economic well-being of the United Kingdom and the strength of sterling. The Commonwealth is not likely to flourish under the leadership of a United Kingdom shut out of growing European markets by tariff barriers and diminishing in economic strength. It was apparent from the discussions at the Commonwealth Prime Ministers' meeting and the preceding meeting of senior officials that there is already a good deal of quiet realisation among some Commonwealth Ministers and officials of this basic position: and certainly no belief that an alternative could be found in a self-contained Commonwealth bloc. But there has been no discussion with them of any specific terms on which we might seek to negotiate a long-term accommodation with the Six.

The USA

13.   It is possible that the attitude of the United States Government may be modified by the failure of the Summit and that they will now be prepared to throw their influence behind early moves to bring the Six and Seven together in order to strengthen the political cohesion of the West. Hitherto that has not been their attitude. Their interest has been to see that nothing impedes the achievement of economic unity by the Six and that may remain their position. But if, at a later date, the Six and the Seven made it clear that their agreed purpose was to secure a single European market it would probably be difficult for the United States Government to do other than to accept the new arrangement with a good grace in the belief that it would add to the economic strength and the political cohesion of Western Europe, notwithstanding the fact that tariff discrimination against United States goods would be *pro tanto* increased. Naturally the height of the external tariff would be very important: the lower the tariff, the less the discrimination would be, and the more acceptable the whole arrangement would be to United States opinion: no doubt, too, their attitude must be affected by the degree of political content of the new association.

14.   Thus our policy should be to maintain close touch with the United States Administration, to recognise that at the present they are the admitted protagonists of the Six, but to do everything possible to persuade them that, notwithstanding any increase in discrimination against United States exports to Europe, their interests will be best be served by the emergence of a strong Western Europe, based on the achievement of a single market, rather than by the continuance of two rival groups.

Domestic Issues

15.   It is right to say that hitherto we have tried to secure the benefit of a European free trade area by paying only a purely "industrial" subscription - i.e. the removal of tariff protection in respect of industrial goods. Almost certainly - even if the political will to a settlement becomes apparent - we shall have to go further than this to secure the sort of settlement which we want. The successful development of the Six in recent months and the increased economic strength and self-confidence of France all point to the necessity of our being prepared to go much further than we have hitherto contemplated. We must put out of our minds the idea that we are so badly wanted by the Six that we can secure our objective on the cheap. But the payment of an increased price will almost certainly involve difficult and unpalatable decisions - in political terms (some surrender of sovereignty, some weakening of our Commonwealth links) and in economic/political terms (concessions

on agriculture, horticulture, a further erosion of Commonwealth Preference, tariff policies, harmonisation of social arrangements).

IV

UNITED KINGDOM OBJECTIVE

16.   Against this background some possible solutions can be summarised.

An Atlantic Free Trade or Preferential Area

17.   This would pre-suppose a free trade or near-free trade association of Western Europe (i.e. both the Six and the Seven) with the USA and Canada.   There is reason to believe that the State Department may have some arrangement of this kind in their minds as an ultimate objective. But quite apart from the very great political difficulties which any such grouping would involve in respect of the countries left outside (Australia, New Zealand, India, Japan leap to mind) there is really nothing in present United States and Canadian policies to give any grounds for realistic hope that such a concept can be practical politics - and therefore our declared objective in place of a single European market - for a good many years.   In any event the initiative for such an Area must come from the United States and not from us.

A single European market between the Six and the Seven

18.   This solution would assume that both groups maintained their identity but agreed to enter into what would be, in effect, a Free Trade Area (possibly confined to industrial goods).

This would really be the old European Free Trade Area concept under another name.   Even if the political climate has changed it seems inevitable that the Six would still reject it, as cutting across or weakening their new-found unity between themselves without (as they would see it) bringing the real benefits of economic union to Western Europe.

A single market with a preferential position for the Six

19.   This solution would have immediate political attractions.   But the more closely it is studied the more difficult it appears from the standpoint of our own interests.

20.   There are three reasons for this view.   Even a 5 per cent margin of preference would appear to British industry as a very poor second-best to a single market.   The attempt to negotiate such an arrangement might well lead to the establishment of a much more privileged position for the Six than is envisaged by thinking of the concept in terms of a preference figure of, say, 5 per cent.   If a substantially larger measure of preference had to be conceded, this would go far to nullify the economic advantages to the Seven.

21.   Secondly - even though the prospect of economic union in Europe would have attractions for them - such a solution would be particularly repugnant to American thinking.   It would involve discrimination against them, and in the most objectionable form. It would be equally obnoxious to other third countries, especially in the Commonwealth, and would tend to be so divisive of outside opinion that it might well founder on that ground alone.

22.   But the most serious objection is that for us to acquiesce in or to encourage the creation of a preferential area in Europe (to which we sent 25 per cent of our exports) would be contrary to our broad interest of maintaining the broadest possible freedom of trade in other markets of the world. The principle of m.f.n. has long been the main instrument in our commercial policy in ensuring that our exports get equal treatment in other countries. It is true that we have been prepared to agree that if two or more countries move very close together in the direction of economic unity the principle of m.f.n. should be foregone. The thought behind this is that the formation of a full free trade area or customs union is very difficult for countries to achieve. But if we were to allow the m.f.n. principle to be breached for an arrangement which permitted of a derogation from free trade of say, 5 per cent, there would be no reason why other groupings might not proceed to devise much greater derogations between themselves. There would be a real risk that we should find other countries grouping themselves together and abrogating our m.f.n. rights with relative ease, basing themselves on the European precedent. In short, there would be a serious danger that the world might break up into a series of preferential areas which would be highly damaging to our trade.

Joining the Common Market

23.   This is the course likely to be pressed increasingly in the months ahead by important sections of United Kingdom industry.   From a straight economic standpoint, it is almost certainly - with the possible exception of the Atlantic Free Trade Area (paragraph 17 above) - the solution which would be most advantageous to the United Kingdom. We should form a part - and an influential and important part - of an economic grouping of great and growing strength. If we were truly competitive we should dominate and lead the group.   We should compete on equal terms with other countries in the group within the rapidly growing European market, and our position in important third markets would only be damaged if Europe became an uncompetitive high tariff bloc, which would be unlikely if we belonged to it. -

24.   Such a course would, however, involve great difficulties:-

(a)   We would hope to negotiate appropriate trading arrangements which would ease the position of those EFTA countries which felt unable to join the Six (e.g. the neutrals like Sweden, Switzerland and Austria).   But in the interim period, while negotiations were getting under way, it would be difficult to hold the position and there is the danger that EFTA might break up. We should be fortunate if there were not a sense that we were going to betray the Seven in pursuit of our selfish interests.

(b)   It is impossible to say to what extent, if we joined the Six, we should in fact be committing ourselves to the acceptance of the ultimate objective of becoming part of a federal state in Western Europe. At the present time, the "federal" objectives in the Six are being tacitly relegated to the back-ground, particularly because of the opposition of General de Gaulle. But that position might not last. And in any event, in the eyes of most people in the United Kingdom and the Commonwealth we <u>should</u> be committing ourselves to an ultimate political objective. This would amount to, or at any rate be represented as, a political *bouleversement*. We should be represented as having chosen Europe in preference to the Commonwealth.

(c)   Joining the Common Market would create political difficulties with the Commonwealth - the links which bind the Commonwealth together might be weakened. In the economic field, there would be the question of whether we could negotiate arrangement which would maintain Commonwealth free entry into the United Kingdom, on the one hand, and our preferences in Commonwealth markets on the other. We might be able to preserve something of the present system, but it would not be Commonwealth Preference in its present form.

25.   These are formidable obstacles, almost certainly decisive against any immediate decision to make this our objective. But the pressures on us in industrial and other circles in this country to adopt this clear-cut solution, notwithstanding the difficulties, are likely to grow in strength and insistence unless it becomes clear that we should have good hopes of attaining the objective of a Single European Market <u>without</u> having to go so far as joining the Common Market.

Near-identification with the Common Market

26.   By this clumsy title is meant an arrangement between the Six and the Seven which would go as far as possible towards acceptance by the Seven of most of the essential features of the Common Market without formal participation in it.   It is obviously impossible to indicate precisely what this might involve, since much would depend on the atmosphere in which final negotiations were started and the extent to which we were trying to carry our EFTA partners with us. But broadly speaking the concept would be (i) a much more general acceptance of the economic arrangements of the Six, as incorporated in the Treaty of Rome, and (ii) acceptance of the political arrangements sufficient both to meet the continental desire to see us prepared to identify ourselves more with Europe and to give us sufficient participation in the institutions to wield an effective influence on policy matters.

27.   A solution on the foregoing lines would be likely to involve acceptance of most if not all of the following arrangements:-

A common external tariff

(a)   This is almost certainly an inevitable condition. We might be able to negotiate some derogation (perhaps in a limited form) for continued Commonwealth free entry (subject to (d) below).

Agreed arrangements on agriculture and horticulture

(b)   We could no longer exclude these from the ambit of agreed and concerted arrangements. But that would probably mean the acceptance of European-wide managed markets (not free trade) for some important agricultural products. On horticulture we should have to be prepared to make tariff concessions in favour of some of the members of the Six (the Dutch, the Italians, the French and the Belgians), and there might have to be managed markets for some horticulture products too.

Harmonisation of social charges

(c)   Almost certainly the French would insist on this as a *sine qua non* of their acceptance of free trade within the association.

Compensation taxes

(d)   If, notwithstanding the acceptance of a common external tariff, we were able to retain some form of Commonwealth free entry as a special arrangement we should have to be prepared to accept the principle of compensation taxes on United Kingdom exports within the group benefiting from such free entry. We could certainly claim that if preferential arrangements were retained within the Six for products from ex-French and ex-Belgian colonial territories which have now or will be assuming independence compensation taxes should apply if exports from the Six incorporating such products came to the markets of the Seven.

Membership of ECSC and Euratom

(e)   We should have to consider whether it would not be appropriate for us to agree to join these institutions as a "natural" part of arrangements bringing us into close association with the Common Market.

Institutions of the Six

(f)   Acceptance of the common external tariff would mean that we should lose our autonomy over the United Kingdom tariff. In other fields where some measure of harmonisation is envisaged, e.g. agriculture, social charges, questions of autonomy would also arise. This means that there would have to be a Council of Association where United Kingdom Ministers could discuss these matters with Ministers of the Six, decisions being taken in appropriate cases by some form of majority voting. In addition some means of effective participation in the work of the European Economic Commission would also have to be found.

Implications of near-identification

(a)   General

28.   It is not possible to say definitely whether - assuming that the political will to have a settlement existed - an "imperfect" solution on the foregoing lines would be negotiable. But given the fact that we so nearly achieved the negotiation of an Industrial Free Trade Area in 1958 it seems likely that a settlement on these lines would be attainable. But it would be dangerous to assume that we could secure our objective by paying a lower price than the sum of the foregoing (though no doubt marginal easements or derogations could be negotiated). The acceptability of such arrangements to world opinion would depend on the height of the common tariff.

(b)   Implications for the Commonwealth

29.   Any material disappearance of Commonwealth free entry or substantial concessions on agriculture would involve a re-negotiation of our trade agreements with other Commonwealth Governments and it might be difficult to retain much of the Commonwealth preferential system. As indicated in paragraph 11, some Commonwealth Ministers and officials appreciate the importance of our securing an economic settlement in Europe. They may not, however, appreciate how substantially they might be affected and they are influenced by a hope that, as part of such a settlement, they might secure better access for their goods in the markets of the Six, particularly agricultural products and low cost manufactures. They might, for example, like to participate in managed market arrangements for some agricultural products. We, on behalf of our dependent territories would like to see any such comprehensive settlement cover agreed arrangements about the sale of tropical products, including a solution of the 'mitigation' problem. All this would be extremely difficult to negotiate and at least some Commonwealth Governments would press to participate in the negotiations, as their interests would be so much at stake. We could not negotiate on their behalf.

(c)   Implications for the United Kingdom

30.   It must be recognised that a solution on the lines summarised in paragraph 27 would involve   formidable political and economic difficulties, and painful problems for some sections of the United Kingdom economy. Acceptance of a common external tariff would involve some surrender of sovereignty. In the field of agriculture managed markets might well mean increased burdens for United Kingdom consumers (though not necessarily for United Kingdom

agricultural interests) and would raise our general level of costs. Concessions on horticulture would obviously involve great political difficulties.

31.   Acceptance of the principle of harmonisation of social charges would undoubtedly involve substantial complications and difficulties although there would be scope for argument about the actual provisions.

32.   Ministers are already aware that the entry of the United Kingdom into the ECSC and Euratom would be opposed by certain interests here.

Conclusion

33.   The Economic Steering Committee has set in train a detailed study of the arrangements set out in paragraph 27 and of their political and economic implications for us. A further report will be submitted on them. The difficulties which they would involve must certainly not be under-estimated. It must, however, be emphasised that the difficulties cannot be quantified. We cannot forecast the amount of trade which we might lose, or gain, by adopting one course rather than another because we cannot say how British industry would fare in the situation which confronted it. The problem is essentially one for a broad political and economic judgment. Officials have come to the conclusion that they should recommend to Ministers that near-identification with the Common Market is the right objective for the United Kingdom to pursue. Indeed they see no alternative between accepting that objective and acquiescing indefinitely in the continuation of the present situation in Europe, with all the economic and political dangers which are inherent in it.

34.   Once our objective has been determined there is a substantial task ahead. We have to prepare public and Parliamentary opinion and we have to hold discussions with industry, our EFTA partners and the Commonwealth. There has already been considerable speculation in the Press and a lot of questions have been asked. Questions of tactics and timing will have to be considered. But it would be helpful if, on the basis of the present paper, Ministers felt able to determine what our objective should be.

There were six Cabinet Ministers present at the Committee to discuss this memorandum, in addition to the Prime Minister. The following is the main body of the record [40].

THE PRIME MINISTER said that the first question was whether "near-identification" was in fact the only alternative to continued acquiescence in the present situation. Was it necessary for the United Kingdom to give up all hope, even as a long term objective, of an industrial free trade area? Might not this solution - which was economically the most advantageous from our point of view - still be feasible once the Six had fully consolidated their economic and political union? Alternatively, was it really against our interests and out of the question to work for a single European market with a preferential position for the Six? How serious in practice would this infringement of the m.f.n. principle be? If we were able to get American support as well as agreement with the Six, would it not be possible to secure at least the acquiescence, if not the approval, of the other parties to the General Agreement on Tariffs and Trade?

If it was right that "near-identification" was the only alternative, then the disadvantages as well as the advantages had to be carefully examined. There were formidable political objections to "near-identification". Harmonisation would require us to surrender our independence in fixing our internal tariff; to that extent we should give up control of the level of our internal costs. Commonwealth free entry would certainly not be fully maintained; any weakening of our trade links with Commonwealth countries would greatly diminish the political cohesion of the Commonwealth and the additional authority we enjoyed as its leading member. Managed agricultural markets would involve drastic changes in the present system of protection for British agriculture and horticulture; farmers, although not horticulturists, might become reconciled to the changes but we would have to weigh carefully the effects on internal price levels and on our competitive power. Finally, "near-identification" would commit us to some institutional arrangements with majority voting. The economic objections were also considerable. We should lose our exclusive preference on industrial goods in the markets of the Seven. To the extent that we were forced to abandon free entry for the Commonwealth our preferential position in the Commonwealth markets, covering some 40 per cent of our trade, would be at a risk. Acceptance of a common tariff might disturb our present access to cheap raw materials to the detriment of our competitive power.

It was true that "near-identification" would remove discrimination by the Six against our trade with them and we should thus avoid direct economic damage. But how far would anything short of full membership of the Common Market meet our indirect economic difficulties? Could we hope fully to participate in foreign investment in Europe and in the expanding European economy? It was for consideration whether, if we were prepared to contemplate "near-identification" with all its difficulties and dangers, we should not do better to go the whole way and secure the full advantages of membership of the Common Market. To "go into Europe fully" would at least be a positive and an imaginative approach which might assist the Government to overcome the manifest political and domestic difficulties. "Near-identification" had less attractions, and not appreciably less dangers.

In the course of discussion the following were the main points made -

(a)   The main economic argument for a close association with the Six was not that we would thereby avoid discrimination against 15 per cent of our exports, but that we should gain an enormously increased "home market" with all the opportunities for economies of scale, and a full share in foreign investment and economic growth.

(b)   Several Ministers thought that a policy of "near-identification" might well involve us in paying almost as high a price as joining the

Common Market but that the rewards would be considerably less. Nevertheless, there were great political difficulties in accepting the Common Market as our immediate objective. "Near-identification" was a more practicable immediate objective and if all went well, might lead ultimately to the realisation of a Common Market. There was, however, some danger that in any step-by-step approach our bargaining position would be weakened as we went along.

(c)   The United Kingdom enjoyed important advantages from being the leading member of the Commonwealth.   Commonwealth preferences were one of the most important elements in existing Commonwealth policy and their loss would greatly weaken our political influence in the Commonwealth.   An association with the Common Market which led to significant inroads on the preferential system therefore raised the grave political question whether it would be right to bring about a weakening of the Commonwealth.

(d)   An association with the Common Market would probably require the United Kingdom to give up more sovereignty in agriculture than in industry. It was extremely difficult to assess what the effect of managed markets would be on British agriculture as compared with the present system of subsidies and protection. It was possible that the farming community might come to accept managed markets and that some special solutions suited to conditions in the United Kingdom might be found. It need not be assumed that we would have to accept precisely the same arrangements as the Six contemplated. But a great deal of work needed to be done on the implications of managed markets for British agriculture and if a change of policy were decided upon, it would be a long process getting the farming community to accept it.

In further discussion there was general agreement that more information was required about the possible consequences of the various courses. Officials should proceed with the study mentioned in paragraph 33 of EQ(60) 27 on the political and economic implications of "near-identification". But other kinds of studies were also needed - e.g. the effects of managed markets on agriculture, and what the United Kingdom would gain as well as lose in terms of industrial costs and other trading opportunities in the Commonwealth and elsewhere by continuing with the present situation. It was recognised that final and complete answers to these questions could not be provided, but that was all the more reason for having the arguments on both sides set out. It was equally important to have the best assessments that could be made of some of the major political issues. There was an assumption that it was bad for us, both economically and politically, not to be part of the "new giant" in Europe. It was arguable, however, that, although we might not gain as big trading opportunities as if were inside the Common Market, we would gain something from having a rich customer on our doorstep. And in political terms it was not self-evident that we would lose influence vis-a-vis the rest of the world. It might be that, because of the necessity of the Six to reach agreement, they would be less able to take a positive approach to world problems and we should be exerting a greater influence in world affairs through being outside.

Summing up, THE PRIME MINISTER said that policies of "near-identification" and of joining the Common Market were so similar that one might well lead to the other, and if we were prepared to accept near identification, it might be preferable to contemplate full membership. The basic choice for the Government, therefore, was between initiating a dramatic change in direction in our domestic, commercial and international policies, and maintaining our traditional policy of remaining aloof from Europe politically while doing all we could to mitigate the economic dangers of a divided Europe. This would be another of the historic moments of decision and would need much careful thought. As a basis for further consideration, officials should prepare answers to, or at any rate comments on, the doubts and questions, both economic and political, which Ministers had raised. He would himself, in consultation with the Chancellor of the Exchequer and the Foreign Secretary, circulate a list of the questions to which thought should be given. The Committee recognised that many of these were primarily matters of judgement which could not be answered definitively.

The Committee -

Agreed that further consideration of the long term relations between the Six and the Seven should be resumed when officials had examined further the economic and political questions to be indicated by the Prime Minister.

APPENDIX C

Association with the European Economic Community

Cabinet Memorandum [42]

NOTE BY THE SECRETARY OF THE CABINET

On 27th May the European Economic Association Committee agreed that the broad choice for the United Kingdom was either to seek a close association with the European Economic Community or to continue to remain aloof from it while doing all we could to mitigate the economic and political dangers of the division in Europe. The Prime Minister subsequently circulated a list of questions about the future of the Community, and about the broad political and economic considerations which should determine the choice of policy, and asked that these should be studied by officials of the Departments concerned. These studies have now been carried out, under the auspices of the Economic Steering (Europe) Committee. A report by that Committee is circulated herewith by direction of the Prime Minister.

(Signed)   NORMAN BROOK

THE SIX AND THE SEVEN: THE LONG-TERM OBJECTIVE

COVERING NOTE TO THE ANSWERS TO THE PRIME MINISTER'S LIST OF QUESTIONS

Introduction

We attach replies to the questions circulated by the Prime Minster in his memorandum of 1st June (EQ (60) 29). They are in the form of fairly short answers with, in some cases, more detailed argument and explanation in annexes [omitted]. We have altered the order of the questions where it made it easier to submit the answers to Ministers in consecutive form. We have also added two questions (Nos. 8 and 9) which we thought might arise in Ministerial discussion as they did in our own.

Reservations
2.   We must make two specific reservations which apply to most, if not all, of the answers:
(a)   On many points the policies of the Six (i.e., the European Economic Community) are not yet firm, notably on matters left open in the Treaty of Rome. Consequently any answers given now might be considerably affected by the policies which will eventually be adopted; and
(b)   If the United Kingdom were to join the Six, we should undoubtedly influence to a considerable extent the development of these policies. Our presence would also inevitably bring about changes in the

structure of the Common Market as it exists to-day. But it is not possible to judge now how great our influence would be and how far therefore our presence would change the eventual outcome and consequently some of the answers we have given.

"Joining" and "Close Association"

3.   We have not discussed in the answers what might be the difference - on particular issues - between joining the Community and close association with it. This is because we think that, if we were to seek to join the Six, the preceding negotiation would bring about modifications in the Treaty of Rome which would be likely to leave us in much the position we should reach if we sought "close association" at the outset. There would be some difference in public presentation, but probably little in substance. The main substantial differences would be:

(a)   "Close association" might well take much longer to achieve than actual joining, and the price we should have to pay would be greater than we should have had to pay for the Free Trade Area, while we should not be members of the inner councils of the Six, and would thus not solve the political difficulties which we think will arise if we remain outside;

(b)   Our willingness to join as a full member would give the other members of the Six a better chance to overcome any French reluctance to accept us; whatever their individual inclinations might be, they would find it much harder to secure French acceptance of any intermediate solution short of full United Kingdom membership, and

(c)   The immediate impact on the Commonwealth would probably be less unfavourable if instead of actually joining the Community we entered into close association with it.

The Issues Involved

4.   In what follows we set out some of the main issues which arise on the answers. But we have not attempted to summarise the answers, and many of the qualifications and reservations which appear in them are not repeated here. This covering note is therefore supplementary to the answers, but not a substitute.

Foreign Policy Considerations

5.   In the first place, it is now apparent that there are strong reasons of foreign policy for our joining the Six. If the Six "succeed", we should be greatly damaged politically if we were outside, and our influence in world affairs would be bound to wane; if we were inside, the influence we would wield in the world would be enhanced; while still retaining in some degree the right to speak on our own account, we should also be speaking as part of a European bloc. If, on the other hand, the Six "fail", there would be great damage to Western interests, and the weakening of Europe which would follow would be a serious matter for the United Kingdom; it would be too late for us to go in to prevent failure when a breakdown was seen to be coming, but if we were already in, we could probably strengthen the European bloc and

prevent its disintegration. Foreign policy considerations therefore require us to be in the inner councils of the Six.

Economic Advantages
6.   In joining the Six, we should be participating in a vigorous and rapidly expanding market, and there would be good grounds for hoping that our commerce and industry would benefit. We could gain a great deal from larger scale production, specialisation, higher efficiency resulting from keener competition and the more rapid spread of technical skills and new developments. All this we should miss - to the detriment of our industry - if we remained outside. If we joined, the inflow of new investment into the United Kingdom would be greater, and the outflow of capital to the Six might be less than if we remained outside.   We should, however, only achieve these advantages of potentialities if we were fully competitive with the Six - which we must be whether we join the Common Market or stay outside it - and if the Government maintain appropriate economic policies at home.

What Joining the Common Market Means
7.   We cannot join the Common Market on the cheap. Joining means taking two far-reaching decisions. First, we must accept that there will have to be political content in our action - we must show ourselves prepared to join with the Six in their institutional arrangements and in any development towards closer political integration. Without this we cannot achieve our foreign policy aims - see paragraph 5. Secondly, there must be a real intention to have a "common market", and this implies that, in so far as the members of the market consider that production inside the market requires protection against outside production, this must also apply in our corner of the market; that is to say, in general we must accept the common tariff.

The Four Main Problems
8.   Joining the Common Market raises four main problems. First, and most difficult of all, are the problems of our political and economic relations with the Commonwealth and the maintenance of free entry which goes wider than the Commonwealth. Secondly, there is the problem of agriculture and horticulture. Thirdly, there is our commitment to, and relationship with, the other countries in the European Free Trade Association (EFTA). Fourthly, there is the question of the reaction of the United States (and indeed other third countries outside the European bloc and outside the Commonwealth).

The Commonwealth and Free Entry
9.   In the political field we believe that we could demonstrate to the Six the importance to them (if we were to join) of our maintaining the Commonwealth political relationship. We believe that we could show the value to the free world generally of our special relationship not only with the old Commonwealth countries, but also with the newer countries (notably India) and the emerging countries (for example

Nigeria). The Six in general are well aware of the attachment of the British people to the Commonwealth concept.

10.   It is in the economic field that we come up against what seems to us the really crucial issue in the problem of whether or not to join the Common Market. This arises from the existence of arrangements for the duty-free entry into the United Kingdom of a range of products which come mainly from the Commonwealth, but also from important third countries like the United States. At one extreme it seems that if we were to insist on the maintenance in full of these free entry arrangements (which are the basis of the whole Commonwealth preferential system), there can be no agreement with the Six, particularly as we could not then accept and take part in their common agricultural policy. At the other extreme, it seems inconceivable that we could accept the common tariff in full and thus give the Six more favourable treatment than the Commonwealth ("reverse preferences") on some products in which there is a strong Commonwealth interest. For example, it is unthinkable that we should apply the common tariff of 20 per cent against wheat from Canada and Australia - and the United States - while allowing French wheat in free of duty.

11.   The Six would expect us to raise the problem of free entry, but we cannot judge whether we could negotiate an acceptable compromise solution. A possible line of approach - though one full of difficulties - is indicated in the following paragraphs.

12.   It might be that we could accept the common tariff on *manufactured goods* without placing intolerable strains on the Commonwealth, provided that we could secure from the Six some easement of their restrictions on imports from the low-cost countries (though our attitude to Japanese goods would be a complicating factor). Even so, the granting of "reverse preferences" in favour of the Six and against the Commonwealth would create serious resentment in some Commonwealth countries.

13.   The treatment of *raw materials* would be a somewhat easier problem, a solution might be found on the basis of acceptance of the common tariff, or on the continuance of free entry coupled with compensation taxes, or possibly through arrangements on a commodity by commodity basis. To accept the common tariff on raw materials as well as on manufactured goods would be a further blow to the Commonwealth.

14.   As regards *foodstuffs*, the problems of tropical products would probably be less difficult than those of temperate products.

15.   As regards the former, our overseas territories and the overseas territories of the Six produce in general the same kind of things, and a broad bargain might be possible under which they would allow free entry to the produce of our overseas territories and we would allow free entry to the produce of theirs. Taken as a whole, such a bargain ought to be acceptable to the Commonwealth countries concerned, whether dependent or independent.

16.   It is on temperate foodstuffs that the most difficult problems would arise. It seems out of the question that we could accept the common tariff or the other protective devices of the Six for these

products, even from foreign sources, because of the impact on the Commonwealth, the damage to our trading relations with third countries - in the case of the United States a breakdown of the Trade Agreement - and the consequences for food prices here. The only possible way out might be to propose discussions with the Six, commodity by commodity, bringing in the Commonwealth countries concerned, the United States and perhaps other major foreign suppliers. But this would involve a most formidable programme of negotiations and at this stage it is impossible to say whether generally acceptable compromises would emerge.

Agriculture and Horticulture

17.   If we joined the Six and accepted their common agricultural policy, our farmers as a whole might not suffer, though some sections would. But the common agricultural policy is radically different from our own, and farmers in the United Kingdom would need to be convinced that this new policy would not work out to their disadvantage. To join the Six while attempting to maintain existing free entry arrangements for foodstuffs would expose our farmers to the full force of world competition. Horticulture would involve difficulties of a different kind. It is not the present intention of the Six to use managed markets in horticulture, but since we rely on the tariff to protect our horticulturists, these would be faced with increasing competition from the Continent from the outset. We might be able (*eg*, through minimum price schemes) to mitigate the damage for some time, but in the longer term some sections at least of the industry would be bound to suffer.

European Free Trade Association

18.   Her Majesty's Government have given repeated assurances that they will abide by their commitments to the Seven and will only proceed in their dealings with the Six in consultation and accord with their partners. If it were to look as though we were not fully honouring these undertakings and were merely out to obtain the best possible arrangement for ourselves, we should be exposed to severe criticism on grounds of bad faith - and not only in the countries of the Seven. In practice, if we were to join the Community and if, as is possible, Denmark and Norway joined with us, it should prove practicable to negotiate an association providing for the avoidance of trade discrimination between the EEC thus enlarged and those EFTA countries who felt unable to enter the Community. The outcome might well be satisfactory, but the handling of the E.F.T.A. countries at the time when we presented our proposals to them, and when we entered into negotiations with the Six, would be very difficult indeed and call for the greatest care.

United States

19.   If the Americans recognised that we were intending to enter Europe politically as well as economically, they could hardly object. Just as they have welcomed the move towards integration brought about by the Treaty of Rome, so they would probably welcome a move by us

to integrate ourselves with the Six. In addition to their interest in the problem of free entry, however, they would dislike the larger bloc from the economic point of view, since it would entail increased discrimination against them. This dislike might be intensified if the arrangements for dealing with the problems of the overseas territories (dependent and independent - the Six's and ours) led to the setting up of what looked like new preferential arrangements discriminating even further against the United States.

Tactics

20.   On all current indications we do not think that circumstances will be favourable for discussions with the Six leading to a mutually acceptable settlement for some considerable time - at least 12 or 18 months. We do not therefore deal in this paper with questions of tactics and handling. They will, however, be of the greatest importance and may determine the nature of the settlement (*eg*, whether we join the Community alone or as part of a wider move involving the other EFTA countries). These matters would need very full consideration. There would be questions of how and when, and in what order, the Commonwealth, the EFTA countries and others with an interest (notably the United States) were consulted, and the further question of how the negotiations should take place and where. All these matters we leave over for the time being. But we do think it right to emphasise to Ministers at this time that, once they have decided on our policy and on the basis on which they are willing to negotiate, an essential step must be to ensure by some appropriate preliminary approach that the Six (and this really means France) would be willing to see us join or move to close association with them on terms which we could accept. To launch another initiative and receive a second rebuff would be disastrous.

THE SIX AND THE SEVEN: THE LONG-TERM OBJECTIVE

Answers to the Prime Minister's Questions

FOREIGN POLITICAL QUESTIONS

QUESTION 1
      Will the Six develop into a powerful and effective unit, both economically and politically, or will it break up or be weakened by internal dissension?

ANSWER
(a)   It is not possible at this stage to be sure how powerful and effective the European Economic Community (EEC) will become, or what shape it will assume. So much will depend on what happens in France and Germany after the disappearance of de Gaulle and Adenauer.
(b)   On the one hand there is a genuine sentiment in the peoples of the Six for closer European unity, even at the cost of surrendering considerable national individuality. This is likely to grow as the Six become more and more a going concern. It will be in the interests of the

Governments of the Six to form a closer-knit community and they will be encouraged by the United States to do so. If things go according to plan, the Community should become a very important factor on the world scene - politically, economically and quite possibly militarily as well.

(c)   But on the other hand if there is a *crise de régime* in France after de Gaulle's disappearance or over Algeria, or if the Germans were, some years after Adenauer's departure, to lose their morale and seek an accommodation with Russia, or if there were to be a major world economic recession, then the Community might well be greatly weakened. Furthermore, one cannot be sure that there will not be Franco-German rivalry for the leadership after the disappearance of de Gaulle and Adenauer, even though in other respects the Community is working very successfully.

(d)   As long as General de Gaulle is in power, his concept of a *"Union des Patries"* is likely to dominate. If the Community develops on these lines, its form may be described as that of a Confederation, rather than the political Federation which remains the objective of the Monnet school. It is more difficult to forecast how far Governments will hold to this concept after the General's departure. There can be no certainty that the strength of the Federalist movement will not reassert itself effectively. But in any event it does not follow that a confederation would be less effective and powerful than a federation.

QUESTION 2
        If it is going to succeed, is it desirable that the United Kingdom should be associated with it so that we can influence its policies?

ANSWER
(a)   Yes. If the community succeeds in becoming a really effective political and economic force, it will become the dominating influence in Europe and the only Western bloc approaching in influence the big Two - the USSR and the United States. The influence of the United Kingdom in Europe, if left outside, will correspondingly decrease. Though we may hope to retain something of a special position *vis-à-vis* the United States, the latter will inevitably tend to attach more and more weight to the views and interests of the Six rather than to those of the United Kingdom. The relative decline in the United Kingdom's status will reduce our influence in the Commonwealth (see also Question 17) and with the uncommitted countries. Quite apart, therefore, from the economic damage which we shall suffer from the consolidation of the Six, if we try to remain aloof from them - bearing in mind that this will be happening simultaneously with the contraction of our overseas possessions - we shall run the risk of losing political influence and of ceasing to be able to exercise any claim to be a world Power.

(b)   On the contrary if we were to be effectively associated with the Community, we should not only be able to benefit from its political and economic influence, but would have the opportunity to influence its policies. This would be particularly the case if, as is by no means impossible, France and Germany dispute for the leadership of the Community. If that should happen it might be the role of the United

Kingdom to hold the balance between the two and exercise a degree of leadership in the process.

QUESTION 3
If it is going to fail, would this be such a setback for economic and political co-operation among the Western Allies and for world trade generally that we ought to go in to prevent failure?

ANSWER
(a)   Yes. Whether failure would occasion a serious setback for world trade may be arguable. However, the collapse of the Community after it had been in existence for some years, would be a grave misfortune not only for Western Europe but for NATO and the Western cause as a whole and therefore for the United Kingdom. It would greatly increase the risk of Western Germany breaking the ties with Western Europe and throwing Germany itself into the arms of the USSR.   It would encourage the spread of neutralism in Europe and would seriously endanger the existence of NATO.
(b)   If the United Kingdom were in a position at the critical moment to exert a powerful influence, these dangers might be overcome. But it must be doubted if the United Kingdom, after the consequences of some years of standing aloof from the Community, would be in such a position. The United Kingdom would be in a much stronger position to prevent the collapse of the Community or to limit its effects if it had been associated with [the] Six from an early date.

QUESTION 4
Alternatively, is the creation of a powerful bloc in Europe - "the third force" - likely to be dangerous in terms of world power politics?

ANSWER
A European "third force" would only be dangerous if it pursued radically different policies from those of its allies. Such differences could only occur if the Community adopted a more aggressive or more conciliatory attitude towards the Soviet *bloc*. It does not seem possible that Western Europe in the foreseeable future could enjoy the military strength to contemplate adventures against the Russians except at the side of the United States and United Kingdom. Neutralism is a little less unlikely but for political and geographical reasons this too seems a remote possibility. The risks of neutralism in any individual country of the Six would certainly be much greater if the Community did not exist or were to disintegrate. There is, however, a possibility that the Six might pursue independent policies (possibly but not necessarily anti-American) which would not affect their basic loyalties but would have some of the disadvantages of neutralism.

QUESTION 5
Who of the Six is likely to control it or have the greatest influence over its policies?

ANSWER
The French will have the greatest influence in the next few years and may be able to retain it. But much will depend on the future of France after de Gaulle's departure and upon developments in Germany. The Germans, particularly if there was a swing to the Right backed by the industrialists, might well make a determined challenge for the leadership.

QUESTION 6
How would our influence with the Six from outside compare with our influence if inside?

ANSWER
(a)   The tendency, already noticeable, for the Six to reach decisions on questions of importance to them by discussion among themselves before meeting other countries in the various international bodies will no doubt grow as the Community develops. As this extends, as seems inevitable, to political consultation, we shall find ourselves increasingly excluded and therefore unable to exert effective influence during the formative stages of EEC policy-making. On matters directly affecting the Treaty of Rome this is already the position and we have already been the sufferers in the last few months from the growth of direct consultation between the Six and the United States. We may find a tendency for the United States and EEC increasingly to concert policy on major issues, political and economic, without proper regard for the views and interests of the United Kingdom.
(b)   The best way of insuring against this would be so close an association with the Six that we take part, from the outset and at all stages, in policy discussions on particular problems. How far it would be possible to achieve this by an arrangement short of full membership is open to question. It would certainly be difficult to achieve it with complete success unless we were regarded by the Six as full and equal partners.

QUESTION 7
How will the development of the Six affect our relationship with the United States and our influence in the rest of the world?

ANSWER
(a)   Although we could still hope to maintain something of a special position with the United States, more particularly perhaps in military matters, and would continue still to benefit from the ties of a common language, the general decline in our influence - especially in Europe - would   inevitably encourage the United States to pay increasing importance to the views of the Community. The corollary is that if we were effectively associated with the Six we should not only improve our position with the United States but in some degree be able to act as an intermediary between the United States and the Community.
(b)   As regards our influence in the rest of the world, this is partly covered by the answer to Question 2. If we stayed aloof from the Six, the relative decline in our status would reduce our influence in the

Commonwealth and with the uncommitted countries. We should run the risk of losing political influence and of ceasing to be able to exercise any claim to be a World Power. On the other hand, if we joined the Community, the initial reaction of the Commonwealth would be that this was turning away from them. Our influence with some of the uncommitted countries, *eg*, in Africa and Asia might in the short term be diminished to the extent that we were felt to be even more closely associated with the colonial rearguard, *viz*, France and the Netherlands, although much would depend on developments in Algeria and what country might currently be the target of the "anti-colonialists". In the longer term, our association with the Six should make us economically stronger and thus improve our capacity to wield influence through trade and aid - factors which will count a good deal with the uncommitted countries.

QUESTION 8
What would be the attitude of the United States to our joining the EEC?

ANSWER
(a)   The initial reaction of the United States to our seeking membership of the EEC might well be one of mistrust of our intentions. But if it was made clear that we were seeking full membership and if - as we should hope - this was welcome to the other members of the Six, the United States Administration could hardly be seen to oppose the joint purpose of the Six and of ourselves. Furthermore, there would be political advantages for the United States to set against any economic disadvantages for them. Public opinion in the United States which favours the concept of a United Europe would in general be on our side. There would, however, be misgivings both inside and outside the Administration. On the economic side, American dislike of a larger *bloc* discriminating against United States exports would be strengthened. Some circles would be disturbed at the thought of their closest ally moving to some extent out of their sphere of influence. These fears would be mitigated by the hope that the accession of the United Kingdom to the Six would increase both the strength and reliability of Europe.
(b)   Membership of all three European Communities (the European Coal and Steel Community and the European Atomic Energy Community as well as EEC) might endanger our bilateral agreement with the United States on atomic energy matters.

QUESTION 9
Would the European Free Trade Association (EFTA) survive United Kingdom membership of the EEC? If not, what would be the consequences for the United Kingdom?

ANSWER
(a)   Not in its present form. United Kingdom membership of the EEC as constituted by the Rome Treaty would not be consistent with the full obligations of the EFTA Convention.

(b)   It can be taken as certain that membership of the EEC would be unacceptable to some of our partners in the EFTA. But, provided we ourselves became members, it might be possible to negotiate for them a satisfactory association, the general effect of which would be avoidance of trade discrimination.

(c)   Even if arrangements of this kind could eventually be made, there would, at the outset, be a good deal of resentment in some of the EFTA countries, particularly Sweden and Switzerland, at the change of policy, and a suspicion that they were going to be let down by the United Kingdom.   But given satisfactory arrangements eventually, these feelings should not endure for long. (See also Question 12.)

TRADE AND ECONOMIC QUESTIONS

QUESTION 10
    What direct trade and economic advantages do we expect to gain from joining the Six?

ANSWER
(a)   The industrial policy of the Six, in contrast to their agricultural policy, is competitive and expansionist. Joining the Six would give large potential trade and economic advantages for British industry. We should be joining an area which is economically the most rapidly expanding in the world and we can reasonably hope that our commerce and industry would be invigorated by this. We would be part of a single market of over 200 million people; and though we should still, compared with our European competitors, be slightly handicapped in much of the area by higher transport costs and different standards and specifications, we could gain much from more specialisation, larger-scale production, higher efficiency through greater competition and a more rapid spread of technical skills and new developments.   The inflow of new investment from both inside and outside the area might be greater, and the outflow of capital to the Six might be less, than if we remained outside, with consequent benefit to our balance of payments. Finally, in its external trade, the area should be at once a competitive seller and an expanding buyer. With rising production, it would be possible, given the will, to invest more overseas and give greater aid to under-developed countries.

(b)   But it should be emphasised that all the above advantages are potentialities that joining the Six might enable us to realise, not inevitable consequences of joining. If our economy and our exports are to grow faster in the future the main changes must come from within the United Kingdom.   Even before union the exports of the Six were growing faster than ours. If we are to prosper, we shall have to be fully competitive with them - whether we are in the Common Market or not - and the removal of tariff barriers against the Six would force greater competitiveness on our industries. But the Government would still have to maintain appropriate economic policies at home.

(c)   Whether we join the Six or not, we shall have to reduce the proportion of our output devoted to consumption, and increase the proportion which is invested or exported. If we join the Six and seek to secure the benefits of association with the Community, we shall have to be fully competitive with them and this may involve changes in our industrial structure which may be both more rapid and of a different character than would be the case if we stayed outside. While these changes were taking place, there would be greater need for mobility of labour in the United Kingdom, and some social hardship might be involved. In this connexion, however, we must remember that changes in the pattern of industry are taking place all the time, and that in an expanding economy they can be accomplished without undue difficulty. Moreover, we were ready to face industrial changes when we originally proposed a free trade area, although the changes required for the Common Market may be a little greater than those which a free trade area would have involved. If, on the other hand, we decide to stay out of the Common Market, we shall not be faced with these particular, short-term problems, at any rate in the same form. But neither will United Kingdom industry have the advantages of our association with the Six, and this may lead to stagnation and the country as a whole being the poorer for it.

QUESTION 11
What are the other important consequences of joining the Six?

ANSWER
(a)   One of the objectives of the Six is the eventual free movement of labour within the area of the Community. If we join the Community, we must expect gradual pressure to adopt a more liberal attitude to this question, but how much more liberal cannot be forecast at this stage. In general, the present practice of the Six is less restrictive than ours, and we should find it difficult to resist pressure to fall into line with them. We should bear in mind that the movement of labour works both ways, and might conceivably be of advantage to us as a method of dealing with unemployment. If we joined the Six, we should be accepting the objectives of the eventual free movement of capital, the removal of restrictions on services, such as banking and insurance, and the harmonisation of labour conditions (equal pay, for example), and of fiscal policies. The future significance of these objectives is quite uncertain, and the Six will certainly pursue them gradually. As members of the Community we should be in a position to exert our influence on what the actual policies should be.

In general, it seems fair to say that most of these possible developments offer potential advantages in the long run (and from some, such as banking and insurance, we should benefit in the short run as well), but they may give rise to some difficulties in the transitional period.
(b)   There would be some change in the pattern of our trade, though how great it would be is impossible to say. There is already a tendency for the proportion of our trade with the Commonwealth to fall; this tendency would be increased, since we should both buy and sell more in the area of the Common Market. We should also expect to buy

proportionately less from the United States and we might sell proportionately less to them as well.

(c)   Very tentative estimates suggest that if we join the Six as full members and accept the common agricultural policy without modification (but see the introductory note to Questions 13-15), the direct effect on the Retail Price Index might be to raise it by about 2 per cent. - some increases in food prices being offset by some reductions in the prices of manufactures. There would be consequential indirect effects on wages and prices, but both direct and indirect effects would make themselves felt little by little over the lengthy transitional period. As a partial offset to the rise in the cost of living, there would be the savings to the Exchequer from the abolition of the agricultural subsidies, and these could be used to reduce the level of taxation.

QUESTION 12
What value do we expect to gain from our preferential position in the markets of the Seven (bearing in mind possible adherents)? If we attempted to bring the Six and the Seven together, how much of this advantage might we lose through:
(a)   sharing the preferences with the Six;
(b)   the possible refusal of some members of the Seven, and any later adherents, to associate with the Six?

ANSWER
We expect to increase our export trade to the Seven (i.e., other EFTA countries) by a useful amount. The total market (over 90 millions including the United Kingdom) is big enough to give us in theory a major increase, and of course we dominate the market as the greatest industrial producer in a way in which we could not hope to dominate the Six. On the other hand, the preferential advantages are small in the richest parts of the area. If we had to share our preferences with the Six we should lose most of our gains, though if the sharing were postponed for a couple of years we could dig in during that time and expect then to retain some of our gains.

AGRICULTURE, FOOD, PRICES &c.

The answers to the following questions (Nos. 13, 14 and 15) about agriculture, food and prices are based on the assumptions -
(i)   that the common agricultural policy of the Six is broadly as at present proposed by the Commission and has become fully operative;
(ii)   that we participate in it without having been able to negotiate any substantial changes, or special exceptions.
But how far these assumptions are realistic is examined in the cover note by the Chairman of the Economic Steering (Europe) Committee.

QUESTION 13
What changes would have to be made for United Kingdom

agriculture, and horticulture, if we joined the Six? Should we have to participate in "managed markets"? What would this involve and how would these changes affect - (a) the Exchequer; (b) the farmer; (c) the consumer?

ANSWER

(a)   Joining the Six would mean a fundamental change in our agricultural policy.   We should be moving from a system which in general combines world free market prices for food with support for the farmer by deficiency payments from the Exchequer, to one of managed markets with higher prices paid by the consumer.   Part I of the Agriculture Act, 1947, and Part I of the Agriculture Act, 1957, as well as the present assurances to the agricultural and horticultural industries could not be maintained. They would be replaced as instruments of support for the farmer by managed markets, which would include a common tariff, supplementary levies and some quota restrictions on imports from third countries and occasional direct intervention in markets for some commodities.

(b)   The maximum gain to the *Exchequer* from these changes in agricultural policy would be the amount of the commodity subsidies (£160 millions per annum) and the proceeds of the common tariff on imports from third countries.   Production grants would go on; and supplementary import levies would not, in general, benefit the Exchequer because they would be pooled and go mainly to the Six. (See also Question 15).   *United Kingdom farmers* as a whole might remain roughly in the same position. Some sections would do better but others concentrating on milk (if this could not be excluded), bacon, eggs and horticulture, would stand to lose quite a lot.   *The Commonwealth,* which at present enjoys quota and duty free entry, would be hard hit. (See also Question 16).   *The consumer* would find the cost of living rising, markedly in bread and butter; as a partial offset reductions in taxation ought to be possible. (See also Question 11).   *Generally,* there would be some interference in our marketing system - particularly in the national and international corn exchanges.

QUESTION 14

How would joining the Six affect our access to cheap foodstuffs and basic materials? What effect would it have on our internal costs and our competitive position in third markets?

ANSWER

(a)   We should, on the whole, have to pay more for food imports. But it is not possible to quantify this or to say what effect on the terms of trade would be.

(b)   The prices of some foodstuffs, including horticultural products, would probably be somewhat reduced.   But these price reductions would be much more than offset by increases elsewhere - especially for bread, butter and meat, where relatively large rises in price must be expected. Food prices as a whole might rise by about 7½ per cent. (See also Question 13).

(c)   The prices of basic materials would probably not be much affected.   EEC tariffs on basic materials are in most cases low. However, since at present most of the basic materials on which we have a tariff come in duty free from the Commonwealth, no reductions in price can be expected.

QUESTION 15
What would be the fiscal advantage to the Exchequer from joining the Six - in particular the revenue from import duties or export taxes, and the effect on agricultural subsidies?

ANSWER
(a)   The net ultimate gain to the Exchequer is put tentatively at about £220 millions per year, on the basis of present levels of trade and income. It should be emphasised, however, that the figure is little more than a guess.
(b)   On the assumption that Commonwealth free entry is not maintained, there would be an increase in revenue from tariffs amounting to about £70 millions (net of the loss from the abolition of tariffs on EEC products and the small reduction, on average, in the level of our protective tariffs against manufactured imports from third countries).   The maximum gain from the reduction in agricultural subsidies is put at £160 millions, but in fact the gain is likely to be rather less than this (see Question 13). No significant gain is expected to accrue from supplementary import levies on agricultural produce (see Question 13) or export taxes. It is possible that harmonisation of social policies might relieve the Exchequer of some of the burden of financing the social services.   However, this is speculative and in any case there would be a strong argument for reducing taxation by as much as was saved in this way.   Hence no gain is assumed from this source.   (See Question 21)

COMMONWEALTH QUESTIONS

QUESTION 16
To what extent does joining the Common Market put Commonwealth free entry and our Commonwealth preferences at risk? Of what value are they now, and how much of that value might we expect to keep over the next 10 or 20 years in either case?   Would compensation taxes on some of our exports to the Six to allow for Commonwealth free entry be practicable?   Could we negotiate any benefits for the Commonwealth in the markets of the Six to compensate for loss or reduction of free entry here?

ANSWER
(a)   Joining the Common Market without any special exception would require us to apply the common tariff to all imports from the Commonwealth, so ending free entry (except for those raw materials where the common tariff is nil) and the preferences we give the Commonwealth, and replacing them by preferences for Europe against the Commonwealth.

(b)   We should lose immediately such contractual rights as we have to preferences and all preferences themselves would disappear within a few years. They cover about 20 per cent. of our total exports. The value varies but major exporting industries attach a good deal of importance to them. They are slowly declining in value and the decline will continue; if we do not by our own action (*eg*, through our arrangements with the Six or because of substantial increases in our own agricultural output) hasten change, our preferences in Commonwealth countries will still be worth having even after 10 years.
(c)   We could accept the imposition of compensation taxes where necessary.
(d)   Commonwealth Governments would not be prepared to let us, in their absence, negotiate benefits in Europe to compensate them for loss or reduction of free entry here. The most important trade affected would be in agricultural items where the Six would be very unlikely to make any significant concession. There might be scope for negotiating benefits for tropical foodstuffs, and possibly for some raw materials and low cost manufactures, as part of an arrangement involving reciprocal benefits for the associated overseas territories of the Six.
(e)   The difficulties for the Commonwealth would be reduced if free entry into the United Kingdom could be continued for basic foodstuffs. But this in turn would give rise to two problems. First, if free entry were confined to the Commonwealth, there would be very serious difficulties with the United States and other foreign countries, quite apart from the consequences for the cost of living. Secondly, the retention of free entry would remove any attraction the Common Market might have for United Kingdom farmers.

QUESTION 17
Is it politically possible to take a course which could be represented as turning away from the Commonwealth? Would it in fact be practicable to join the Six without substantially weakening the Commonwealth connexion?

ANSWER
        The initial reaction in Commonwealth countries to our joining the Common Market would be difficult to dispel, and there would possibly be a continuing fear that we had altered our traditional policy and had turned away from them. Furthermore, in course of time the Common Market may develop into a federal European State, though such a development would be contrary to present trends among the Six. The closer the Six moved towards a federal State, the more difficult it would become for us - if we were members of the Community - to maintain our relationship with the Commonwealth, at any rate on its present basis.
        The indirect political effects, ie, the political repercussions of the economic consequences, would depend on the extent to which the terms we were able to negotiate with the Six in fact damaged particular Commonwealth countries. Any withdrawal of free entry would create great difficulties with them. They would insist on re-negotiating their

trade agreements with us, and we should stand to lose the preferences we enjoy in their markets. If we were unable to preserve free entry for foodstuffs, the economic consequences for the Commonwealth would be so serious as to endanger its very existence, particularly since we should be admitting imports of foodstuffs from Europe duty-free. On the other hand, if we remained outside a successful European common market our influence with the Commonwealth would be affected by the relative decline in our political status and economic strength. (See also the answer to Question 2).

QUESTION 18
If the Commonwealth connexion were substantially weakened, how would this affect our influence in the world?

ANSWER
The Commonwealth association (including the use of sterling as a reserve and trading currency) is an important buttress of our position as a Power with world-wide interests and influence. It goes some way to offset our loss of stature in the economic and military fields. Without it, or were it substantially weakened, our standing in the world would suffer and our ability to influence the policies of the United States be affected. A unique bridge between the West, i.e., the older white countries of the Commonwealth, and the new countries of Asia and Africa would be broken. Our political influence with Asian and African countries might well diminish with consequent increased opportunities for the Communist Powers and a weakening of our trading potential in these parts of the world.

SOVEREIGNTY QUESTIONS

QUESTION 19
To what extent would joining the Six require us to give up sovereignty, i.e., to give up such control as we still have over our domestic economic policies including agriculture and our social policies?

ANSWER
Between now and 1970 there would be some progressive loss of sovereignty in a number of matters affecting domestic policy, of which agriculture is likely to be an important example. It is difficult to say how much would be involved in any single field. The terms of application of the generally imprecise provisions of the Rome Treaty affecting the issues other than tariffs have still to be agreed between the Six in many cases. If we were to join the EEC at an early date we could take part in the formulation of these provisions, and influence the extent to which they affected freedom in domestic policy. The effects of any eventual loss of sovereignty would be mitigated:
(i)   by our participation in majority voting in the Council of Ministers and by our being able to influence the Commission's preparatory work;
(ii)   if resistance to Federalism on the part of some of the

Governments continues, which our membership might be expected to encourage.

QUESTION 20

To what extent would joining the Six limit our freedom to act independently in matters of foreign policy, including external commercial and financial policy?

ANSWER

(a)   Our power of independent action in many fields is already limited by our alliances, our Commonwealth obligations and indeed by our own reduced circumstances. The concept of "interdependence" recognises this, but places no constitutional brake on our power of independent decision nor does it call in question our status as a sovereign nation with an identity of our own. If we were to join the Community, we would accept treaty limitations on our sovereignty of a more precise and definite character than any existing alliances impose. How far these limitations would prove to be of such a nature that in our external affairs we would find ourselves unable to take independent action and thus prejudice what we might conceive to be a vital United Kingdom interest is hard to foretell. The stake we would acquire in the success of the Community as a whole might change our concept of what were vital United Kingdom interests, whether in domestic or external relations. Progress towards integration is bound to be gradual. All the members would still have special interests to reconcile, and each would take their full part in the evolution of Community policy towards particular problems.

The possibility of further erosion of the power of independent decision and perhaps ultimately of some loss of national identity must nevertheless be faced.

(b)   At present we have independent control of our tariff (up or down) though in practice our freedom is limited by many considerations. In accepting the common tariff of the EEC we should forfeit this freedom though we should gain a voice in settling and adjusting the common tariff. We should have to move our tariffs up or down to the common tariff level; we should be able to exempt imports, wholly or in part, from this common tariff only in certain closely defined circumstances and subject to approval by the organs of the Community; autonomous reductions in the common tariff would, with limited qualifications, require unanimity; and it would be the Commission, subject to control by the Council (by unanimous vote at first and subsequently by qualified majority vote), that would be responsible for negotiating in respect of the common tariff with outside countries. In addition to losing from the outset independent control or our tariff, we should be committed to achieving, by the end of the transitional period, a common commercial policy generally in relation to outside countries.

(c)   Our prime objective in the financial field must be to maintain the strength of sterling. The Treaty of Rome provides specifically for independent action by a member country in emergency to defend its balance of payments. The institutional provisions appear to be such as to give us adequate opportunity to make our influence felt if ideas emerged which would be harmful to sterling. In general, any loss of freedom of action would be a change of degree, being an intensification of methods of economic co-operation which we have fostered since the war, unless and until common monetary institutions are evolved as part of more complete political unification.

(d)   As regards capital movements, the Six have already shown signs of being ready to move faster towards complete liberalisation among themselves than we have been ready for generally. To allow complete freedom of capital movements would be a large departure in United Kingdom policy, which we have not hitherto felt able to afford because of the inadequate size of our reserves; the difficulties of complete liberalisation at present would be formidable, but should not, over a period of years, be insuperable. If we were to join the Six it would eventually be impossible to prevent movements of capital out of the United Kingdom for new industrial investment in Europe in order to achieve the best economic siting of plants; if on the other hand we were outside the Six there would nevertheless be a strong demand for capital movements in order to surmount the tariff barrier which in our own general economic interest it would be difficult to resist. Liberalisation *vis-à-vis* the other members of the Common Market would involve for us virtually complete liberalisation world-wide since several of the Six already have no barriers against capital movements to the rest of the world.   The special position which the sterling Commonwealth countries have had in the London market would in time have to be shared with the other members of the Common Market.

QUESTION 21
How important is it to maintain our present independence in fixing the level of our tariff and our present freedom of choice of economic policies, including the freedom to decide whether to join new economic groupings?

ANSWER
(a)   Our independence over tariffs is already severely restricted in practice - see Question 20 - and our economic freedom limited. Further limitations of the kind to which we would be likely to have to submit would not necessarily prove dangerous to us, having regard to the degree of economic interdependence we have already found it advantageous to accept.

(b)   The main reductions in sovereignty, which we should have to expect in fields other than tariff-making if we accepted the obligations of the Treaty of Rome, are set out in answer to Question 19. The importance or otherwise for economic policy of maintaining sovereignty in the fields of agriculture and capital movements are discussed elsewhere (Questions 13 and 20 respectively). The abolition of restrictions on the movement of persons and the implementation of equal pay for equal work would probably not have any serious economic effects, but would give rise to serious difficulties with labour. In particular, the acceptance by Her Majesty's Government of a commitment to establish equal pay would, as we argued in the Free Trade Area negotiations, violate our principle of not interfering with free negotiations between employers and workers. Harmonisation of social policies might ultimately entail a shift towards the continental system of financing social services, i.e., higher contributions by employers and insured persons and lower contributions by the Government. This would make possible a reduction in general taxation which would largely but not wholly offset the effects on wages, prices, income distribution, &c., but there would doubtless be hardship and difficulties in particular cases.

(c)   As regards general economic policy, the Treaty of Rome provides only for consultation and collaboration and, though external pressures in favour of particular policies might thus grow, our institutional sovereignty would be unimpaired. However, we should undoubtedly be less able than we are at present to insulate ourselves from the effects of the economic policies of the Six, and these policies might sometimes be different from our own. In recent years, for example, the Six have tended to emphasise price stability more, and full employment less, than the United Kingdom: to the extent that such differences in attitude persisted the achievement of the aims of United Kingdom policy might prove to be considerably more difficult.

(d)   In practice, our freedom to join new economic groupings is already limited, as these answers have shown. If we were to accept a common tariff we could not independently seek to establish an Atlantic free trade or preferential area. But if all members of the Community so agreed, such a development would not be precluded.

OTHER QUESTIONS

QUESTION 22

What has changed in the situation since Ministers decided on the basis of full review in 1956 and again in 1959 against joining the Common Market?

ANSWER

There have been five main changes in the situation:

(i)   Earlier on it seemed very doubtful if the European Economic Community would ever see the light of day owing to the inability of a weak France to withstand increased competition from her future partners, especially from Germany.

(ii)   We thought that, even if the Common Market did come off, we should be able to make our own terms for associating with it. The Free Trade Area negotiations proved us wrong.

(iii)   France - and Western Europe generally - is no longer weak. The Common Market is becoming a powerful and dynamic force, economically and politically.

(iv)   In 1956 we thought that joining the Common Market would weaken our special relationship with the United States. The position has now changed and the United States are attaching increasing importance to the views of the Community. It is by no means clear, therefore, that the best way of retaining our influence with the United States would be by staying outside the Community, rather than by becoming a leading member of the group with a powerful influence on their policies.

(v)   In so far as our previous attitude was influenced by our desire to do nothing which might prejudice the Commonwealth relationship, this consideration is now matched by the fear that the growing power and influence of the Six will seriously affect our position in the world - if we remain outside - and this itself will be damaging to our relationship with the Commonwealth.

QUESTION 23
     What are the chances that the Six, once they are consolidated, would be prepared ultimately to enter a free trade area with the Seven?

ANSWER
     We find it impossible to think of circumstances in which the Six would ever agree to joining a free trade area of the pattern we attempted to negotiate in 1956-58. The arguments on political grounds and on grounds of economic interest for the EEC Governments declining to enter such a free trade area are too strong. These arguments, and the ability of the EEC countries to sustain a policy of refusal, will become stronger as time goes on. On the other hand, there are also forces working in the direction of an association with other European countries. The French may become more worried about their ability to dominate the Germans. At the same time, increasing French confidence in their economic position and the consolidation of the Community may make them more disposed to accept the possible risks involved in an arrangement with the Seven. It is therefore possible that, if the Seven remain firm and united, the Six may in a few years be prepared to enter into some association with them. But it would be very risky to gamble on this.

Record of Cabinet Discussion [43].

     The Cabinet had before them a note by the Secretary of the Cabinet (C. (60) 107) covering a report by officials on the future of the European Economic Community (EEC) and the broad political and economic considerations which should determine whether or not the United Kingdom should seek to join the Community.

     The Chancellor of the Exchequer recalled that the Prime Minister had previously said that the Government would eventually have to choose between (i) initiating a dramatic change of direction in our domestic, commercial and international policies and (ii) maintaining our traditional policy of remaining aloof from Europe politically, while doing all we could to mitigate the economic dangers of a divided Europe. The report now before the Cabinet clarified the issues which would arise in making that choice. A decision to join the Community would be essentially a political act with economic consequences, rather than an economic act with political consequences. The arguments for joining the Community were strong. If we remained outside it, our political influence in Europe and in the rest of the world was likely to decline. By joining it we should not only avoid tariff discrimination by its members against our exports, but should also be able to participate in a large and rapidly expanding market. However, the arguments against United Kingdom membership were also very strong. We should be surrendering independent control of our commercial policies to a European *bloc*, when our trading interests were world-wide. We should have to abandon our special economic relationship with the Commonwealth, including free entry for Commonwealth goods and the preferential system, and should instead be obliged to discriminate actively against the Commonwealth. We should have to devise for agriculture and horticulture new policies under which the burden of support for the farmers would be largely transferred from the Exchequer to the consumer, thus increasing the cost of living. Finally, we should sacrifice our loyalties and obligations to the members of the European Free Trade Association (EFTA), some members of which would find it impossible to join the EEC as full members.

There were four possible courses for the United Kingdom. The first would be to seek full membership of the Community on the terms of the Treaty of Rome. This was wholly unacceptable, if only because it involved discriminating against the fundamental trading interests of the Commonwealth and in favour of Europe. Secondly, we could seek to negotiate membership of the Community on special terms. Though we should have to accept in general the common tariff of the Community, we could seek to preserve some free entry for Commonwealth foodstuffs. But, if we were to pursue this course, we should have to accept the fact that our preferential position in the Commonwealth (which affected 20 per cent of our total exports and was considered by industry to be still of substantial value) would be progressively eroded. Thirdly, we might seek some form of association with the Community falling short of full membership. This course might be easier for the other members of EFTA but it would not enable us to exert as much influence in the Community as if we were members of it. Finally, we could stay outside the EEC and consolidate the EFTA. In the end we might have to accept this last course, but we had never visualised it as more than a second best to a wider European system.

The Chancellor said that his personal conclusion was that we should be ready to join the Community if we could do so without substantially impairing our relations with the Commonwealth. We might seek to persuade the other Commonwealth countries to relinquish some of their special advantages in the United Kingdom market in order to enable us either to accept membership of the Community on special terms or to enter into some form of association with it. But we should not press that persuasion to the point where it threatened the Commonwealth relationship. In spite of the pressures for an early decision it would be wrong to be rushed into hasty action. We should try to carry our partners in the EFTA with us. We should also consult the principal members of the Commonwealth: the forthcoming meeting of Commonwealth Finance Ministers would provide a suitable opportunity for testing their reactions. We should also try to find out what attitude the French were likely to take towards any proposal for membership on special terms or association. Finally, if it were ultimately decided to move in this direction, careful action would need to be taken to prepare public opinion in this country for such a move.

The President of the Board of Trade said that the Community was based fundamentally on the principle of common policies, determined in common and carried out by a common institution. We should find it difficult to renounce our national control of policy, especially in respect of agricultural and commercial policies and our special relationship with the Commonwealth. On the other hand, the development of the Community was a serious economic threat to the United Kingdom, as regards both our trade to Europe and our competitive position in the world. As our economic influence declined in comparison with that of the Community, we should find that the United States and other countries would increasingly attach more weight to the views and interests of the Community.

In any negotiation with the Community we should have to seek an agreement which preserved the fundamental trading interests of the Commonwealth. It would, however, be disastrous to enter into negotiations until there was a political will in the countries of the Community to reach an accommodation with us. France and the United States held the key at the moment. Although the French were not now so much concerned at the prospect of industrial competition from the United Kingdom, they feared that our membership of the Community would threaten their leadership. The present United States Administration favoured the development of the Community, regardless of the difficulties which this would cause for the United Kingdom.

The Government should not allow themselves to be pushed into hasty decisions by the campaign in some parts of the Press. There was need of an authoritative statement in which the Government would make it clear that this was not a suitable moment for negotiations with the Community and, while expressing readiness to work towards a single trading system in Europe, would emphasise the fundamental objections to United Kingdom membership of the Community.

The Commonwealth Secretary said that from the point of view of our future political influence in the Atlantic Community there were strong arguments for joining the EEC. We might hope eventually to achieve leadership of it and we could use our influence in it to keep West Germany independent of the Soviet *bloc*. On the other hand our wider interests and influence throughout the world depended to a considerable extent on our links with the Commonwealth; and if, by joining the EEC, we did fatal damage to these we should lose our power to exert our influence on a world scale. An association short of membership would not secure for us enough influence in the Community to make the price worth paying. We should therefore consider full membership, but seek special terms to meet our fundamental interests and those of the Commonwealth. We should associate the other Commonwealth countries with our negotiations at all stages. As a first step, we should take advantage of the presence of Commonwealth Finance Ministers in this country in September to see how far they would be prepared to give up their special position in the United Kingdom in the interests of a wider European settlement.

Discussion showed that the Cabinet fully agreed that the United Kingdom could not accept membership of the Community on the terms of the Treaty of Rome. There was also general agreement that, while it was not possible at this stage to distinguish completely between membership on special terms and some looser form of association, the latter course would be likely to entail most of the disadvantages of joining the Community while denying us the main political and economic advantages of membership.

On the question whether the United Kingdom should seek membership of the Community on special terms, rather than remain outside it, it was argued that there was no ground for alarm that membership would commit us to close political integration. As a member, the United Kingdom would be able to influence the political development of the Community and strengthen the forces in it which already preferred a loose confederal arrangement. Although the time was not yet ripe for negotiations with the Community, we should prepare the ground for later negotiations by discussion with the other Commonwealth countries and by strengthening the EFTA.

On the other hand, it was argued that the considerations which were decisive against full membership of the Community on the terms of the Treaty of Rome weighed almost as heavily against seeking membership on special terms. Even if a solution to the problem of free entry for food could be found, any such settlement would be bound to inflict damage on the Commonwealth and upset United Kingdom agricultural policies. Moreover, it was far from clear that a satisfactory settlement could be reached. There would be the greatest difficulty in reconciling the interests of the Commonwealth, United Kingdom farmers, the EEC and other foreign countries including the United States. *The Minister of Agriculture* pointed out that the negotiations concerning wheat alone would present formidable difficulties, and would entail a system of import levies, the reorganisation of our trade agreements with the United States and Commonwealth producers, the establishment of a United Kingdom cereals marketing board and the control of production by United Kingdom farmers. There was little possibility of producing a settlement which would at the same time be fair to the other Commonwealth countries and acceptable to farmers in the United Kingdom.

In further discussion it was suggested that the advantages of joining the Community and the dangers of staying outside had been exaggerated. Many other parts of the world besides Europe were expanding rapidly; and as a country with world-wide trading connexions we were in a good position to exploit these wider opportunities. To become a member of the EEC could be positively harmful to our position in the world, since some of the political and economic policies of the EEC countries did not inspire respect. France and Belgium had colonial difficulties, Germany was following an ungenerous credit policy, and the EEC countries generally were seeking to expand their production of primary commodities at the expense of the less-developed countries. In trying to negotiate a settlement with the Community we might run grave risks of impairing the unity of the Commonwealth and undermining the confidence of its other members in the United Kingdom, with serious financial and economic consequences to ourselves.

On the other hand, over a period of years our relationship with the Commonwealth would in any case change, as would other factors in this problem, including the agricultural difficulties. It would therefore be necessary to adapt our policies to new situations. It would be desirable in any case to bring about a greater awareness of the problem and of the choice which would eventually have to be made, by consultation with the Commonwealth, by discussions with the agricultural and horticultural industries, and by informing public opinion generally.

The Foreign Secretary agreed that the future development of the Community might not necessarily entail any close political integration. It could not be ascertained for some time whether the Community would accept the United Kingdom as a partner on terms which would enable us to satisfy our existing obligations, particularly towards the Commonwealth and EFTA. It would certainly be unwise to try to secure satisfactory terms in protracted bilateral negotiations with France. Our aims should therefore be to strengthen EFTA, to work for the reduction of tariff discrimination through the General Agreement on Tariffs and Trade, to seek the full co-operation of the Commonwealth countries in finding the best solution of the whole problem, and to improve political relations with European countries, especially France, so as to create a favourable climate of opinion for an eventual accommodation between EEC and EFTA.

The Prime Minister said that it was important that the Cabinet as a whole should be kept closely in touch with the development of policy on this question. The forthcoming debate in the House of Commons, probably on 25th July, would provide a useful opportunity for a further authoritative statement of the Government's attitude. This statement should explain that there were insuperable difficulties in the way of our accepting membership of the Community under the existing provisions of the Treaty of Rome, especially in relation to our responsibilities to the Commonwealth; but that we fully accepted the establishment of the Community and, with our partners in EFTA, would continue to seek for a mutually satisfactory arrangement between the EEC and the EFTA. The President of the Board of Trade should prepare a draft statement on these lines, in consultation with the other Ministers mainly concerned, and should circulate it for consideration by the Cabinet.
The Cabinet -

Invited the President of the Board of Trade, in consultation with the other Ministers concerned, to draft a statement of the Government's attitude to the problem of political and economic relations with Europe, and to circulate it for consideration by the Cabinet.

APPENDIX D

Report on Washington Talks

Record of Cabinet Discussion[86]

First Meeting

The Prime Minister said that these discussions had strengthened his view that far-reaching decisions would have to be taken soon about the United Kingdom's relations with Europe. In recent years the Communist *bloc* had been gaining ground at the expense of the West and, if this was to be checked, the leading countries of the Western world would need to draw more closely together. There was, however, a risk that current developments in Europe would tend in the opposite direction; for, if the countries of the Common Market formed a close political association under French leadership, this would create a further political division in Europe and would also have a disruptive influence within the Atlantic community. This might be averted if the United Kingdom, together with some of the Seven, could join the political association of the Six and help to build in Europe a stable political structure which would prevent France now, and Germany later, from attaining too dominant a position. Difficult economic adjustments would be involved, both for the United Kingdom and for other Commonwealth countries; but it was arguable that both we and the other Commonwealth countries would in the long run gain greater economic advantage from access to a wider market in Europe. The Cabinet must now weigh all the relevant considerations and determine its future course. If they decided that it was right, on balance, to draw closer to Europe, they would have to consider what economic price might have to be paid and what were the tactics by which this objective could be attained. Nothing would now be gained by delaying a decision. And, if the decision went in favour of closer union with Europe, the practical steps to that end would have to be taken before the end of the present Parliament.

The Prime Minister invited his colleagues to express their general views on this issue.

The President of the Board of Trade said that in 1954 we had under-estimated the strength of the forces working for unity between the countries of the Six. The Common Market was now firmly established and, as it developed, our economic interests would be gravely prejudiced if we remained outside it. We should be excluded from one of the largest and most dynamic markets in the world; and, as time went on, the trade and investment of the United States would be drawn increasingly towards Europe. It was therefore in the economic interest of the United Kingdom to be associated with the Six. Our attempt to form a European Free Trade Area had failed largely because the French opposed it. The French would also be reluctant to accept our participation in the Six - partly, no doubt, because they wished to retain its political leadership. We should have therefore to fashion a line of approach which the French would find it difficult to resist. For us the main difficulty in joining the Six would be, not the common tariff, but the concept of a single commercial policy. From this we should need to obtain some derogation, if our special relations with other Commonwealth countries were to be preserved. As regards foodstuffs, the main burden was more likely to fall on consumers, than on farmers, in this country - though British horticulture was bound to suffer. It should however be remembered that the agricultural policy of the Six had not yet been finally determined; and, if we joined, we should be able to influence its formulation. British industry was increasingly aware of the advantages which it would gain from our association with the Six. The other members of the Seven were more apprehensive about the future. Economic association with the Six would present them with no great difficulties, but for some of them political association would be impossible. A system might perhaps be devised which involved equal economic obligations but differing political obligations.

The Commonwealth Secretary said that, if the United Kingdom joined the Six, awkward adjustments would have to be made in our economic relations with other Commonwealth countries. Canada, as an exporter of manufactured goods, would be seriously affected, and there would be special difficulties for New Zealand. On the other hand, it should be possible to devise arrangements for tropical foodstuffs which would safeguard Commonwealth interests. Moreover, to the extent that our economy was strengthened by our participation in the Six, this would serve the long-term interests of other Commonwealth countries. He himself believed that, if we stood aloof from the Common Market, we should get the worst of both worlds; and that the right course on balance was to go fully into partnership with the Six. If we could take this decision in principle, we should be better able to discover by negotiation how far our difficulties could be mitigated and what price we should need to pay. We ought then to be able to persuade the other Commonwealth countries to acquiesce in that course; but it would be a mistake to get into further consultation with them before a decision of principle had been taken.

The Minister of Agriculture said that, in measuring the effects on British agriculture, it was right to consider, not merely the short-term disadvantages of joining the Common Market, but also the long-term results of standing apart from it. In the countries of the Western world surpluses of agricultural production were increasing, and all our traditional suppliers were expanding their production. The countries of the Six were now net importers of agricultural products. It was true that they were not planning to produce surpluses; they were planning merely to be self-sufficient. But there was no doubt that improvements in the structure and efficiency of their agriculture would lead inevitably to increased production, and they would ultimately be able to supply all their needs and possibly to produce a surplus. Then, with our open market, we should be exposed to the surplus production of many countries in the Western world. Meanwhile, the production of British agriculture would expand; and, as world prices of foodstuffs fell with the greater quantities available, the Exchequer cost of maintaining the existing system of support for agriculture in this country might in a decade rise to something like double its present figure. All this suggested that we should be thinking in terms of moving over to the continental system of supporting agriculture. If this were the right policy for us, it would make it easier for us to join the Six. But, if we were to do so, we should move in good time, before the agricultural policy of the Six had been finally settled, so that we could play our full part in influencing it in directions convenient to ourselves. He had arranged for a study to be made of the effect which the adoption of the continental system of agricultural support would have on food prices in this country and on the balance of payments. The effect of such a move on opinion in farming circles should not be under-estimated. At the time of the last General Election, the Government had undertaken that the present system of support for agriculture would not be changed in this Parliament. The immediate effects of such a change would also be serious - especially in relation to pigs, eggs and horticultural products. Moreover, most farmers were content with the present system and would be apprehensive of change. They would have to be convinced - and this would not be easy - that they would suffer even more serious damage in the long run if we stood aside from the Six. Even so it must be recognised that, if we joined the Six, the net income of British agriculture would be lower than at present and our trade with other Commonwealth countries would also be reduced. For the countries of the Six would certainly insist that there should be some increase in our imports of foodstuffs from Europe. Our task would be to ensure that the policies adopted by the Common Market were so designed as to do more economic damage to third countries than to British agriculture and Commonwealth trade. The French and other members of the Six realised that we should have to safeguard some of our Commonwealth interests. They would expect us to insist on special arrangements in respect of butter from New Zealand and wheat from Canada and Australia; and, if they wanted us to join them, there should be no difficulty in working out satisfactory arrangements for temperate foodstuffs for the next seven years or so.

In further discussion the following points were made:
(a)   Political association with the Six might ultimately involve a significant surrender of national sovereignty. Adherence to the Treaty of Rome would limit the supremacy of Parliament, which would be required to accept decisions taken by the Council of the Community.
      It would restrict the right of the Executive to make treaties. It would also involve a final right of appeal from our courts to the Supreme Court of the Community. A major effort of presentation would be needed to persuade the British public to accept these encroachments on national sovereignty.
(b)   The immediate effects on our relations with other parts of the Commonwealth would be serious. Apart from the reactions in other commonwealth countries whose economic interests would be damaged, public sentiment about the Commonwealth in this country must also be considered. There was at present a growing recognition of the part

which the Commonwealth could play, as a multi-racial association, in the world of to-day. Opposition to this European venture would develop if it were thought that it would undermine the cohesion of the Commonwealth and impair its value as a factor for preserving world peace.

(c)   It would not be easy to secure adequate safeguards for Commonwealth production of tropical foodstuffs. On this particular point we could not look for assistance from the United States Administration, who were interested to safeguard the position of our competitors in Latin America.

(d)   Canada would suffer special economic damage if we joined the Six. There might be advantage in repeating our earlier offer to negotiate a Free Trade Area with Canada at once.

(e)   The disadvantages from the point of view of the Commonwealth might be mitigated if our joining the Six could be presented as a necessary measure to draw the countries of the Western world more closely together in order that they might be better able to compete with the rate of economic growth in the Sino-Soviet bloc. From this point of view it would be valuable if our association with the Six could be presented as a first step towards a wider assimilation of trading areas on both sides of the Atlantic.

(f)   Need it necessarily be assumed that, if we joined the Common Market, the trade in foodstuffs between the United Kingdom and the countries of the Six would result in a net increase of imports into this country? British agriculture was, on the whole, more efficient than that of the Common Market countries, and we ought to be able to export foodstuffs into those countries.

(g)   Even so, the political difficulties of justifying this policy in agricultural constituencies would be very great. From that point of view its presentation would need careful consideration.

(h)   The special difficulties in respect of agriculture should not be allowed to obscure the undoubted advantages which British industry would derive from the wider market opened to it by our association with the Six. Modern industry needed to operate in a large economic unit. This was strikingly illustrated by the output per worker in the United States and the Soviet Union, which was far greater than that in the United Kingdom. British industry could not afford to miss this opportunity of access to the wider market of the Six. If we stood aside from this we should fall behind industrially; the Common Market and the United States would forge ahead and we should be increasingly excluded from our markets overseas. From this point of view it was gratifying that the new Administration in the United States were in favour of our joining the Six.

Second Meeting

The Prime Minister said that the time had not yet come to take a final decision on the question whether the United Kingdom should accede to the Treaty of Rome. Many important aspects of this problem would have to be further considered in detail, and full consultations would have to be held with our partners in the Commonwealth and in the European Free Trade Association (EFTA). The question to which the Cabinet should address themselves at this stage was whether it was to our advantage to work towards a solution by which the United Kingdom (preferably with some of her partners in EFTA) would join with the countries of the Common Market in forming a wider political and economic association in Europe. The question for discussion now was whether, on a balance of advantage, it was in our interests to try to bring this about.

The following is a summary of the main points made in the Cabinet's discussion:

(a)   The countries of the Common Market, if left to develop alone under French leadership, would grow into a separate political force in Europe. Initially this would tend to have a disruptive effect within the Western Alliance. Eventually it might mean that the Six would come to exercise greater influence than the United Kingdom, both with the United States and possibly with some of the independent countries of the Commonwealth. This development was therefore a threat to the political position of the United Kingdom as a world Power. It would be consistent with our traditional policy to seek to   prevent the concentration of undue strength in a single political unit on the continent of Europe. Politically, our interests would be better served by working for a wider European association in which we could play a prominent part.

(b)   The Common Market also represented a serious economic threat to the United Kingdom. The countries of the Six, with a population of 160 millions, would together constitute a market comparable in size to the United States; and, under modern conditions of industrial production, this must lead to a great increase in the efficiency and productivity of industries within the area. The larger industrial units which were already being formed in the countries of the Six would be in a stronger position - by reason, not only of their size, but of the degree of standardisation which could be developed within the area - to compete successfully with British industry in the export markets of the world; and this would be even more damaging to our interests than our exclusion from the European market itself. Moreover, as the economic strength of the Common Market grew, other European countries would be attracted to it and, against its attractions, we should find it difficult to hold EFTA together. If, therefore, we stood aloof from the Six, we should find ourselves in a position of growing economic weakness.

(c)   Hitherto we had been thinking in terms of an economic settlement between the Six and the Seven. It was now apparent that this alone would be neither practicable nor sufficient. A   solution was needed which would prevent political, as well as economic, division in Europe. Moreover, the United States Government would not lend their support to a purely economic settlement: their main concern was to prevent the Six from developing as a separate political force in Europe. In these circumstances a political initiative was required.   Our economic objectives could not be attained unless we could find a means by which we, together with some of our EFTA partners, could join the political institutions of the Treaty of Rome.

(d)   Public opinion in this country had in the past been preoccupied with the difficulties and dangers of a closer association with Europe. Recently its advantages had been more clearly seen. Many of the leaders of British industry were in favour of our joining the Six: indeed, there was now some risk that the difficulties would be under-estimated. In political circles also informed opinion was moving in the same direction. On the other hand it must be remembered that a great weight of sentiment could easily be aroused against any policy which could be represented as a threat to the Commonwealth and to British agriculture. In the Conservative Party, in particular, this could evoke strong emotional reactions comparable to those which had recently arisen over Colonial policy.

(e)   In respect of our relations with other Commonwealth countries a number of difficult questions would need to be considered. Thus, if we acceded to the Treaty of Rome, could we secure acceptable derogations in respect of Commonwealth preference and free entry? Would it be possible to assess, before entering into detailed negotiations, the nature of the derogations which we were likely to secure on these and other matters? Should we have to forego our right to make agreements with other Commonwealth countries? Would they have to forego their right of free access to the London money market? If we joined the Six, would European interests come eventually to weigh more with us than Commonwealth interests in formulating our general political and economic policies? Finally, we were under obligation to consult fully with other Commonwealth Governments on this question, and the timing and the method of such consultation would need careful thought.

(f)   *The Home Secretary* recalled that, at their meeting on 13th July 1960, the Cabinet had agreed that there were insuperable difficulties in the way of our accepting membership of the Six under the existing provisions of the Treaty of Rome. The Cabinet had then particularly in mind the difficulties in respect of the Commonwealth. But there were other difficulties too. In the Cabinet's last discussion on 20th April reference had been made to the surrender of national sovereignty which would be involved; and this point would certainly require careful thought in the light of reports by officials which were coming forward for consideration by Ministers. The Cabinet must also weigh the likely reactions of British farmers. The National Farmers' Unions had now published a pamphlet which came out strongly against association with the Six; and the Government had themselves undertaken that they would not alter the existing system of support for agriculture during the present Parliament. In the discussion on 20th April the Minister of Agriculture had indicated the general lines on which the existing system might be adapted; and it was possible that a new policy on those lines might, at the cost of some increase in the cost of living, protect the interest of arable farmers. So far, however, nothing had been suggested which would provide similar safeguards for horticulture or for the producers of pigs or eggs. Much further thought would need to be given to the agricultural aspects of this problem. The Government would be in very grave political difficulties if they could be represented as having broken their pledges to the farmers.

(g)   *The Minister of Agriculture* said that the pamphlet published by the National Farmers' Unions was concerned with the results which would follow if the United Kingdom joined the Six without any derogations in respect of agriculture. The Government were not contemplating such a course; and he fully agreed that they must avoid putting forward any new policy proposals which would expose them to the charge of having broken their pledges to the farmers. In general, the alternative policy which he had outlined would have the effect of transferring from the Exchequer to the consumer some of the financial burden of supporting British agriculture. This would not in itself be a betrayal of the farmers. It was true, however, that difficult problems would arise on particular commodities and these were now under examination. A wider common market in Europe must inevitably mean some changes in the pattern of agriculture, both here and in other countries; but it need not necessarily mean any reduction in the net income of British farmers.

(h)   *The Minister of Education* asked whether the countries of the Six would be content with changes in our agricultural policy which, while varying the pattern of our production, left the net income of British farmers unchanged. Would they not expect that in return for taking more manufactured goods from the United Kingdom, they would have opportunities for increased exports of foodstuffs to this country?

The Minister of Agriculture said that our existing system of agricultural support, because it reduced the price of food to the consumer, resulted in a lower level of wages. It was primarily for that reason that the countries of the Six would expect us to adopt a different system. It did not follow, however, that the net income of British farmers need be substantially reduced.

(i)   *The Minister of Labour* said that he agreed with the view, expressed by the Minister of Agriculture in the discussion on 20th April, that in the long run British agriculture was likely to suffer more severely if we stood outside the Common Market than if we joined it. He also agreed that the balance of logical argument lay on the side of joining the Six, with suitable safeguards for agriculture. But the political difficulties of this course should not be under-estimated. British farmers were content with the present system of support, which insulated them from the effect of world prices; and they would be reluctant to consider an alternative system which lacked that obvious attraction. Moreover, though it should be possible to devise safeguards for most commodities, there would be some for which it would not be possible to provide protection. Horticulture, in particular, was bound to suffer serious damage. The political pressures from areas specialising in these commodities would be very severe.

(j)   *The Lord Privy Seal* said that the French Government had indicated that they were willing to discuss with us how we could join the Common Market, or enter into a special association with it, so long as we were ready to make some concessions on Commonwealth trade and on British Agriculture. They had made it plain that, while it was

open to us to consider either course, they would greatly prefer
membership to association. Hitherto, we had not been able to tell the
French how far we were prepared to go, either on Commonwealth trade
or agriculture. If we could disclose to the French the sort of conditions
which the Cabinet were now considering it was possible that further
progress could be made in negotiation.   Even so, it was doubtful
whether it would be expedient for us to declare at the outset that we
were prepared to accede to the Treaty of Rome before we had
negotiated the necessary derogations. Such a declaration would involve
us in political difficulties in this country: it would also leave us less
room for manoeuvre in negotiation. It would be preferable to make
further progress with the detailed negotiation of the necessary
derogations before taking any final decision. The obligations which we
had undertaken to consult with our partners in the Commonwealth and
in the EFTA were a further reason for preferring that course. It was
evident that we could not accede to the Treaty of Rome without some
economic damage, at least in the short term, both to this country and to
other countries of the Commonwealth; and, before a final decision was
taken, the Cabinet should have before them a statement showing the
balance of advantage and disadvantage in the course ultimately
proposed.

  The Prime Minister, summing up the discussion, said that this
question must be viewed in the wider context of the East-West struggle.
In this the Communist bloc were gaining ground and the Western
countries were in some disarray. It was an article of Communist faith
that capitalism would in the end destroy itself; and, given competing
currencies and conflicting trade interests, there was a real risk of a
growing economic weakness in the Western world unless its countries
could find means of drawing more closely together. For some time after
the war, in her years of political and economic weakness, Europe had
been dependent on American aid and content to accept Anglo-Saxon
leadership. Europe had now regained her strength, and a new situation
had arisen. Different means must now be found for binding Europe
within the wider Atlantic Community. The United Kingdom, as the
bridge between Europe and North America, had the opportunity to take
an initiative in this. We could of course decline that responsibility. It
would be easy for us to put forward, as excuses, the need for preserving
our special relations with other Commonwealth countries and protecting
the interests of British agriculture. But, if we decided to stand aloof
from inner Europe at this time, might we not find that the eventual
damage to our interests would be even greater in terms of the secular
struggle between East and West? We should not forget that in this
struggle half of our Commonwealth partners and half of our partners in
EFTA were neutral. Moreover, as the economic strength of the Six
increased, other members of EFTA would certainly be under strong
temptation to join it; and, to the extent that this happened, the economic
position of the United Kingdom would be progressively undermined.
The older members of the Commonwealth, though they would stand
with us now, might then be obliged to turn increasingly towards the
United States; and new world groupings would arise, as a result of

which the United Kingdom would lose much of her influence in world affairs. These considerations suggested that, on a balance of advantage, it was in our interest to join the political and economic association of the Six if we could gain admission on terms which would be tolerable to us. A political initiative would be necessary, and France was certainly the key to the situation. Hitherto, General de Gaulle had not wished us to join the Six - presumably because he wanted France to retain the leadership of inner Europe. But his attitude might be changed if he could be brought to see that the West as a whole could not prevail against the Communists unless its leading countries worked together towards a wider unity in the free world as a whole.

The Prime Minister said that at the present time France was, in more respects than one, a main obstacle in the way of creating a closer unity in the West. This had been a main theme in his recent discussions in Washington. He believed that he had persuaded President Kennedy that, if the free world was to present a united front to the Communists, General de Gaulle must be brought to see that France must co-operate more fully and effectively with her Western partners. First, she must take her full share of responsibility within the North Atlantic Alliance and accept its principle of interdependence. Secondly, if she was determined to continue with her nuclear programme, she must aim, not so much to create an independent national force, as to make a contribution to the strength of the Western deterrent as a whole, which should increasingly be regarded as held in trust on behalf of the free world as a whole. Thirdly, she must make it possible for the United Kingdom and some of the other members of EFTA to join with the Six in creating a wider political and economic association in Europe. If, in all these matters, she were willing to work for Western unity, she could take her rightful place with the United States and the United Kingdom as one of the pillars of the Western Alliance and thus earn the right to participate in the system of tripartite consultation which General de Gaulle demanded.

The Prime Minister said that he hoped that President Kennedy would speak to General de Gaulle along these general lines in the course of his forthcoming visit to Paris. If so, we should be able to judge, in the light of the General's response, whether there was a basis for seeking wider political and economic association in Europe. If General de Gaulle was willing to consider this problem in the wider framework of the world situation, it should be possible to find a solution of the special economic difficulties which the United Kingdom Government would find in acceding to the Treaty of Rome as it now stood.

The conclusion reached by the Cabinet, in the light of this discussion and the earlier discussion on 20th April, was that the right policy for the Government to follow at this stage was to work for a solution by which the United Kingdom (preferably with some of her partners in EFTA) would join with the countries of the Six in forming a wider political and economic association in Europe. It would be necessary, in negotiations with those countries, to secure special arrangements to preserve the main trading interests of the Commonwealth; a satisfactory relation with other members of EFTA;

and special provisions for British agriculture to enable it to be brought into harmony with the general agricultural policy of the Six on a basis adequate to support the interests dependent on it. If, however, these points could be covered satisfactorily, either in a protocol to the Treaty or otherwise, there seemed to be no reason of principle why the United Kingdom should not accede to the Treaty of Rome, including its political institutions.

The Cabinet -

(1)   Took note that, in the course of his visit to Paris, President Kennedy might be able to ascertain whether the French Government were willing to co-operate more fully with their Western Allies on the general lines indicated by the Prime Minister in summing up the Cabinet's discussion.

(2)   Agreed that, if President Kennedy's approach elicited a favourable response from General de Gaulle, the United Kingdom should be ready to enter into further negotiations with a view to finding means by which the United Kingdom, together with some of her partners in EFTA, could join with the countries of the Common Market in forming a wider political and economic association in Europe.

APPENDIX E

Report of Conversations at Birch Grove [113]

The Prime Minister began by saying that at Rambouillet:-
President de Gaulle had asked if England was prepared to enter the European Community or not. Since then, Great Britain had taken her decision to apply for membership. The economics could really be arranged if there was a will; political questions were perhaps more important. After the war, British Conservative leaders had taken a lead in the European movement; they had been somewhat frightened off by the activities of the federalists, and had not wanted an integrated Europe. Now it seemed more possible to enter Europe on a confederal basis. The Commonwealth did not really present a political obstacle to this. The Commonwealth was not a political organisation. The new countries of the Commonwealth were very similar to the French African territories, and the old Commonwealth countries were bound by ties of blood and loyalty, but conducted a quite independent political life. Consequently, it was fairly easy for the United Kingdom to accept the French view of Europe. We had not seen the text of the Fouchet Plan, but had a very good idea of its broad terms and it seemed to pursue the same theme as the United Kingdom wanted. Consequently, this seemed a good moment to make a European union now, when President de Gaulle and Dr. Adenauer were still in power. It was certainly important to hold Germany to the West and to accomplish this quickly. Integration was not practical politics at the moment; it was absurd to imagine holding elections in five or more languages. But it was not true to say that the United Kingdom was not interested in the politics of the European Community. We had seen Germany attack us twice in 50 years, and were quite clear that France and the United Kingdom had a basic community of interest in dealing with this problem. The United Kingdom saw dangers in Germany being either chauvinist or neutral. We wanted to enter the Community for political reasons. The economic difficulties could be solved and in any case led on to the possibility of a wider European influence through the Commonwealth. Europe could not forever rely upon the Americans, who would find increasing difficulties in the Americas. It was therefore important that Europe's economic power in the world should be as widely extended as possible.
President de Gaulle said that he entirely agreed that the aim should be to bring the four main countries of Europe, that was the United Kingdom, France, Germany and Italy, together. This was Europe's last chance, or at least her last chance but one, because the final chance was Russia joining with Europe. This might be possible, because as Russia changed so the conflict with the rest of Europe would become less dramatic. He was against an integrated Europe; this was neither practical, sensible nor desirable, and the result would be a materialist, soulless mass, with no idealism left. He therefore believed that the national identity of the European nations should be preserved. The Community had started on an economic basis, because common ground was easier to find in this field. Nevertheless, the Rome Treaty

had a political reason. It was very important to create economic interests between Germany, France, Italy and the others, because one could not tell what the attitude of the Germans would be in years to come. If there were strong economic links between Germany and the rest of Europe, it would be more difficult for Germany to break loose. Nevertheless, this structure was still new and fragile; its effects should not be exaggerated, since there were still basically different economies in each of the countries of the Six. So it was that he had difficulty in seeing how the United Kingdom would fit into this beginning of Europe. The Prime Minister had said that there was not a great deal of difficulty in this, because the economics would follow the political, but in the case of the Six, the economics were the only political element which existed. In any case, there would be problems hard to overcome. *The Prime Minister* interjected that the French had made arrangements for their Community. *President de Gaulle* agreed, but said that this had been less difficult because the client States of France in Africa had had nothing to sell. Countries which had something to sell, like Canada or Australia, were in a different category. Perhaps the United Kingdom could manage to find a way to enter the Community, but it would not be easy. But even if the Brussels negotiations did not work out the first time, there might be a later opportunity because the United Kingdom changed and the Commonwealth was changing. There was a danger that if Europe did not have a real economic policy, all the members, including the Germans, would look elsewhere for a solution. It was true that countries like Nigeria, Ghana and Kenya could be compared to Senegal and the other African countries of the Community, but the existence of countries like Canada changed the situation. How could the United Kingdom join the Common Market if these countries were excluded, and how, if they were included, could the United States be kept out? If the United States were included, however, she would be too strong and Europe would not be re-formed. *The Prime Minister* said that in Europe the agricultural difficulty would be a surplus of production. It would soon be necessary to work out a system for giving under-developed countries food instead of money.
On the next day:-

The Prime Minister said that he had reflected deeply on their conversation of the previous day and would like to speak quite frankly to General de Gaulle.

European civilisation was what we must at all costs preserve. It had survived for 3,000 years, but it was menaced from all quarters, by Africans, Asians and Communists and, in a quite different way, even by our Atlantic friends such as the North Americans and New Zealanders and Australians. More than ever there was a need of real political unity in Europe. He had worked for this ever since the war and had taken some political risks in trying to turn the ideas and opinions in Great Britain towards European unity. At first, he and his friends in the European movement had met with great difficulties because they had had to battle against the ideas of the Federalist movements which were unrealistic and had no appeal in this country. When President de Gaulle came to power, the Prime Minister realised that his ideas were very close to our own and that progress was possible towards a united Europe based not on integrationist ideas but on confederal ideas. The traditionalists in the United Kingdom were still reserved and were fearful of weakening Commonwealth unity. But the young people, and those who had fought in the war, were determined that Europe should not once again tear itself to bits and wanted to draw closer to Europe.

A great step had now been taken; The United Kingdom had applied to join the EEC. The Prime Minister accepted that European unity must be built on an economic base, because that was the only one which existed. But though he accepted this, he felt that it was nevertheless a fragile base; this was partly because it appeared too small to catch the imagination of peoples who had played a world role not only in Europe but overseas generally. Secondly, he felt that the European countries must think in broader terms than trade in Europe alone, they must look outwards towards their old empires and aim to become the most powerful trading body in the world. It was for this reason that the British relationship with the Commonwealth was of such importance. If the United Kingdom came into Europe it would broaden the base and provide added strength to the Community.

It was argued that the balance of the EEC would be upset if the United Kingdom joined and her requests for special treatment in the Commonwealth were granted. This problem tended to be exaggerated. In fact, the United Kingdom had only asked for special treatment in respect of 20 per cent. of her total imports, which amounted in all to £4,500 million. Half of this 20 per cent., or 10 per cent of the total, was wine or food stuffs which would have to be covered by the agricultural arrangements which were being discussed separately. This meant that the United Kingdom was asking for exceptional arrangements over a range of only 10 per cent. of her total imports. He could not believe that if satisfactory arrangements were made to cover this relatively small category the internal equilibrium of the EEC would be destroyed. Australia, New Zealand and Canada would be prepared to make reasonable arrangements which would meet most of their demands. They would not press for satisfaction on all points. The politicians in these countries had made a lot of propaganda but in fact they were playing politics; but the Press and the intellectuals there thought that in the long term the Commonwealth countries would be better off if the United Kingdom joined the EEC. A wider market would lead to increased prosperity and the losses temporarily incurred in the United Kingdom market would be made up elsewhere in Europe. If they could be offered good terms, he was confident that they would accept.

Agriculture was another problem, but surplus food production was something which had to be dealt with anyway. If there was too much food in one part of the world, it was far better to give it to people who were short of it, instead of providing them with armaments and means of making war.

The problem was admittedly exceedingly difficult, though it was of vital importance that progress should be made, and seen to be made, towards a solution. *President de Gaulle* claimed that there was no great hurry; if the present negotiation was unsuccessful the matter could be adjourned and another attempt made later, say in 1964.

The Prime Minister said most earnestly that the President should understand that this was a turning point in history and for Europe. If the United Kingdom could not enter the EEC in 1962, the chance would not recur. The circumstances were uniquely favourable; the President was in power in France; Dr. Adenauer had been re-elected in Germany for a further period, and he, the Prime Minister, was in power in the United Kingdom. In a manner of speaking, they were men of destiny. If no progress could be made in the negotiation at present under way, or if they failed, he would have to go to his party and explain the reasons. If he had to say that the failure had been caused by the impossibility of making arrangements about New Zealand which would not shatter her economy, or because agreement could not be reached over a few thousand tons of wheat, people would think that the real cause of failure was that the United Kingdom was not wanted in Europe. Her Majesty's Government would then be forced to set out on another course, which would mean turning away from Europe. People would not be able to understand why it was necessary for Britain to abandon her commitments all over the world in the defence of Europe if the Europeans did not want her in Europe. Nor would they agree to go on paying vast sums of money, amounting next year to something like £100 million, to keep British troops in Europe. The United Kingdom would have to withdraw from these commitments and this would have the effect of shattering the organisation of the defence of Europe. Certainly Britain could not maintain her obligation under WEU which would not survive in any case. But if the idea was to set up a new empire of Charlemagne, obviously it must defend itself. The United Kingdom could not be called upon to help only when times were bad.

The Prime Minister could not say what new course the United Kingdom might follow. It might be an arrangement with the United States, or an attempt to draw the Commonwealth closer together, or there might be a reaction towards isolation. There might even be an attempt towards an accommodation with Russia.

On the other hand, the Prime Minister felt that there was no fundamental reason why negotiations should fail. Everything pointed to the need for success. Economic and political arrangements in Europe at the moment needed to be improved. WEU had no reality and as time went by NATO would change. If economic unity in Europe could not be created, the political and military reality of NATO would disappear as well. He felt moreover that the tide in the United Kingdom was flowing strongly in the direction of Europe, and he reminded President de Gaulle of the quotation: "There is a tide in the affairs of men which taken at the flood leads on to fortune". In addition, success was important from the point of view of wider French and British interests. They must remain friends and allies not because they feared a common enemy as in 1914 or in the case of Hitler, but because their basic political interests were alike. The future of Germany was uncertain. After the disappearance of Dr. Adenauer, the country might be torn by conflicting interests and might be under great pressure from the

Russians. He agreed with President de Gaulle that the only way to hold Germany was in a framework of European unity. Nothing else had any reality. In order to give stability to Europe, it was necessary for the United Kingdom to be tied in economically and politically to the new structure which was being created.

The Prime Minister repeated that if the solution was not found in 1962 the idea of the restoration of Europe would fail. History would regard it as a repetition of the story of the city States of Greece which could not unite or could only unite occasionally as at Marathon. The dream of French and British leadership of Europe would be gone forever as would all hope of giving Europe a strong and individual personality which would enable it to survive as an independent force in the world.

President de Gaulle said he was very impressed by what the Prime Minister had said. He agreed that Europe must be made to live. There was no point, politically speaking, in living in a world where only the United States and the USSR remained. *The Prime Minister* interjected that the disappearance of Europe would be a blow for the Americans too; after all, they were Europeans by descent and in spirit. *President de Gaulle* agreed and added that the Australians and the New Zealanders were in the same category, although the Indians were not. As for the British, they had a long history and they were also Europeans in their own special way. They were a part of Europe and at one recent time indeed, they alone had been Europe. But Great Britain had many extensions which were of far-reaching importance. These were much more than purely commercial for they involved great political, economic and psychological ramifications as well as trade links. The whole combined to form a complex of great importance. Canada, Australia and New Zealand may have been Europeans once but they were no longer Europeans in the same sense as the British. He and the French wanted the British in Europe. But they did not want to change the character of their Europe, and therefore did not want the British to bring their great escort in with them. India and African countries had no part in Europe. British relations with the Commonwealth countries were a matter of great importance from the political point of view.

President de Gaulle was not saying that one could not build a system which included both Britain and the Commonwealth. This was conceivable but difficult, but it would not be Europe and it would inevitably weaken the spirit of Europe. What would the Americans say? Either they would be opposed to this new system or they would want to join it and the British and their friends would inevitably want to let them in. A lot of people in France would want to do likewise. People were constantly saying to him that there was no need to have a French foreign policy since there was an Atlantic foreign policy, or a French army since NATO existed. In short, if Europe let the rest of the world in it would lose itself; Europe would have been drowned in the Atlantic. It was not the British themselves who were the stumbling block. France wanted them in; so did he personally. He realised that France could not contain Germany and even Italy by themselves and Europe had everything to gain from letting serious-minded people like the British in. British entry was certainly in the common interest; it would hold Europe together and it would add enormously to its influence in the world. But if Europe was to be created it must have a political, an economic and also a defence basis. This latter was important and had not been mentioned by the Prime Minister. (*The Prime Minister* agreed that it was important). *President de Gaulle* concluded by saying that he understood the British position very well and that a compromise must be found. *The Prime Minister* said he would try to put the position as fairly as he could: the United Kingdom would come into the political organisation on President Gaulle's basis, ie, on the basis of a confederation not an integration, that is to say "*l'union des patries*". *President de Gaulle* said that he was not responsible for the expression "*l'union des patries*". This had been invented by the journalists. What he said he had favoured was "*co-operation entre les états*", in other words a union of States. *The Prime Minister* said that Her Majesty's Government did not want to bring Canada, New Zealand and Australia into Europe politically but at the same time they did not want to weaken their influence with them. They considered that this influence had a beneficial effect both in peace and in war. Experience had shown, for instance, that the British Dominions had come into the last war more readily than the United States. It was not the intention of the British Government to change the political character of the new European structure which was being created. The individual countries of the Commonwealth might remain much as they were, but they should be no impediment to the United Kingdom joining the Community. The Commonwealth was not a political organisation. On the other hand, if the links which united the Commonwealth were severed, it was difficult to say what the results would be. After Nehru, India might lapse into chaos or it might gravitate towards Communism. Canada, Australia and New Zealand would probably turn towards the United States. It was, therefore, clearly important to try to preserve the Commonwealth political links as they were. The Prime Minister was very glad to know that President de Gaulle believed that the technical problems of British entry into the Six could be overcome. The United Kingdom could not enter Europe if it involved abandoning the Commonwealth. It was neither in their interests nor in the interest of Europe. But he agreed that it was not right to destroy the political and economic equilibrium of Europe. Europe did not and could not live inside a wall and its influence on the world in general would be immeasurably strengthened if its economy were enlarged by the addition of the United Kingdom and if its influence abroad could be exerted through British connexions overseas. As for the Indians and the Africans, the British aim was to avoid a vacuum which could be filled by the Russians. Both politically and economically this would be dangerous. Admittedly, it was expensive to try to keep these countries on the right path but on the whole it seemed worth while. *President de Gaulle* suggested that it was necessary to give more thought to all these problems. The British were on the move, and so was the Commonwealth. *The Prime Minister* said that he could see President de Gaulle's fears but that the experts could and must overcome the problems and that the way must be found of including Britain in Europe. *President de Gaulle* repeated that the attitude of Great Britain towards Europe was changing. *The Prime Minister* agreed that this was so up to a point but this evolution could not be counted upon to provide a solution to the problems. *President de Gaulle* said that one should not be pessimistic; more time was needed. The problems would become clearer. They could not be settled tomorrow. Equally he did not think it was necessary, as *The Times* had suggested that day, to wait for a generation. The Canadians were cross, the Americans were anxious, the Europeans were nervous.

Everything was changing; this was in the nature of things, and the process would go on. The idea of Europe was new for the British and so the problems had to be approached without haste. The process of negotiation was bound to take more than six months. Things were moving. The United Kingdom only applied to join in October. This was an act of very great importance, and the resultant technical questions were still being studied. These were inevitably subordinate to the political ones, but the problems were not yet clearly defined and on some of them, for instance on agriculture, he was not sure himself of the French position. For instance, it might even be that the problems of agriculture could not be overcome, and that in January 1962 it would appear that the Common Market could not go forward. None of these things could be settled quickly and one should not, therefore, talk in terms of ultimata or time limits.

The Prime Minister said this was where he differed from General de Gaulle. The problem must be settled next year or the courses of the two groups would begin to diverge. In the United Kingdom, other people with other policies would take control. He had felt that de Gaulle would be able to help the United Kingdom to get closer to Europe. The Prime Minister himself could carry through the present policy only if the tide was flowing in his direction. He might be wrong, but he knew his country. He was asking President de Gaulle to think about the answers, not to give them now. But the President should understand that, if present negotiations failed, a reaction against Europe would set in in the United Kingdom and all possibility of agreement might be lost for a generation.

President de Gaulle asked how the smaller countries such as Denmark, Sweden, Portugal or Ireland, would fit into the scheme of things. The Prime Minister said that he thought that some distinction could be drawn on the basis of defence policies. Some of the smaller countries were neutrals, such as Sweden, Switzerland, Austria and Ireland. Others, for instance Norway, were not, and they could find a place in the new organisation.

President de Gaulle suggested that Norway was in a difficult position because of Soviet threats. *The Prime Minister* agreed that Soviet pressure was likely but thought that the Norwegians were courageous and could be relied upon to stand firm. *President de Gaulle* asked whether, if one looked at Europe from the point of view of politics and defence, it would be possible to leave Spain out indefinitely. *The Prime Minister* thought that it would be too difficult to bring her in while Franco remained in power but after he had gone there might well be some form of monarchic régime in Spain which would be more respectable and could be brought into a European structure without too much trouble. In general, he thought that Europe could be organised in concentric circles. There could be a political and military core around which there would be an economic organisation. Some of the smaller countries could be associated to this and special cultural associations were also conceivable. In fact, relations of different orders between all the participating countries would gradually develop.

President de Gaulle was attracted by this thought and mentioned that if the British came into Europe this would add a certain flexibility and suppleness to political thought which was lacking among the French and the Germans. He was optimistic about the future and about British membership. The profound change which was taking place in the facts of the situation and in the necessities with which nations were faced would inevitably cause opinion to change too. He believed that all the problems would be successfully solved.

Fig1 197

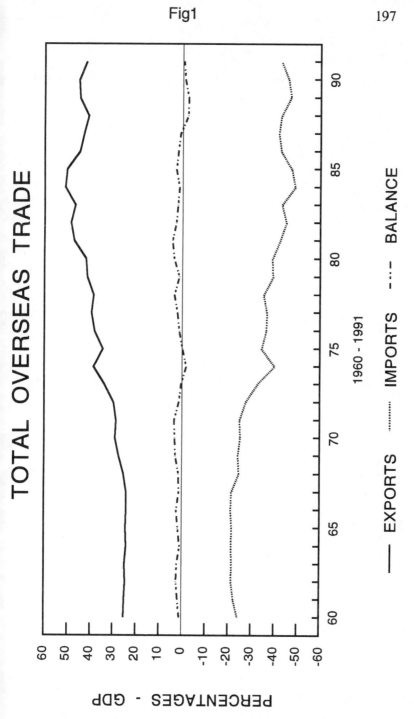

TOTAL OVERSEAS TRADE

1960 - 1991

PERCENTAGES - GDP

—— EXPORTS .... IMPORTS - - - BALANCE

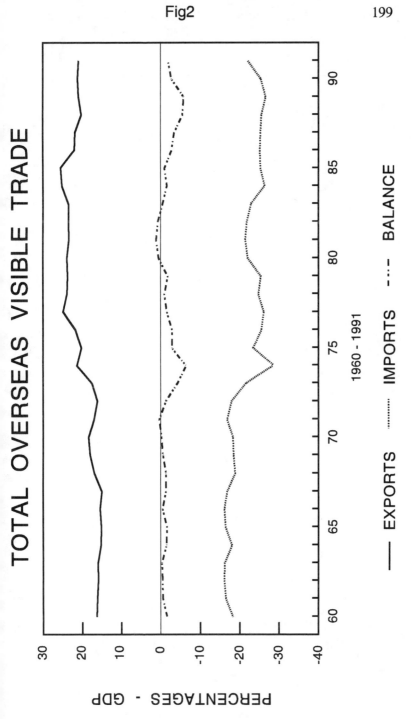

Fig2

TOTAL OVERSEAS VISIBLE TRADE

PERCENTAGES - GDP

1960 - 1991

—— EXPORTS   ········ IMPORTS   --- BALANCE

Fig3

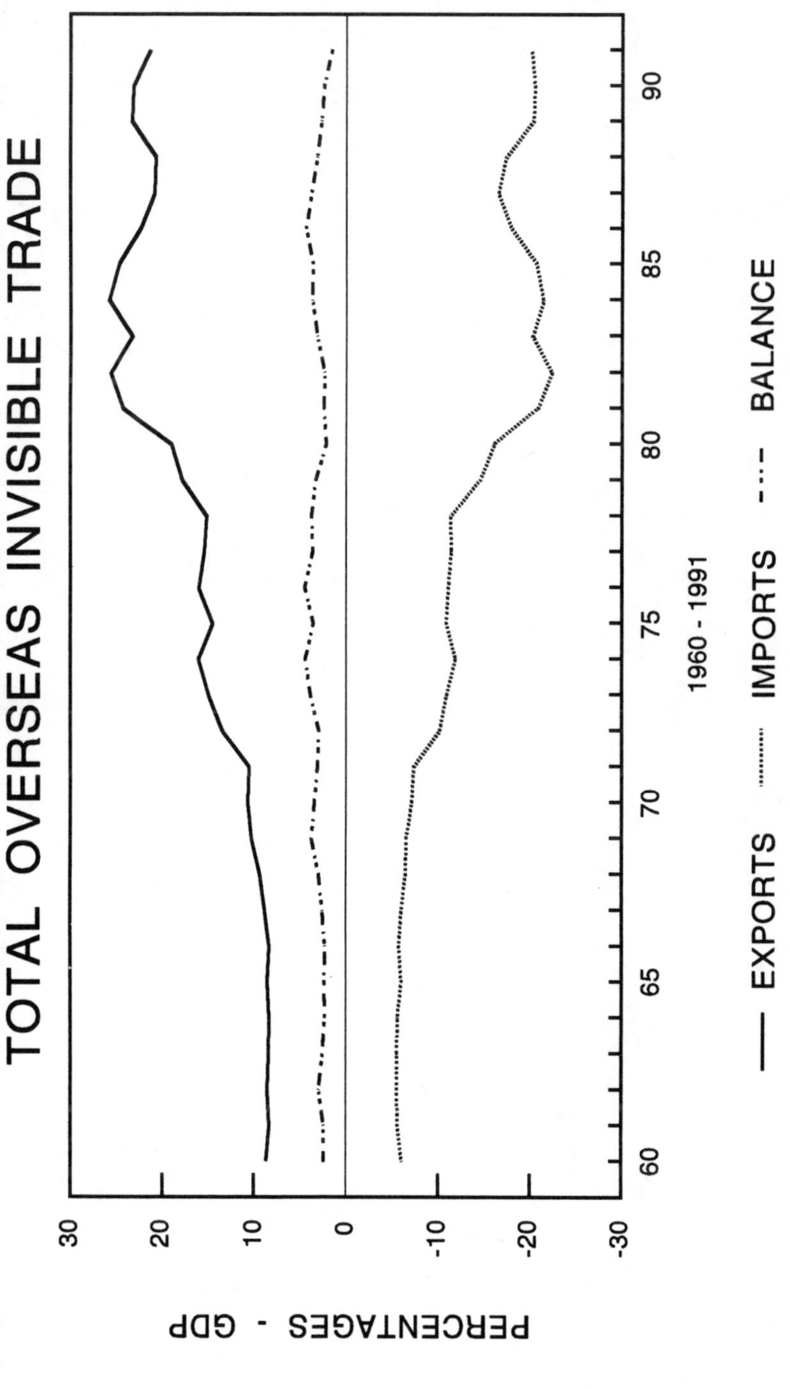
TOTAL OVERSEAS INVISIBLE TRADE
1960 - 1991
EXPORTS
IMPORTS
BALANCE
PERCENTAGES - GDP
30
20
10
0
-10
-20
-30
60
65
70
75
80
85
90

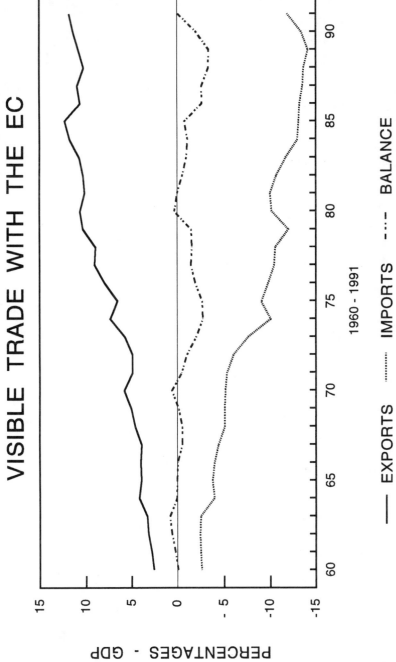

Fig4

VISIBLE TRADE WITH THE EC

1960 - 1991

PERCENTAGES - GDP

—— EXPORTS .... IMPORTS --- BALANCE

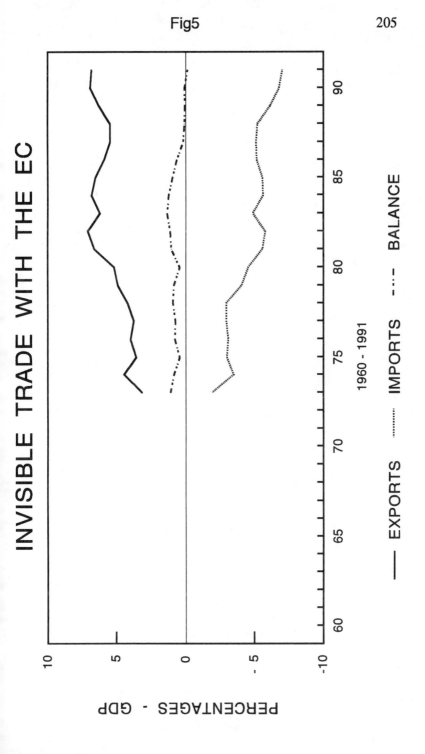

INVISIBLE TRADE WITH THE EC

Fig5

205

1960 - 1991

—— EXPORTS   …… IMPORTS   --- BALANCE

PERCENTAGES - GDP

Fig6

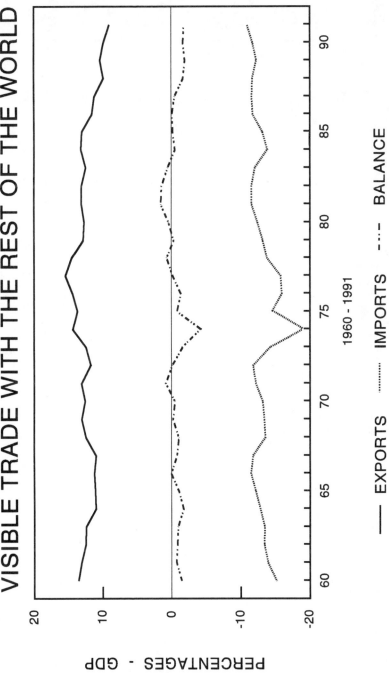

VISIBLE TRADE WITH THE REST OF THE WORLD

EXPORTS   IMPORTS   BALANCE

1960 - 1991

PERCENTAGES - GDP

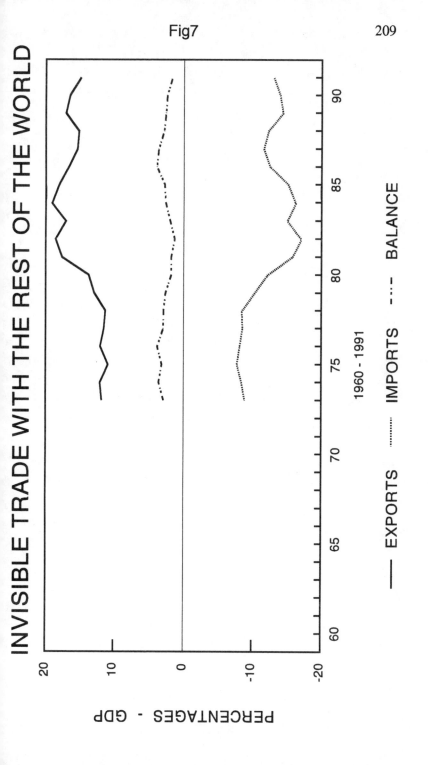

Fig7

INVISIBLE TRADE WITH THE REST OF THE WORLD

1960 - 1991

PERCENTAGES - GDP

— EXPORTS   .... IMPORTS   --- BALANCE

References: Those in code form are to documents in the Public Record Office.

1   Quoted in M Laing, Edward Heath, Prime Minister, p.127.
2   FO 371/150363, M 6136/29.
3   Quoted in M Camps, Britain and the European Community 1955-1963, p.86.
4   T 234/720, Chairman's memo.
5   Camps op.cit. pp.78-9.
6   FO 371/150363, M 6136/29.
7   CAB 129/91, 27.
8   CAB 129/92, 65 and 67.
9   CAB 129/95, 229.
10 CAB 128/32, 80(8).
11 Camps op.cit. p.133.
12 CAB 128/32. 5(5).
13 Maudling, Memoirs p.233 and Camps op.cit. p.123.
14 T 234/720.
15 CAB 128/32, 80(8) and FO 371/150363, M 6136/29.
16 CAB 129/96, 27.
17 Camps op.cit. p.216.
18 FO 371/150366, M 6136/87.
19 FO 371/150363, M 6136/29.
20 Quoted in Macmillan, Pointing The Way, p.54.
21 PREM 11/2985.
22 CAB 129/99, C.(59) 188.
23 CAB 130/157, Gen. 671/51.
24 CAB 128/33, 63(3).
25 CAB 134/1819, EQ (60)11.
26 T 234/721 on EQ (60)11.
27 Macmillan op.cit. p.313, PREM 11/2998.
28 FO 371/150268, M 6114/114; 150270, M 6114/158.
29 T 234/667.
30 PREM 11/2978.
31 CAB 134/1819, March 1960.
32 Macmillan, op.cit. pp.313-16.
33 CAB 134/1852.
34 Ref. cit. ESE (60)3, cf. FO 371/150268, M 6114/114.
35 FO 371/150282.
36 CAB 130/173.
37 CAB 134/1820, EQ (60) 27.
38 FO 371/150363, M 6136/29.
39 CAB 130/173, EQ (60) 26.
40 CAB 134/1819, 8th Meeting.
41 CAB 134/1820, EQ (60) 29.
42 CAB 129/102 pt.1, C(60) 107.
43 CAB 128/34, CC 41 (60).
44 FO 371/150360, 26 June.
45 FO 371/150361, M 6136/18.
46 FO 371/150363, M 6136/29.

47   FO 371/150363, M 6136/33.
48   Camps op.cit.
49   Design for Europe, a pamphlet. I am obliged for this quotation to J Obdam's pamphlet The Rape of Britannia.
50   FO 371/150363, M 6136/33.
51   CAB 134/1820, EQ (60) 33.
52   CAB 134/1819, 9th Meeting.
53   Camps op.cit. p.107.
54   PREM 11/2905.
55   CAB 134/1820, EQ (60) 35.
56   FO 371/150223, M 619/102.
57   CAB 134/1822, 14th Meeting.
58   PREM 11/3131.
59   CAB 134/1822.
60   FO 371/150338, M 6121/78.
61   FO 371/150369, M 6136/118.
62   FO 371/150363, M 6136/38, 39.
63   FO 371/150363, M 6136/27.
64   FO 371/150224, M 619/108.
65   FO 371/150369, M 6136/118.
66   FO 371/158160, M 614/1.
67   FO 371/150369, M 6136/107, 139.
68   FO 371/150270, M 6114/168.
69   cf. FO 371/158264, M 634/2.
70   FO 371/150364, M 6136/47, 62.
71   FO 371/150369, M 6136/165.
72   FO 371/158160, M 614/1.
73   ditto, M 614/14.
74   PREM 11/3322.
75   PREM 11/3553.
76   ditto and FO 371/158264, M634/12.
77   PREM 11/3345.
78   PREM 11/3554.
79   CAB 134/1821, 2nd Meeting.
80   FO 371/158265, M 634/22.
81   FO 371/158160.
82   PREM 11/3284.
83   CAB 133/244, PM (W) (61) 1 and 3.
84   FO 371/158163, M614/69A.
85   PREM 11/3555.
86   CAB 128/35 pt. 1, C.C. 22 (61) 4, 24 (61) 3.
87   CAB 128/35, C.C. 26 (61) 4.
88   CAB 130/176, p.732.
89   CAB 134/1821.
90   Annexed minute.
91   PREM 11/3555.
92   CAB 134/1821, EQ 21.
93   CAB 129/105, (61) 84 and (61) 87.
94   Camps, op.cit. p.341.
95   CAB 128/35 pt.1, C.C. 35 (61) 4.

96   CAB 134/1821, EQ 25.
97   CAB 134/1821, 5th Meeting.
98   FO 371/158277, M 634/225.
99   CAB 129/105, (61) 96, 129/106, (61) 104 and 111.
100 CAB 128/35, pt.2 C.C. (61) 42 (1).
101 PREM 11/3558.
102 CAB 134/1852, 19 May 1960.
103 PREM 11/3559.
104 CAB 128/35 pt.2, C.C. (61) 44 (1).
105 Camps op.cit. p.359.
106 CAB 134/1821, mem.26.
107 Cmnd. 1565.
108 FO 371/158304, M 634/720.
109 FO 371/158305, M 634/739.
110 Macmillan, At the End of the Day, p.30.
111 FO 371/158302.
112 cf. Camps op.cit. pp.367 et seq.
113 PREM 11/3561.
114 Macmillan, op.cit.
115 Pollard, The Development of the British Economy 1914-1967,
     p.434 et seq.
116 Jones, British Industrial Regeneration, in Britain in
     Europe, ed. Wallace, p.116 et seq.
117 CAB 129/106, (61) 110.
118 A Lamfalussy, Europe's Progress: Due to a Common Market?
     in Lloyd's Bank Review, Oct.1961.
119 K Young, Sir Alec Douglas Home, p.129.
120 J Moon, European Integration in British Politics 1955-63,
     p.180 et seq.
121 FO 371/158277, M 634/222, 229.
122 FO 371/158278, M 634/236.
123 FO 371/158301.
124 FO 371/158302.
125 FO 371/158283, M 634/330.
126 Macmillan, Pointing the Way, p.316.
127 John Murray, Conservative Concern, p.4.
128 BT 213/148.
129 Camps, op.cit., pp.236-7
130 ditto, p.336.
131 Schlesinger, A Thousand Days: John F Kennedy in
     the White House, p.845.
132 ditto, p.357.
133 Not used.
134 Moon, op.cit. pp.171 et seq.
135 FO 371/158265, M 634/22.
136 Horne, Macmillan Vol II, p.258.
137 cf. Camps, op.cit. p.369.
138 Kitzinger, Diplomacy and Persuasion, p.27.
139 Moon op.cit. p.37, 169.
140 Horne, op.cit. p.315.

141 Jenkins, Mrs Thatcher's Revolution, pp.44 et seq.
142 Wallace ed, Britain in Europe, p.7.
143 FO 371/158169, M 614/190.
144 Cairncross and Eichengreen, Sterling in Decline, p.187.
145 K Young, Sir Alec Douglas Home, p.129.
146 cf. J Young, cited in Sked, Time for Principle, p.49.
147 Pollard, op.cit., pp.411-12.
148 Sked, Time for Principle, pp.29 et seq.
149 eg Howarth, in The Cost of Europe, (ed Minford),
    pp.51 et seq.
150 eg Ritson, in Britain in Europe, (ed Wallace),
    pp.91 et seq.
151 Cmnd. 4289 (1970) para 27.
152 ditto, para 42.
153 Cmnd 4715 (1971) para 42.
154 Wallace op.cit. p.178.
155 Howarth op.cit. pp.60-61.
156 Burkitt, Baimbridge and Reed; From Rome to Maastricht,
    pp.14-15.
157 Crafts, Can De-Industrialisation Seriously Damage Wealth?
    pp.12 and 39 et seq.
158 ditto, p.19.
159 Kitzinger op.cit. p.286.
160 Cmnd 3269 (1967).
161 Kitzinger op.cit. pp.46 et seq.
162 Jay, review of Lacouture in New European, Vol.5 No.1 (1992)
    pp.46-7.
163 Sked op.cit. pp.50 et seq.
164 Wallace op.cit. pp187 et seq.
165 ditto, pp. 5 et seq.